Smoke on a Summer's Day

ISBN-13:
978-1533115850

ISBN-10:
1533115850

By same author

Into Splendour
Finding One
Universal Glue
Forever Yours Forever Free
All The Way Home
The Ascent of Awareness

"unnamed sources"
As we journey through life we encounter and accumulate
sources of wisdom the origins of which stretch into the mists of
time.
I am so happy to gratefully acknowledge the many gifts of
knowledge and opinion
so many people have bestowed upon me in countless ways.
From client feedback to personal observations and a myriad of
material in the common domain, common practice and common
sense.
To you who have made this book a reality, *"Thank you"*

Tony Beckett-Hester

A Penmeera book

Smoke on a Summer's Day

By

Tony Beckett-Hester

"Stand still, look down and find
the happy path beneath your feet."
From "Standing Still"*

"Find yourself.
And you will know what there is to know.
You will know who you are and what you are.
Help another to do likewise.
From "That Is All."*

"You are a link,
All people are links
Instrumental in the fulfillment
Of a universal destiny"

*First published in Forever Yours Forever Free

Contents

(A grandfather's thoughts)

If there were just one gift that I could give you, a gift which could be passed from old to young and age to age, it would be a gift that frees the mind from fear and fear's unwelcome grip.

If it were in your power to give and in my power to take, I would take from you your fear.

Yet how could I take from you something inherent to all who are born into the body? How could I take from you that which is essential to your survival in this life? Without making you afraid, how would your mind protect you from the dangers and hazards of the world?

Without imagination and the powers of the mind, how would you know the wonders of inspiration, the magic of fantasy and the joy of creation? How would you grow? No, I could not, nor would I seek to take away from you this notion.

I would take from you only the kind of fear which has no reason and no sense about it; that brought only misery and torment. I would take from you the fears which dogged your days and hounded you at night; which robbed you of happiness and denied you the vision of the wonderful future which lay ahead of you.

I would ask, "Of what are you afraid?" And you would say, "I am afraid of this or that." and I would say, how you need not be afraid. The time you fear will be more bearable and pass more quickly than the hours you now spend fretfully awaiting its arrival and reassure you that all would be well.

For if you could, just for a moment, be without that sense of fear, then you would touch again the freedom of your birth.

You would not be without fear but you would also know the love in which you were held. That no matter what lay ahead, the love would hold you, envelope you, sustain you and carry you when you were unable to carry yourself.

I would tell you how, in time all fears fade and the day would come when you would look back and see that your fear existed only in your thoughts, fears then blown away like smoke on a summer's day which, only for a moment obscures the sun.

My love would reach out and I would say to you, "Why wait?" and with one bold stroke you would bid farewell to fear. You would call fear's bluff, demand to know its substance, which you would find most surely lacking and fear would lose its grip and slink silently away like some unworthy foe.

This is the gift I would give you, of a love that brought you joy and gave your spirit wings.

Tony

Introduction

My years in practice as a Counsellor and therapist offered my patients/clients and I opportunities to find and explore roads we then journeyed together. When I retired my thoughts turned to writing.

My initial thoughts were to publish separately a selection of the leaflets and explanatory notes that I had written for clients over the past twenty-five years. However, the importance of presenting them in a way that they could be read progressively soon became obvious.

The result, *Smoke On A Summer's Day,* is offered as a companion guide to the reader seeking better understanding of him or herself: to identify and overcome personal problems, including: anxiety, fears or phobias, relationships, jealousy, guilt, communication, eating, work and stress. Problems and other personal problems commonly encountered.

It is important to understand the principle of a matter as much as its detail. In understanding the 'bigger picture' we allow the mind to embrace individual details in context before knowing all other details.

When we see how a problem can be accounted for and understood we can look at the problem with the benefit of that understanding. The more that is known, even if only in principle, the easier it becomes to allay fears based upon 'the unknown'.

It also offers a framework around which a practitioner new to counselling may shape his or her own disciplines and beliefs.

How both practitioner and patient view each other, and themselves relative the rest of creation, is of great importance, no matter how sketchy that view may be.

Beginning with some basic observations about working as a practitioner just setting out, the book goes on to suggest ways of opening a conversation with prospective clients.

These 'prompts' are equally effective as a starting point for the reader who is invited to 'self-question'. Questions he or she likely encounter at a professional consultation..

What follows is the distillation of my years of counselling practice, study and perhaps most important of all, a privileged insight into the lives of other people. The diversity of patients' lives, their experiences, private thoughts, fears and insights is beyond imagination but surprisingly widely shared. You are not alone and for the most part must remain so. Suffice it to say that life is truly stranger than fiction.

The book continues with examples of behaviour and ways of thinking which can limit our options and choices. How, by understanding ourselves, and other people, we broaden our vision and open ourselves to new possibilities, and enrich and enhance our lives and those of other people

A practical and philosophical book, *Smoke On a Summer's Day* combines elements of psychology, physiology, spiritual and paranormal elements of life to aid the human search to find ways in which body, mind and spirit work harmoniously together.

An overcoming of irrational fears and realization of the happy Self.

Matters understood simply and simply presented.

There are always gaps in one's understanding. Where detail is known, it is given, where only principle is known that too is what is given.

Love and Light

Tony

1. Counselling-Counsellor

Rudiments, techniques and objectives

Before attempting to offer to counsel someone, the would-be counsellor should have a clear understanding of his or her relationship with the intended beneficiary and an equally clear notion as to his or her role in that relationship.

The counsellor may consider him or herself a friend of the recipient but there is a clear distinction between being a personal friend and being a professional friend. True friendship, of whatever kind, is sincere, constant and if it is to be of lasting value, must also be honest.

The purpose of counselling is to help someone resolve a situation satisfactorily. The situation in question may be one of simple practicality; may involve the client alone; may be hypothetical or imaginary; may be to do with the emotions; may relate to previous experiences; may be of the utmost urgency; may be of a most serious nature; may be anything at all......

The first duty and responsibility of the counsellor is to identify, understand and accept the subjective reality of the problem as presented by the client. During which time to also establish a rapport that allows the client to feel that he or she is understood and is being taken seriously.

The counsellor may view the problem or situation described as one of fearful imagination, or not supported by the facts as they are presented, but even so the client must be heard out fully. The client must be allowed to express fully his or her fears and concerns, without hindrance. At this stage it is perfectly in order to make notes, and be seen to make notes. Clients find this reassuring but be sure also to continue to maintain eye contact. A counsellor who gives his notepad more attention that he gives his client is sending the wrong signals.

A counsellor may analyse but he is not necessarily a clinical analyst.

A counsellor should examine, question and practically analyse the client's circumstances and the problem in order to understand them. Apart from raising singular points essential to continued clarity, questioning is best left until the client 'had his say'.

A counsellor should preferably have at least a rudimentary knowledge of the effects and side effects of any medication the client may be using, also the effects of any medically diagnosed conditions. Appropriate reference books should be considered essentials by the professional practitioner. The internet is a valuable reference source outside consultations but use during what is supposed to be a counselling session is distracting and inappropriate.

The client may be using drugs, prescribed or otherwise, or suffer from mental or physical conditions affecting his or her outlook and judgement. Without taking these into consideration counselling may be misplaced or ineffective. An initial consultation where all these factors can be noted allows for their deeper investigation prior to the onset of a course of counselling sessions.

The counsellor must be imaginative on behalf of his client and to do so he *must* have a good understanding of the problem. Take an interest – imaginative questioning is essential. Without taking on board the problem, the counsellor must see and feel the problem as does the client – more use of the imagination.

While not offering advice, the counsellor can then explore avenues of action, word, thought or deed, aimed at bringing the client to his or her solution. At all times the counsellor must be positive. Even negative outcomes represent progress and can be presented positively. Ultimately, if all avenues seem to have been explored without resolution, in validating the problem, the need of further counselling will become obvious, as will the value of that which has already taken place. Progress will always be made. Even when a problem may not appear to have been resolved when a counselling session ceases, clients will have benefited by the processes of effective analysis and dissemination of their situation. Ultimately, with or without the counsellor's presence, any decision that leads to a resolution satisfactory to the client will be a decision taken by the client.

Counselling is a process of restoring confidence and self-empowerment to the client.

Preliminaries to counselling.

Where, when and how?

Having the rudiments of counselling in focus the question of where, when and how will the counselling best proceed?

The 'where' will depend for the main part on what facilities are at the counsellor's disposal. Each counsellor will work in ways with which he/she feels comfortable but I suggest the following arrangements would prove productive.

Privacy is very important. A room which offers a high degree of visual and audible privacy is essential. If the sounds other people in the building make cannot be heard your client will feel insulated from prying ears and eyes. The room should not be too large; one measuring 3 metres by 3 metres is adequate. Nor should it be cluttered, having room for a small desk is helpful but the essentials are a comfortable sofa or settee for the client and a matching easy chair for the counsellor. These should be positioned with clear space between the settee and the entrance door – the client be made to feel welcome but also see that there is no physical barrier to his/her leaving the room.

The counsellor's chair should face the settee, slightly offset, to allow comfortable direct eye contact while avoiding the feet of counsellor and client pointing at each other.

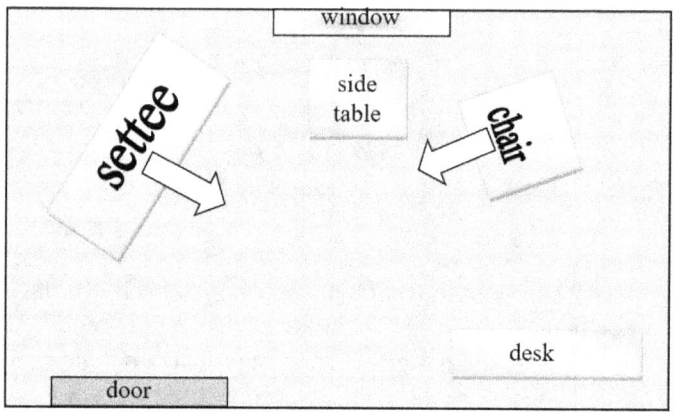

A small table, set with water and glasses, placed just off centre but not between client and counsellor forms a common contact point without forming a barrier.

While one-to-one counselling has been my own general rule I have found it sometimes necessary to see two people together and a comfortable settee accommodates such need. Also, the space afforded the single client adds to the air of openness and freedom, leaving plenty of room for bags, coats and other personal effects to be close by and not put on the floor.

Overall the room should feel 'warm' but uncluttered. A few pictures and ornaments are fine, and should be representative of his or her approach.

It is important you feel comfortable with *your* room but you must also remember the use to which it is to be put. The ambience should be such as to enhance communication and offer few distractions without being austere. Even a small room is capable of being made to feel warm and welcoming without a feeling of being cramped. An atmosphere of intimacy is not out of place.

The 'when' will be determined by the client and the counsellor's diary. Beware the client who attends at a partner or friend's insistence who then also provides transport and so dictates the time. The client must want or feel a need for help.

The 'how' is down to you. The rules of engagement must be established from the outset, uppermost being an assurance of confidentiality. Cost and payment details should also be dealt with before counselling begins.

The client should be asked to complete and sign a short questionnaire providing essential background information. This should include any disclaimers you feel appropriate and, if not covered elsewhere, the cost of the consultations. At your discretion a copy can be given to the client, though I never felt the need to do this or was ever asked.

Sit facing the client, holding good eye to eye contact, with facility to make notes on your lap. Throughout the session it is important to remain non-judgemental, or at least appear so. You should appear interested without either seeming to agree or disagree, approve or disapprove of anything presented to you by the client. This may sound easy but some things you will hear, or indeed see, may catch you by surprise, can disgust you or send your thoughts off into space. You may think you have heard it all and that nothing could shock you but if you intend to pursue the role of a counsellor, you will find this could not be further from the truth.

The knack is to show interest while remaining objective and to respond imaginatively without becoming involved. People want to feel understood and when they feel this is the case, and you show no sign of disapproval, you will most likely be thought to be in agreement. That you are not in agreement is less important than what the client thinks. What is important is the rapport you establish with each client and the openness enabling them to speak freely.

Questioning should relate to elaboration, not to induce doubt, for example.

"Do you think that was wise?" may introduce doubt, while-

"What effect did that have? Does not, and brings the client to think about the consequences of his/her action.

You may come across a situation that troubles you, because of moral or legal implications. Incestuous relationships, fraud or

5

theft, client's with-holding information from the police are just a few of the less serious ones you may encounter.

Finally, you will almost certainly encounter paranormal situations. From 'possession' by an evil spirit, or not so evil, to clairvoyance, prophecy and various forms of religious mania to drug induced psychosis.

Be ready, be aware, and in your response, be bomb-proof. Beyond this let your gut-feelings and your conscience guide you.

Before counselling commences the client should provide the counsellor with some basic information about him or herself, his or her circumstances and the problem in question. The client's response to initial questioning, which can be by way of a simple questionnaire, may be sufficient to enable counselling to begin. If it is not the counsellor is faced with the task of eliciting more information from the client.

Prompts to help identify counselling objectives, including relationships.

Is there a particular problem or is it difficult to put into words?

Do you want to:

1   To communicate more effectively?
2   To identify problems?
3   To discuss a particular problem? (Might be of an intimate nature not yet broached openly)
4   To identify and resolve partner (or other relationship, boss etc.) difficulties?
5   To identify common goals? (Business, marital..)
6   To establish some ground rules enabling problems to be discussed?
7   To find a way of living happily with an existing situation?

What are your personal objectives?

8   To establish personal goals and find ways in which they may be pursued?
9   To feel free to decide your own future?
10 To make a relationship work?
11 To break or change a relationship amicably or safely?
12 To have greater freedom, to have your own friends, pursue a hobby, etc.?
13 To have fewer responsibilities?
14 To have more say in decisions which affect my life (work, home, political etc?)
15 To feel more confident in yourself and to be respected more (by colleagues, partner, etc.)?

Prompts to aid self-appraisal and identify sources of disharmony.

1　To what do you look forward or anticipate? (Good, bad, inevitable etc.)
2　What is the best time of day for you? (Why?)
3　Is there something that you dread, imminently, or at some future time? (When did it start..)
4　Is there a person you go out of your way to avoid? (Explore reasons)
5　Is there a place you dislike particularly? (Is reason known, people, feel of place etc..)
6　Do you enjoy driving?
7　What do you enjoy doing most each day?
8　What would you say has been your happiest time until now?
9　Is there something you regret having done, or not done?
10　If you could live anywhere you wanted, where would that be?
11　What is the most important lesson you have taken from life?
12　What piece of advice would you give to someone just setting out in life?
13　Have you done or said something about which you feel guilty?
14　What is your most important achievement in life so far? (NOT what have you achieved).
15　What does success mean to you, how would you describe 'being successful'?
16　Is there someone whose lifestyle you envy or admire or you would like?
17　Do you gamble? (Explore all ways of gambling, see solutions to problems etc..)
18　Are you concerned about what other people see in you, how you appear to others?
19　Above all else, what do you want for yourself in life?
20　Do you feel lonely?
21　Is there something or someone about who makes you feel sad?
22　Is there someone whom, you cannot forgive?

23 What, or who, do you see as a barrier to your happiness.

24 If you could make just one law, what would that law be?

25 Do you trust people, just some people, or not trust anyone completely as we are all fallible?

2.   Shared commonality and individuality

Establishing common ground

Before approaching a patient it is important to have an understanding of the make-up of a 'human-being'. Without an oversight of the human mind and body and of humanity as a whole it is difficult to help the patient find a solution to his or her problem.

Your overview need not necessarily be one that is universally agreed upon but it must be one that will help the patient understand how his or her condition can be accepted, treated and managed, even when the outlook is dire. Unless you and the patient are able to confront the patient's 'worst case scenario' you will be unable to properly help your patient and your patient will be unable to help himself.

Your initial approach could be a gentle, verbal exploration of the patient's physical and mental condition and of his mental and spiritual outlook. While all people are in themselves unique there are certain themes, traits and characteristics of which a counsellor should be aware. Physical and mental make-up and development follow certain pathways and so restrained by particular parameters.

The fat man cannot become thin simply because he wishes to be so. There will be reasons why physical change is not possible, but a change of perception is possible.

The mind is capable of change to allow the patient to see his position more objectively and optimistically than perhaps at present. This is where your skill in encompassing your patient's needs within your own thinking and imagination is of paramount importance.

Having established clearly in your own mind how you think your patient wants to precede it is essential you embrace and encompass his wishes, no matter how much they contradict your own. If you are to be imaginative on your patient's behalf, you must allow for this contradiction. You are there to guide your patient to a solution that is relying on your expertise and greater understanding to enable you to do so.

In the process you may find your own knowledge expanding. Every patient teaches.

You do not have to agree or become like your patient, only accept him and his needs as part of your expanding view of humanity as a whole. If you do not do this at the beginning, you could find it difficult to introduce suggestions broadening his outlook at a later stage and inhibiting progress.

You will find within your patient at least a little of yourself. Perhaps a piece you do not like to be reminded of. Your challenge is to not turn away but use this as an opportunity to accept a part of yourself that you have previously denied. Forgive yourself for whatever it is you feel bad about and silently thank your patient for the opportunity he or she has provided you.

I believe there to be a very strong element of serendipity in life, not least in the people we are destined to find as we journey through this world. Paths cross in symbiosis, each leaving us the better, wiser and greater for the meeting, though the way in which one has benefited may not always be obvious.

In looking for commonalities, categorizing traits and in identifying human characteristics it is important not to lose sight of the patient's individuality. We all have commonalities of one kind or another and everyone behaves predictably to some degree. The knack is in using commonly shared strengths and weaknesses to embrace the patient to a degree where he feels that you do truly understand him and his condition. Albeit in truth, only to a small degree or in generality.

From this spring's a mutual respect enabling you to talk simply and honestly to your patient. A respect that encourages your patient to accept what you say because he feels he has your support, even perhaps your compassionate love. He might feel he can speak to no one else about his fears, his guilt, his needs and secret desires but now that he can speak to you, he is no longer alone.

This is the responsibility your position carries.

The first few chapters of this book concentrate mainly on establishing an overview of humankind and the conditions by which he lives.

The broadest brush is used with many generalizations, deliberately so, for this is merely the canvas on which the picture, the representation of the individual, or patient, will be painted. A landscape may consist of trees, hills, river and sky with perhaps the addition of a figure or two. Well this is the way of it. We do not need to know the species of every tree, the geological nature of every hill or mountain, the source of the river or what fish it might conceal in order to know the context in which the figure is placed. That is made obvious by the painting as a whole.

So it is with the theoretical, imaginative or abstract picture, or landscape, into which you place your client. He will tell you where he lives, what he does for a living, whether he is married and has children: here is much of your picture. You will discern much more from his demeanour, dress, speech and appearance. Combining these elements you can begin to paint a picture that will be filled out with ever increasing detail. Ultimately placing your client in the context of a far bigger picture than you and your patient presently see.

As an artist you will work with flair, inspiration and care to build up a work of art of which you will be proud. All the while inspired, led and reflecting the 'model' you see before you.

Let us never forget, without the model we would remain uninspired, unchallenged and ignorant of that which he brings to you.

3.   Body, Mind, Spirit - an holistic approach.

Realisation, freedom and responsibility.

Humankind exists on earth as a multi-layered life form comprising integrated and interconnected physical, mental and what are termed paranormal levels. Individual human beings each comprise millions of cells each one fulfilling specific tasks.

As part of their physical make-up, human beings have a central control unit comprising several separate parts and collectively known as 'the brain'. As well as controlling the function of the physical body, the brain is also capable of producing abstract thoughts and images; a function known as the imagination. At which point it is necessary to make a distinction between the terms Brain and Mind

The Brain, creator of the Mind and responsive to it, is responsible for action of neurological processes and sensory interactions necessary for bodily functions.

The term Mind is taken to mean the mental aspect of brain function; processes which often, though not necessarily lead to physical activity. This is closely linked to another function of the brain, the memory.

In simple terms, the MIND thinks, the BRAIN does.

There is also a view, widely held among human beings, that there somehow exists an additional Self, housed or contained within the physical self. That this additional sense shares the space occupied by the human body, existing in an other-worldly or parallel state: widely referred to as the Spirit Self. Some argue that this is no more than an extension of the human mind; a supra, or higher mind that provides an overview of our individuality, independent of other 'Mind' functions.

The existence of electrical energy fields created by brain function extend the abilities of the human mind to the dynamics of telekinesis.

The brain has innumerable functions, some of which reveal abilities beyond the simple physical processes of day to day living and the mental and emotional reactions and responses associated with them. When we talk about these functions we use the terms Mind and Brain to signify these differences and that of the Supra or higher mind as the Spirit. Body, Mind, Spirit.

From this point we may draw our own conclusions as to where we think we stand as sentient beings in the world of our birth. Here I build a picture supported by commonly held beliefs.

Humankind stands between two worlds, the world seen and that unseen. In humankind's possession are the tools, the senses and faculties from which we draw this conclusion.

Beyond which we speculate. There may be an infinite number of alternate realities or views, states of being and physical worlds.

Where does one world end and another begin? The answer is neither obvious nor clear for while mankind does have sufficient sensory reception to allow for their possibility, without subjective sensory compatibility their precise natures remain elusive. A single thought is all that is necessary to bridge the gap between that which *is* and that which *seems* as if it is.

Thoughts may originate from the processes of the physical organ of the brain. Equally they may come into the awareness of the brain from the spirit self or an external or *paranormal* source, such as telepathy. Experiments have shown that the electrical stimulus of particular parts of the brain result in the production of memory patterns, internal visualisation and emotional states.

In the main these responses to electrical stimulation are retrospective, that is to say from memories recalled in visual imagery. When it is not, and the images are uniquely new, then it may be that the mental picture is from an external source. Yet this is still not original thought, the creation of something completely new. Precisely where truly original thought comes from is unclear.

A thought exists as an abstract mental concept experienced by he or she whose thought it is.   There are exceptions though including occasions of shared imagery or visions, often of a religious or spiritual nature, which occur spontaneously.

Use of the term Mind implies and acknowledges the existence of a state beyond physical reality as we otherwise see it. Part of the Mind's function is to enable us to see these differences and separate its functions: to enable us to handle these different states of reality. Not only to accept that which is explainable but to accept that which is inexplicable but that which never the less exists.

The passage of time is one way in which we separate the real from the unreal. Environmental cycles give us a sense of the passage of time, which we have measured and regularised through calendars and timepieces. This has had the effect of stabilising our historic and predictive perspectives. Combined with our capacity to memorise experiences, this regulated passage of time extends a dimensional sense of being to humankind.

The scale by which the passage of time is measured is determined by naturally occurring cycles, planetary, seasonal and so on, the finer points of measurement being determined by choice.

Reality exists in the singular, momentary point of NOW, beyond which, speculation is an imaginary picture of anticipation created by the memory, or paranormal insight. In either case the intention is a protective one. Preparing us to meet a (possible) potentially harmful situation.

The Brain responds and reacts to stimulus from the body *and* from the Mind. In this process there is little difference between the real and the unreal. An erotically stimulating encounter can have the same effects on the body as the sight of an erotic picture or an erotic thought or memory.

Around these phenomena lies an interesting point of discussion.

If it is the Brain which creates the Mind and it is the Mind that creates and holds the thought, (which is unreal and abstract rather than concrete and may have no basis in reality), why cannot or does not the Brain distinguish between that which is real and that which is unreal, itself having been responsible for the creation of the unreal?

Within this paradox is the basis for inner-conflict, anxiety and the adoption of self-destructive and anti-social behaviour.

The One who is *real* sitting beside the One who *thinks* and therefore *acts* as if he were real.

The Brain. In simple terms the Brain comprises two hemispheres, left and right, joined by nerve fibres called the *corpus collosum.* Each hemisphere is capable of conscious thought and automatic reaction. One Hemisphere, usually the Left, thinks in terms of words and details, analysing and breaking down problems in their component parts: it is critical and judgemental in its function. The other Hemisphere thinks in terms of images, pictures, rhythms and sees the greater picture, its function being scanning and blending in nature.

Each Hemisphere is capable of working separately and independently and when doing so expresses it characteristically. For, coordination and balanced body movement, a sense of perspective and even-handed decision making, both sides of the Brain must work simultaneously and communicating with each other.

The Mind. While the way in which the Mind works may be termed *abstract*, there are further ways of distinguishing or describing Mind function. The Mind can be divided into two parts or spheres of operation. This division is between what are described as the Conscious Mind and the Subconscious Mind. The parts played by the Conscious Mind and the Subconscious Mind are responsible for most human behaviour; the differences between which, may be observed easily.

The Conscious Mind perceives environmental, personal physical, mental and imaginative realities, from which it draws reasoned, logical responses and conclusions. Each situation is taken in context and with regard to present circumstances.

The Subconscious Mind also perceives these things and, drawing upon its immense memory facility, provides automatic, unreasoned reactions based on previous behaviour in similar situations. Situations are constantly and automatically monitored to detect similarity to one previously experienced with two main objectives. Firstly to alert the Mind to something new and therefore potentially threatening; secondly, in finding a similarity between the present situation and one previously experienced, to provide reactions based on past behaviour, which may or may not be presently appropriate.

The Conscious Mind is capable of expansive, multi-directional thought and able to allow for "may-be's" in arriving at a conclusion. Responses are flexible and accommodating of changes circumstances.

The Subconscious Mind seems to work in a repetitive 'yes/no' mode producing an inexhaustible supply of 'what if?' questions. The product of the Subconscious Mind remains inconclusive: however, in apparent contradiction, in also producing automatic reactions, it is singularly conclusive and inflexible.

The way in which communication is given and received involves the Brain, left and right hemispheres, and the Mind, conscious and subconscious. All aspects of the real and the unreal may be encompassed and all levels of brain and mind function involved.

The following table illustrates in an ascending scale, human communication experiences, beginning with the most basic, that of touch.

TOUCH	Simple physical contact.
GESTURE	Physical movement conveying mental activity but without physical contact. Includes body-language.
SPEECH	Physical movement producing a secondary effect, i.e. sound, without physical contact.
EXPRESSION	Physical movement conveying meaning or emotion without secondary effect or contact. Includes body-language.
INDIRECT SPEECH	Physical movement producing a secondary effect, i.e. writing, drawing etc., without physical contact.
COMPLEX	Combining any or all of the foregoing to produce effective and comprehensive communication.
TELEPATHY	Abstract contact, of (likely) mental origin, achieving (mental) contact with another Mind.
CLAIRVOYANCE	Abstract contact of (possible) mental origin and/or (possible) para-normal, with another mind source.
PRECOGNITION	Abstract contact of mental/paranormal origin containing an element of time distortion.
SPIRITUALITY	Abstract, multi-dimensional understanding.

All of these experiences are naturally occurring phenomena of great complexity, even those seemingly most simple and direct. All forms of communication involve a degree of interpretation by the originator before the means by which the communication is to be transmitted, can be engaged.

All forms of communication involve a degree of interpretation by the recipient before the content can be understood.

A communication is only effective when the understanding of the recipient duplicates that of the originator. This may never be wholly possible.

Communication between human beings is a complex structure often using *all* of the above elements. Not all aspects of communication are consciously recognised but can still be acted upon subconsciously. The result can be apparently illogical reactions brought about by the subconscious Mind's great sensitivity to anything potentially life threatening or new.

Another dimension of reactive and unreasoned behaviour and that is the 'gut-feeling' or intuitive guidance attributed to some sense of inner knowing. The most common source of this inner-knowing may be attributed to the subconscious mind drawing upon its memory-store of minutiae and there are occasions when paranormal sources of insight occur.

Whatever the case, when we are unaware of the precise source of our understanding and despite being unable to reason the case for our decisions, we remain convinced of their validity and attribute it to intuition, sixth sense, gut reaction, spiritual guidance etc..

In considering what we have referred to as the real and the unreal aspects of human existence, four distinct levels of functional awareness become apparent.

1   The purely physical, i.e. The body, including the brain and its role in controlling body function.

2   The amalgam of physical and mental, i.e. The (right) Brain, the Conscious Mind, questioning, reasoning, responsive to change.

3   The amalgam of physical and mental, i.e. The (left) Brain, the Subconscious Mind, reactive and resistant to change.

4   The Spiritual or inner-self, i.e. Self-recognition enabling paranormal function beyond physicality and mentality.

The latter may be open to debate but paranormal or spiritual phenomena exist and occur.

When humankind is affected by dis-ease, through physical injury, mental anxiety or inner or spiritual conflict, no matter what part is subjected to the immediate trauma, all parts are subsequently affected.

In the human body's spontaneous reaction to heal itself, all resources are drawn upon, to support and compensate for, the affected part. Very simply, if the right hand is injured, the left hand does more work, the brain has to adjust its thinking to achieve this and musculature throughout the body is adjusted to accommodate the new balance.

Recovery from physical injury is accelerated by the Mind taking decisions to create and live in an environment conducive to healing and to holding a positive *healing* state of mind.

Overcoming worry, anxiety or depression is assisted by the body being placed in a relaxing and harmonious state and environment; being properly nourished and subjected to loving care.

Loss of spiritual awareness can occur following preoccupation with physical, mental and worldly matters of almost any kind but can be rekindled through silent meditation or being opened by a *loving outreach*, physical, mental or spiritual.

Humankind exists as an homogeneous life form made up of millions of individuals, interconnected by physicality, mentality and spirituality. Every individual human being has the capacity for self-determination; comprises of millions cells each one of which is programmed for a specific tasks; the whole set up for both purpose and duration. Humankind is collectively and singularly self-determining and in the immediacy of its existence, responsible for its fate.

As human beings, our search for happiness is in effect a search for self control and self determination – in short FREEDOM to act in the responsibility of the individual. There is no criteria for the *right* to be able to do this. Freedom of the individual is not only a right but is an inevitability. Regardless of an individual's circumstance, he or she still chooses to act and behave according to belief, desire and ability.

The notional reality of self-control and self-realisation must therefore take into account many factors. Without understanding something of human make up, the way in which the mind works and how mind and body heal, how shall we know

21

best how to survive, let alone achieve fulfilment?

In order to restore harmony, we must be able to understand how sources of disharmony have arisen. To remove barriers to personal (and collective) progress, the source or cause of all matters problematic must be identified, isolated, embraced, overcome or corrected.

Failure to identify the true cause of a problem results in either mismanagement of the problem, treatment or mistreatment of a symptom and failure to address the problem at all.

4.   Analysis, Psycho-analysis & Regression

There are many ways in which techniques of analysis can be used in the management of anxiety and other states of emotional and reactive imbalances. Because the processes of analysis vary according to the theory on which they are based, their means of application and the techniques of the counsellor or therapist I offer only basic definitions.

For therapeutic purposes the objectives of analysis are loosely these.

To identify present time situations that are or might be the cause of the problem presented; to then re-examine those situations in order they are no longer considered problematic.

To identify past experiences in order to understand how the patient may have been affected by such events and personalities. To re-examine and re-appraise these causal factors with a view to normalising their effects.

To identify subconscious 'misinformation' held over, especially from childhood, that is directly associated with present time behavioural reactions and prejudicial assumptions.

To determine the course of therapeutic or analytical action most likely to prove effective in revealing and dealing with of the cause of the problem; to bring the patient to mentally distance him or herself from the problem or situation, to bring him or her to be relative to and separate from that situation or cause in order to effect its management.

Analysis: to examine the structure minutely and distinguish precisely the function of each part. To examine critically, to separate, to distinguish the true from the false, to test soundness. The purpose of analysis is to resolve. Analysis is a natural function of the conscious mind.

Psycho-analysis: a method of investigation of mental processes and the motives of conduct. Devised principally by Freud and Jung and based upon a (supposed) conflict between conscious and subconscious impressions which give rise to various *repressions* and *complexes.* Most psycho-analysis starts from a point of presumption and is not personalistic. With an adherence to basic patterns and causal assumptions, the basis of psycho-analysis is objective rather than subjective, even though the application is deemed to be subjective.

There are reservations about the foundations of classical psycho-analysis and as time goes by alternatives will be proposed.

Regression: is to move backwards, to return to a former state of place. Often used in conjunction with hypnosis, regression therapy is based on revisiting and confronting an event mentally, with a view to its re-evaluation.

The term is also used in the context of revisiting a (supposed) previous life, again often in conjunction with trance-inducing or hypnotic techniques.

A **Personalistic focussed Psychological Analysis.**

Where emphasis is on the personal world of the individual.

The patient and his or her story is the point of departure around which analysis and study of the patient's behaviour is concentrated.

There are several techniques but broadly speaking the methods fall into these categories.

Methodology in the therapeutic application of analysis, based upon my own applications.

1   *ASSOCIATIVE CONSCIOUS ANALYSIS.*

a]   **Subject experience** related.

Where the analyst asks the patient to recall experiences and feelings towards certain subjects presented by the analyst and of which the patient has no prior knowledge. The patient is therefore more likely to react spontaneously, rather than respond. The process encourages a broad use of the mind, helping overcome the patient's preoccupations, and prompts unrecognised or forgotten trouble sources, not all of which will be relevant to the problem in question, but contributing to overall improvement. Essential to the success of this technique is the counsellor's ability to discern changes in the patient's demeanour and the subjects to which those changes may be associated.

A very important part of this process is the list of subjects offered to the patient. The subjects should be varied and subjects likely to be causes of emotional disturbances as well as abstract themes and 'happy' words. Part of the exercise is to stretch the patient's mental and emotional parameters. The knack then is to pick up on those which pull up negative reactions and/or memories. Remember this is only the first stage of 'treatment'. It is not to be rushed but the patient must feel that it is productive.

Samples of subjects/words might include: clouds, porridge, touching, seaside, mathematics, girl-friend, trees, feet, runways, boy-friend, and so on. The list can be extended according to need and patient response.

Some patient's enjoy the ride, the combination of excitement and reminiscence, always with the thought and promise of unearthing something hitherto un-revealed. Remember though this kind of analysis must always be productive – if it is not, drop it in favour of an alternative route.

b]   **Emotional experience** related.

Where the analyst encourages the patients to recall occasions when or where he or she experienced certain emotions. This is a variation of 1-a] above using the effect of an experience or encounter rather than the encounter itself. Here it is not just a case of speaking a word but rather seeking to elicit a reaction (Tell me about a time when you felt....).

A prepared list of emotive, emotional triggers words could include: uncomfortable, hot, tearful, self-conscious, confused, aroused, angry, rejected, very happy, and so on.

c] **Word association** related.

Where the analyst offers single words to the patient who is asked to reply spontaneously with a single word. Patient responses are noted by the analyst who is looking for patterns, for example defensive reactions or unusual associations, which may then be explored. The process can be lengthy and results open to many interpretations or no interpretations at all.

This process is my least favoured but can provide an interesting 'interlude' where therapeutic investigation is proving difficult or lengthy.

d] **Free association.**

Where the analyst guides the patient to focus and then concentrate on a particular train of thought that eventually becomes a consuming visualisation. This can result in a semi-dissociated hypnoidal state where, in detachment from present time, experiences can be relived.

This technique relies upon the analyst having a notion as to the likely source of the problem and then his or her intuitive and imaginative abilities in taking the patient back to that point. It is a bit like informal hypnosis, a useful technique easily leaned. It requires, encouraging and supportive words spoken softly, almost monotonously and with a gentle persistence that brings the patient to concentrate on his or her remembered world, almost to the exclusion of the analyst.

2   RANDOM CONSCIOUS ANALYSIS.

This process relies heavily on confidentiality. The establishment of a relationship of trust is essential to the patient's willingness to talk openly. Through informal 'conversation' between analyst and patient, significant experiences, relationships and inner-fears can be identified. Identification is not always in the presence of the analyst, commonly patients would arrive for a appointment saying how, following the previous consultation, this or that had 'come to mind'. Almost always painful or fearful traumatic events, incidents that had been forgotten.

The effectiveness of this process is in part a result of the patient becoming less fearful in outlook. It is therefore essential to explain the working relationship of the subconscious and conscious minds and place clear distance between potentially painful memories and 'safe' present time reality.

Then, following gentle, conversational stimulation, the patient's mind will reveal underlying causes of present time inhibitions and irrational behaviour. It will by now be obvious that to avoid unnecessary delays, the analyst must suspect or have some indication as to the direction the conversation takes.

In the absence of a likely cause, conversation may focus on how present time 'life situations' can be usefully managed. From this, problematic situations can be identified which in themselves may need dealing with but may also lead to other fruitful area of investigation. A one step at a time technique leaves the patient feeling he or she has 'wrapped up' a matter of concern no matter how small. It is all confidence building.

3   HYPNO-ANALYSIS.

This technique is designed to access the enhanced memory of the subconscious and reveal experiences hitherto locked away from conscious recall. The patient is taken into a trace state, where, free of conscious control, the subconscious mind is engaged. Recall may then be from the following levels. This process requires the analyst be trained in the therapeutic use of hypnosis.

a] **Recall.**

The analyst asks the patient to, "Recall a time when you felt/you saw/you heard/etc.." The patient's response may be a simple oral account of a past event, or its re-enactment with or without emotional reaction.

The patient can then be invited to look again at the incident and be brought to a point where any fear or other emotional association with it can be set to one side. The objective is to bring the patient to be an dispassionate observer, even of his or her own behaviour, in the knowledge that it is now 'safe' to do so.

b] **Regression.**

Where the trace state is deepened resulting in a dramatisation memories.

c] **Abreaction.**

Going beyond [b] above and guiding/allowing the patient to live again a remembered episode with full emotional release.

d] **Revivification.**

Where, in deep trace, there is a form of recall in which the patient actually relives a past experience while uninfluenced by life knowledge accumulated **after** the experience.

It will be obvious that care and sensitivity is needed when using hypnotic techniques in analysis. It will also be obvious that there are fine lines between each of the states described and it is essential that patient feedback enables the analyst to know what state the patient is experiencing.

The results of deep trace analysis can bring the patient to re-live dangerous and life-threatening situation AS IF THEY WERE REAL. The need for hypnotic techniques must be questioned in the light of practical alternatives. Hypnotic techniques are used widely and extensively in support of behavioural therapy but I have seldom found need for the use of deep trance hypnosis. Furthermore, I believe that it actually robs the patient of a sense of achievement, any gain being down to the skill of the therapist. My preference is for the introduction of an informally induced light hypnotic state to aid patient focus and objectivity.

The circumstances where hypno-analysis can prove helpful is when, despite all other efforts and having allowed sufficient time for other techniques to 'work-through' there is no sign of breakthrough. (I suggest at least two, preferably three months),

It is a basic truism that life is a process of learning. Learning about the way in which one's mind works is essential to enabling conscious domination of subconscious reactions; knowledge which is at the heart of conquering one's fears.

Overcoming fear in this way opens the mind and allows therapy to access more. A further element, which usually involves some type of hypnosis, is that of past-life recall.

e] **Past-life recall.**

This is where the subject recalls (supposed) pre-birth experiences. The phenomenon may be spontaneous or under the guidance or direction of the analyst.

The basis for this work is questionable. The mode of operation must scrupulously 'clean', that is to say, unguided in any matters of detail. Recollections must be recorded without any assumption as to their veracity and subsequently carefully examined. There must be no rush to conclusion for reasons which will now become clear.

In all matters of past-life recall the following possibilities should be taken into account.

i   CRYPTOMNESIA.

Here, recall is as a form of eidetic memory where the patient (especially when a child) has read a book, seen or heard something relative to the subject or 'target' in question. For example, in response to the analyst saying, "Go back to a time before this lifetime." This literally means, think of a time before you were born. In so thinking the patient's mind may open to all manner of images, none of which may have anything to do with a past-life experience.

(Eidetic is a term used primarily for a type of vivid imagery which is, as it were, projected into the external world and not merely in one's head, frequently the characteristic of children.)

ii   WANTING TO PLEASE.

Under hypnosis, the patient wishes to please the analyst and in his or her assumption of what the analyst wants to hear, produces a fantasy on re-incarnation. A desire to please can be conscious or sub-conscious and in the case of the latter neither the patient or the analyst will be aware of the deception.

    iii GENUINE RECALL.

Revealing the images and/or experiences of the subject or of other people's lives, living or dead. The ability to do this has many possible explanations.

A. An inherited basic memory, transferred from mother while child still in womb.
B. An inherited memory transferred genetically.
C. An inherited maternal trauma impression. An emotional implant from mother to child, between conception and birth, following a trauma to the mother.
D. Reincarnation – access to a previous existence through spiritual/soul memory.
E. Clairvoyance. Where there is spontaneous contact between the patient and a spirit entity who then communicates impressions to the patient.
F. Possession by spirit entity. While in an open, hypnotic state, the patient submits to a spirit entity resulting in that entity 'invading' the patient. The invading spirit is indistinguishable from that of the patient and identifies itself AS the patient, with a view to misleading the analyst. This can be scary but be assured that it can happen.
G. Possession by spirit entity. Where submission to an external force results in that force or entity making itself known and using the opportunity to make contact with the analyst.
H. Retro-cognition. The reverse of pre-cognition occurring when the patients enters what I can only describe as a 'timeless state'. This may also lead to precognition and if precognitive experiences are not recognised as such, it can lead to some interesting times.
I. Telepathy. A phenomenon more likely to occur during hypnosis and the telepathic connection may not be with the analyst.
J. Other unknowns.

There are many variants of response which, when added to personality traits, hidden agendas and desires, mean that caution must be exercised in approaching the subject.

iv   NARCO-ANALYSIS.

Because of the difficulty or inappropriateness of inducing an hypnotic state in patients, clinical psychiatrists and other medical practitioners may use drugs to similar effect.   Under   the influence of a hypnotic drug, inhibitions are removed and the patient can be induced to give vent to feelings otherwise suppressed. The process has been given the name Narco-analysis by which repressed, suppressed and forgotten experiences may be restored to memory.

These drugs have the advantage of expediency and make the most of treatment time when time is limited. However, as with all drugs, their use is limited by their toxic effects on the body and the body's ability to accommodate or 'get used' to them.

Also, whilst these drugs are useful in breaking resistance they fail to elicit the more subtle feelings and emotions of the patient. Because of their mood changing properties, they may prevent full or complete recall responses.

DREAM ANALYSIS.

There is much not yet understand about the true nature of the mind and how it works. For the purposes of counselling and therapy, I offer this framework of understanding dreams.

There is little doubt that some dreams do have meaning beyond simple mind function, but most dreams are no more than the result of nocturnal brain activity. It is suggested that during sleep, the brain/mind sorts and records to memory recent experiences. Snapshots produced during this activity are thrown into the 'viewing' area of the mind providing a basis for imaginative dreaming. A sleeping-conscious attempt to make sense of these snapshots. A bit like standing behind someone filing photographs, the mind and imagination is stimulated by seeing picture after picture without the ability to put them into context.

Dreaming may be:

a) A natural; process of mental activity.
b) A subconscious presentation of a preoccupation. Something feared or desired.
c) An answer in response to self-questioning; to a question posed consciously in the   knowledge that one's own mind contains a solution to the problem.
d) The answer to a wakefully and consciously posed question, that comes from an external/paranormal source, i.e. telepathic, spiritual, and prayerful.
e) A precognitive flash. Dreaming of an event yet to happen.
f) A combination of any or all of the above and/or other unknowns, resulting in   partially accurate recollections and partially correct predictions.

To extricate the salient features in order to make use of dream analysis constructively is no easy task. A string of unconnected images and thoughts can be connected using a little imagination. and some analysts use dream symbolism as a kind of analysis.

Dream analysis is something which is at best extremely subjective and intuitive. If the message is not obvious then it may be that there is no message!

SELF-ANALYSIS.

Self analysis can use any of the foregoing techniques to reveal significant but consciously forgotten experiences. The difficulty is in holding an objective perspective while undergoing a subjective experience, that is to say, sufficiently removed from oneself from that part of the self that is being observed.

Another disadvantage is in not having the benefit of an experienced guide speaking from an independent standpoint.

There is also a danger of raising or creating unwanted or irrelevant questions, or of experiencing something quite unexpected that proves too much to handle, especially if using a self-induced trance state.

For newcomers to trance or meditative state, commonly encountered sources of anxiety include the following.
a) Spontaneously releasing something from the sub-conscious

that the conscious mind is unable to handle. Something the searcher is or has been unable to come to terms with.

For example, death, a sense of loss, a traumatic incident in the past, the unexpected awareness of (a part of) one's body.

b) A psychic experience.

For example, spontaneous clairvoyance, pictures coming into mind telepathically or from other sources, Spirit possession.

The conscious mind is analytical by nature and is the primary driver to increasing personal knowledge and self-understanding. The ego is part of this consciousness and there is always a danger that analysis, the need to examine every aspect of life, and in particular one's own life becomes ego-driven and all consuming. To seek to resolve some personal inhibition or other mental barrier to life advancement or enhancement is laudable and to increase personal knowledge and self-understanding is right and proper. To go beyond this point requires personal insight, sense of purpose and clearly identified goals – plus the guidance of someone experienced in the field of enquiry

Summary.

Analysis is, or at least should be, a process of self-realisation. Even when guided it should remain a completely subjective experience. It may also result in characterisation or personality profiling by the analyst or counsellor. None of this must detract from the immensely personal experience of self-revelation: the moment of realisation when inner minds communicate to each other. The sense of wholeness resulting from such inner communication cannot be over estimated.

The secret to overcoming destructive and self-destructive thinking and the attainment of happiness through peace and contentment lies within each of us.

If life itself is held to be a process of learning and of progress, part of that progress must be the management of one's reactive self. At some stage this will undoubtedly include recognition of a spiritual or superior Self, to which other parts of the mind and ego-self become submissive.

The search for the spiritual or 'real' self is something undertaken by most people, in one way or another. I believe that it is an important element of therapy and counselling and an aspect of life often ignored by clinical psychologists and psychiatrists. It is so important that a failure to include this fundamental element of human make up may result in the failure of truly effective therapy.

When all else fails, faith, belief or strength of inner reserve and resolve may be the only thing that sees us through a crisis.

Life itself, in all its forms, is an overcoming of obstacles; physical and mental, and indeed spiritual. It may be true to say that we develop, mature and grow stronger from finding our capabilities stretched and our personal frontiers expanded.

It is also true to say that we unwittingly or rashly create obstacles for ourselves in many ways, not least by failing to broaden our outlook and embracing what we might loosely call 'the unknown'. Those improbable and unprovable elements of our existence which underlie spirituality and which involve our dealing with the mysteries surrounding death.

Life offers us many distractions. From meeting the essentials of daily existence to the exploration of its many pleasures. Life presents our senses with painful challenges and pleasurable opportunities and in self-centred preoccupation we can lose a sense of proportion and also of personal responsibility.

That is not to say the self is unimportant, quite the contrary, individually it is of the uttermost importance. If we do not regard the Self as our centre of existence, how shall we place ourselves relative to the rest of creation? More importantly, unless we know ourselves intimately, how shall we know or begin to understand other people? It also follows that unless we understand ourselves and control ourselves, how shall we understand the struggles and challenges of others who, in their earnest attempts at self-betterment, cause distress to those around them?

Self acceptance and Self-understanding is essential to personal development and the development of a cohesive social structure built on tolerance and mutuality.

Self-centred too easily becomes self-absorbed, leading to selfishness. Here we find an abdication of personal and social responsibility. This form of social isolation comes in many guises as individuals 'drop-out' of mainstream society, ostensibly to live an idyllic existence they feel society denies them. This is an extension of the restless rebelliousness found in all people, and especially in the young, that is essential to the growth and development of all people.

Unfortunately, a society intolerant of the antics of its younger elements provides ample opportunity for rebelliousness to turn to anger, frustration and violence.

The waters are muddied, the way ahead unclear and a sense of world-weariness leaves us unmotivated, powerless to fight the social machine we see at the root of our ills. What then are we left with?

What we are left with is an undeniable presence of The Self, from which all else flows. A Self that is, in itself, all-powerful and all-knowing, a theme that will be developed in coming chapters.

In short, within our reach is the person **who** we truly want to be and to be able to live a life that is free from groundless fears and in goodness of conscience and inner-knowing.

5.   Practitioner-Patient Relationship

The problem of dependency

A problem facing all practitioners is that of patient dependency. For many reasons and especially when counselling and where interaction is prolonged, the patient may come to feel increasingly dependent of the practitioner; he or she who provides solutions, answers and who is kind and who offers comfort.

The risk of client/patient dependency can be increased where a definable and perhaps intimate psychological problem has to be approached sensitively or when a matter of spiritual belief is addressed.

Here I stress the need for clear thinking and self-awareness on the part of the practitioner. The practitioner must neither take advantage of the client/seeker nor leave him or her confused.

The client must come to his or her personal clarity of thought and meaningful understanding alone. The practitioner may lead, show, invite, instruct and explain all manner of things but it is the client-seeker who must find for himself the understanding that proves most satisfactory.

It is immaterial whether the information sought concerns a psychological problem, a physical ailment or a spiritual belief. The seeker alone must find that which has meaning from the infinite number possibilities he may explore. You, the practitioner, are simply an avenue down which he has chosen to walk at this time. Offer him what you can, allow him to take what he needs and what he is able grasp and let him go the richer for the encounter.

If the seeker finds in you something he values greatly, and comes to see you as a means of salvation, he will look up to you. There is a risk that in not separating what you say from what you are, the seeker may become emotionally attached to you. This is one form of dependency.

When the presented problem is in dealing with a physical ailment, it may be necessary to introduce a psychological element to treatment. In this way bringing the seeker to see his problem in a new light, leading him from fear to a more peaceful and fruitful acceptance of his state. This approach might spill over to a discussion on his, and your own spiritual understanding.

The practitioner becomes the teacher, the client the pupil. There may follow a natural level of attachment, of mutual love and respect that is in essence a joint exploration. Counsellor and client travellers sharing the same road, neither feeling dependent on his or her companion. The love is pure, the relationship idealistic but the risk for dependency is obvious. Equally for the teacher who gives way to a self-centered ego, indulgent needs and desires, and/or a pupil whose loving attitude and gratitude becomes a path to mutually emotional indulgence.

Ultimately it is the responsibility of the counsellor alone to maintain a state of integrity within which the client-practitioner relationship is maintained. A clearly defined space shared mutually, within which both can work freely, honestly and with professional intimacy. A relationship only possible through exercising rigid personal integrity and self-discipline.

Do not underestimate the perils of entering this emotionally charged sacred space.

6.   The Conscious and Subconscious Minds

A view of reaction and response mechanisms

For the purposes of counselling, the following working hypothesis offers a simplistic overview human brain/mind functions. This paints a picture to which most patients can relate and help engage them in examining their own behaviour.

1   The physical brain – a body organ.
2   The working Mind – an abstract entity, wholly or partly the product of the brain.

The BRAIN - a physical component of the body with control functions at three basic levels.

1   The **Hind brain**, closest to the top of the spinal column and comprising:
Medulla Oblongata containing vital centres regulating basic activities including heartbeat; Cerebellum which governs many reflex actions including balance.

2   The **Mid brain**, a short cylinder connecting the Hind brain to the Fore brain spheres   and which acts as a relay station for the senses of sight and hearing and the coordination of movement – a 'switchboard' for the entire brain.

3   The **Fore brain**, the largest parts of which are the two main cerebral hemispheres.
Definite functions can be ascribed to certain areas of the spheres but those responsible for   reason   and   memory remain elusive.

The Left and Right Hemispheres of the Fore brain are linked by a bundle of nerve fibres called the **Corpus Collosum**. In the human brain there is a division of labour between the left and right hemispheric, each hemisphere having its own special function and delineation of the sensory input it handles.

In most people the Left Hemisphere deals with language, numbers and details; it is critical, judgemental and analytical. We engage the Left Hemisphere whenever we 'try' to do something. The Left Hemisphere 'learns' primarily through repetition.

The Right Hemisphere deals with rhythm and feel, scanning and seeing the whole picture and is used to recognise faces, maps and whole words. We use the Right Hemisphere when we act responsively and smoothly 'without trying'. The Right Hemisphere 'learns' by absorbing experiences.

The purely physical picture is complicated by the complex cross-over mechanism by which the brain/hemispheres are connected to other organs in the body. About 80% of sensory signals to and from the left side of the body are directed to the Right side of the brain, the remaining 20% going to the Left: and vice-versa.

The Brain is the control centre for physical responses and reactions, the effects of which govern our state of health and well-being. The effects most likely to cause concern are those relating to fear and anxiety and stress. Such effects are shown below, together with the combating effects of relaxation.

The Physical Responses to Stress and Relaxation.

	Under Stress	When Relaxed
Heart action-pulse rate:	Up	Down
Blood flow to muscle:	Up	Down
Blood flow to skin:	Down	Up
Blood flow to organs:	Down	Up
Oxygen use/need:	Up	Down
Cortisone output:	Up	Down
Energy/food reserves	Depleted	Increased
Blood pressure:	Up	Down
Muscle tension:	Up	Down

The immune system is adversely affected by stress reactions because of raised cortisone output. This can give rise to an increased incidence of allergic reactions and depletion in immune responses leading to a higher incidence of infection – colds, flu etc..

The Brain/Mind can also be looked at from the way in which it works, thought patterns, reactions and so on – and opinion varies with different interpretations; and each new physiological discovery adding to our knowledge.

From the counselling therapist's point of view it is important to have a reasonably firm, if flexible structure on which to base reasoning and treatment. To this end here is a simple pattern of the working mind.

The MIND – an elaborate reasoning and reactive structure that has three distinct inter-relating areas or levels of control.

1   The **Conscious** or **Reasoning Mind** and its memory access. This mind function accepts, and sorts, analyses and questions the information it receives. It is logical and selective in the amount of information it stores/remembers.

2   The **Sub-conscious** or **Unreasoning Mind**, a memory bank in itself. This mind function does not function analytically and accepts unquestioningly, information in great detail. A vast store of minute details and experiences relating to every aspect of life and the physical and emotional changes that have taken place. A habit cultivating, reactive, unthinking process.

3   The **Imagination** or area of the Mind, where mental images are 'seen'. This mind imaging facility does not itself produce the images; the conscious and subconscious Minds or other source* does that.

Paranormal input may be regarded as a separate source regardless of whether it comes through the conscious or subconscious mind before being seen on the 'imagination's' viewing screen.

Understanding the ways in which the various parts of the mind work and how they work and interact affects human behaviour offer the counsellor/therapist a valuable tool. The most basic of these tools is the ability to recognize and distinguish the differences between rational and irrational thoughts and behaviour. From this can be found ways in which unwanted thoughts and behaviour can be modified and controlled.

The **Conscious Reasoning Mind** receives sensory information through the body's neural network constantly and continuously. This information comes from the outside world via the senses of sight, sound, taste, touch and smell most obviously; and inwardly and less obviously from the body itself, also through the central nervous system as deeper mind functions monitor the body's state.

Information from all sources, internal and external, come together to provide the brain/mind with information essential to our survival. As time passes, minute by minute information is updated and replaced, the displaced information becoming the basis of our memory. It is here that mind function reveals the presence of our existence in the fourth dimension, time. Memory gives us a sense of the passage of time, a sense that can be distorted easily by focus and circumstance. Time may 'fly' or 'drag'.

The living mind records everything we experience, including our physical and emotional reactions and responses to those experiences. Moment by moment a vast store of mental pictures and sensations is built up as we journey through life. Where there is repetition, a route of easy-access is formed whereby certain memories and our associated reactions become prominent.

We become creatures of habits which usually make life easier as we need to think less about the 'ordinary' yet often quite complex things we do day after day. So much so that if we try to think about these mundane things we find ourselves confused by their complexity.

Our memories are selective, giving easy recall to those things of special interest or that have happened recently. Incidents of little importance, may be less easy to recall.

A reason for this selectivity is that of all the details recorded, the actual number we will need to recall to ensure survival and progress is in fact very small. It has been suggested that at any single moment, the human Mind collects about fifty separate pieces of information. Of these one may be conscious of only a few, those most likely to be needed, or recalled, for a special reason. Our lives are remarkably repetitive and we may not be exposed to anything that is really new to us or which holds our interest deeply.

The greater the interest, the greater the importance or

relevance a matter had, the easier and more detailed is its conscious recollection. Recreating the mood present at the time of the original incident often enhances the ability to recall it.

Memory or recall is generally reliable. Inaccuracy or distortion of recall can be introduced at a conscious level by our interpretation of the memory *as it is recalled*. With ageing, the function of far or distant memory seems enhanced while recent or short-term memory capabilities may become limited. The reason is thought to be changes in the brain which are a natural part of ageing and these differ from person to person.

The mind can be tricked, leading us to believe that we really did see or experience something that was in fact illusory. Partial perception invites speculation, assumption and false conclusion. Brain cells can be destroyed and memory distorted or made incomplete by chemicals, including drug, alcohol and tobacco use.

We may introduce into our memory something we are mislead into believing is factual when it is not; that is to say our senses are deceived in some way, a trick of the light, a confidence tricksters ploy, and so on. Similarly, bias and assumption can both lead to a misinterpretation of recollections.

Given the foregoing it is reasonable to suggest that memory can be relied upon within the parameters outlined. That is, when we say and believe that we are telling the 'truth', it is a subjective truth and not an absolute truth.

Arguably the absolute truth of any matter remains distant from human resolution, the best we can ever hope for is the sum of our singular and subjective views.

If our minds are so reliable, we are aware of their limitations and can be logical and understanding about our relative predicaments, why do we still have wars, suffer from psychosomatic illnesses and behave irrationally? Perhaps part of the answer lies in the way in which the subconscious part of the mind works.

The **subconscious** part of the mind functions mainly outside the immediate and direct influence of the conscious part. The subconscious is a part of the mind that works automatically, rather than by an individual's expression of will or desire.

A major role of the subconscious seems to be that of acting as a protective mechanism to enhance basic survival. The part that develops habitual behaviour.

Patterns of behaviour that have proved themselves to be 'safe', demonstrated by our subsequent survival, can therefore be repeated 'safely'.

The process is entirely reactive, and unreasoning.

The principle behind this function seems to be, that if you survive a particular experience, then, should a **similar** situation present itself again, behave as you did before and you will survive again.

However, similar does not mean 'identical', nor does the process distinguish whether or not previously we acted in the best way that we could, only that we have survived. Perhaps, on re-examining the incident in question we might feel that we could have handled things differently and so in future, should the situation arise. When we come to do so, we seem to be fighting ourselves as our conscious mind, expressing our desire to change, comes up against the subconscious that wants us not to change.

By this process we develop habits, routines that seem to work for us and which we come to take for granted. In the main, habitual behaviour is helpful, but some of the things that we do without thinking, may not be carried out in the best way, just *our* way.

Some habits result in patterns of behaviour that appear pointless but we live with them and we come to be known for our idiosyncrasies and 'funny little ways', some of which can drive other people nuts!

The subconscious element of the mind is essential to the human learning process. Every experience of change alerts the subconscious, no matter how small the change. Is a new habit to be adopted or the new experience to be challenged? By this simple, fundamental process, the subconscious brings something 'new' into our conscious awareness and in doing so, invites our assessment of its potential benefits or hazards.

To the subconscious, **everything** new is potentially

hazardous and to be resisted or rejected in favour of established **safe** routines. Hence our resistance to change and dislike of the unexpected, even surprises intended to be nice surprises .'Old habits die hard.'

Unpleasant experiences, embarrassment, humiliation, anxiousness and so on, make an especially deep impression on the subconscious. Similar situations are subsequently avoided as the subconscious, prompted by what it sees as a potentially threatening situation, throws painful reminders of that earlier time into consciousness.

An example of how automatic subconscious reactions can be a great benefit is when we are faced with a sudden and unexpected emergency while driving. We have both consciously and subconsciously learnt how to drive; when there is sudden demand for urgent and immediate action it is the subconscious which acts first. Spontaneously triggered by the circumstances with which it is presented our subconscious mind provides us with what it has learned would be the appropriate action. This happens far faster than we can consciously think about what we should do. In short we REACT rather than respond.

This example illustrates very well the essential difference between the conscious and subconscious minds.

The Conscious Mind RESPONDS to a situation. Having given logical consideration to the type and nature of action to be taken and by remaining in full control, the conscious mind responds.

The Subconscious Mind REACTS to a situation. Immediately and uninhibited by thought, the subconscious initiates action based either on a previous experience OR by what it has learned to do fearfully, should the circumstances in question arise. Such as is the case in military training when the repetition of certain actions prepare and subconsciously program the would-be combatant to produce the desired effect in battle. Actions that are actually *reactions* that over ride the considered conscious response that might inhibit the militarily and speedy reaction desired.

Important differences between the conscious and subconscious minds must be taken into account when

46

understanding their various, inter-related functions.

Because the conscious mind is the logically controlled element, the information it receives is screened to ensure that only that which it decides is important and relevant is acted upon. We experience this as concentration or preoccupation, in which circumstance we may be unaware of someone talking to us, background noise or anything which might be considered intrusive. Subsequently, consciously we remember only that part of our experiences on which our attention has been placed; this is our 'truth'. We can never know the 'whole' truth, only that which is relevant and particular.

By contrast the subconscious mind is eager to see the fullest picture possible seems to have no screening mechanisms to distort its memory. In the absence of conscious resistance and screening, subconscious memories contain far greater detail than those of our conscious awareness.

At this point it is worth remembering the part our subconscious reactions play in providing us with so many of our actions. It is why we may sometimes have a sense of inner-conflict in wanting to behave in a certain way only to find we have acted differently, perhaps with regret. Or that we have acted in a way we find difficult to understand or explain. One reason for our inability to understand our behaviour is that we have reacted and the subconscious memories causing the reaction are not in our conscious memory.

In its recognition of a situation, because the subconscious needs only similarity, not duplication, it can misread situations resulting in inappropriate reactions. Every situation we encounter contains many tiny parts or details that are memorised subconsciously. The recurrence of only a few of these component memories may result in misidentification and subsequently misguided and inappropriate reactions.

Whenever we want to change something about ourselves, our subconscious mind offers only resistance. Working on the assumption that our best chances of survival are in repeating 'yesterday', any deviation from behaviour found previously to be 'safe', is to be discouraged. Change then comes only with conscious insistence or unavoidable circumstances. The more a pattern of behaviour is repeated and the longer it goes unchallenged, the more likely is its continuance.

As we have seen then, the subconscious mind is responsible for bringing thoughts, feelings and reactions unexpectedly into conscious awareness. This may occur for no obvious reason, an important clinical principle when dealing with cases of acute anxiety or panic attacks and phobias. Also almost any repetitive patterns of behaviour that are damaging socially or individually.

A good example is the onset of panic attacks, the first of which occurs for no obvious reason. Commonly expressed as coming 'out of the blue', because its occurrence is inexplicable, the panic attack itself becomes a source of anxiety. This increases the likelihood of further attack and which can lead to limiting patterns of behaviour. The underlying cause is likely to be the resurrection of a reaction associated with a distant or traumatic subconscious memory.

Some time in the past, possibly in childhood, the sufferer experienced a time of great anxiety. The subconscious mind absorbed the experience in great and minute detail, impacting greatly on the open mind of a child: a fearful and traumatic experience that left a deep and powerfully reactive impression.

Years later, a situation arose containing elements of that past, fearful time. Elements sufficiently similar to prompt a subconscious reaction, preparing the sufferer to meet that same challenge. Unfortunately the subconscious may not make the conscious mind aware of what it is doing and so to the sufferer, not remembering the childhood experience and unaware of anything fearful at present, the feelings of anxiety – rapid heartbeat, cold sweat, stomach churning, trembling and so on – seem to come 'out of the blue'.

When I talk of the 'elements' of the experience I refer to the myriad of minutiae contained in ANY experience and which are captured in their entirety at subconscious levels of the mind. Consciously we are aware of about fifty separate pieces of information at any moment. These range from body states, temperature, light levels, sounds and so on. The subconscious on the other hand, unrestricted by any need to understand or interpret the information it receives, absorbs hundreds, if not thousands, of items simultaneously.

Different experiences and situations in the memory can share common elements which, when mirrored with a present time situation, can trigger reactions based on subconscious misidentification and false comparison. In the remembered incident there are also elements, or factors, which the subconscious ignores in its quest to compare present with past. These include date and location; also an individual's capacity to better deal with situations which might once have posed problematic.

So, while it might be 3.00 pm on a sunny day in Margate and we are standing on the corner of a certain street, to our subconscious mind it suddenly becomes 3.00 pm on a sunny day in Margate 30 years ago when we were lost and felt anxious! Yesterday becomes today and now, today, we feel anxious.

Panic attacks and other reactions can only be controlled AFTER they have begun to occur. Once the process by which they arise is understood attacks can be controlled and their effects minimised until such time they no longer present a problem.

The **Imagination** is a part of the mind where images are viewed. These images may originate in the memory, the conscious or subconscious mind, paranormal/telepathic sources or be deliberately created fantasies. Images viewed on an inner screen of mental creation.

Imagination is subject to the rules of conscious and subconscious thought. When we choose to think about a certain thing, then images of that thing will come into view. These images in turn act as a trigger to the subconscious, spontaneously providing a barrage of further mental images, not all of which may be to our liking. These are no more than reactions and responses to thought association.

The subconscious is tuned in to preserving life and so holds a great store of associated memories relating to all manner of things that we have been told are potentially life threatening. Unfortunately, much of this information is false, based on snippets we have heard, propaganda, sales pitches, scaremongering and so on. Our fears are more fiction than fact and most of what we 'fear' is without true foundation.

The body reacts to whatever catches our attention. Outwardly this can be on the reality of the moment or inwardly as we day-dream in our preoccupations. This is as a result of the conscious and subconscious controls that automatically take place. Because these, and other reactions are beyond our control until we experience them, if we wish to avoid predictably unpleasant reactions known to accompany certain subjects, we avoid thinking about them. We avert or displace our attention to avoid the full force of the reaction. Just thinking about something can bring us out in a cold sweat.

It is important to remember that the subconscious does not simply remind us of something or tell us how to act. The subconscious institutes reactions. There may be no conscious memory of why these reactions exist within us, only that we experience a change of state of mind and body as a result of their resurrection.

The subconscious does not differentiate between past and present, thought and reality, fact or fiction. The subconscious contains a vast array of 'trigger' memories and is in a constant state of awareness, ready to prompt us to act should a trigger be activated.

The conscious mind is capable of discrimination and of questioning the information it receives. Processes which are developed and improved with age and experience.

The subconscious is unquestioning, nor does it discriminate between the false and the true, that function is left the conscious mind. The subconscious accepts every experience to which it is exposed. We must rely on our conscious judgement to determine what, of the vast amount of information presented to us, is factual and true.

7.　　Conscience and Conflict

Choices and decisions

Moment by moment, as we journey through life our minds ask us to choose between consciously responding and subconsciously reacting to whatever situation presently confronts us. We do so while maintaining the state of equilibrium at the heart of all that exists and reliant on one of nature's fundamental laws: that of action and reaction.

For the human being, part of this process involves an interaction between the conscious and subconscious minds (see separate chapter). Prompted by the presence of a potentially threatening situation, the subconscious urges us to react and take a course of action IT feels will enhance our survival prospects.

For example. Consciously presented with an opportunity to steal something, a sense of guilt and wrong-doing makes us hesitate – this is our conscience at work (an aspect of both the conscious and subconscious minds). We might then choose to justify the act in question by saying that it is not really stealing, or that it is simply compensating for a loss we have suffered. However, we are also faced with the prospect of the consequences of being found out and the punishment we might suffer – this is the subconscious at work, drawing on all the possibilities we hold in that memory, raising our level of fear.

The balancing act is between the conscious excitement at the prospect of gain on one hand and a sense of guilt and the fear of punishment on the other.

Within a particular culture, broadly speaking most people behave with common predictability. While it is impossible to predict *exactly* what an individual will do in *every* situation, there is sufficient commonality to predict what most people might be expected to do in a given situation. Variances of individual patterns of behaviour are determined by personal experiences; their upbringing, sense of right and wrong, rules of social acceptability and so on.

Also, the number of times a certain influencing experience is repeated, the greater the impression it makes on the subconscious; the more frequently subsequent subconscious reactions are revived the more likely the pattern of behaviour in a given circumstance will embed and persist.

In the variation of these and other factors, an individual evolves as a unique being. Sharing common experiences and behavioural similarities, whilst retaining a sense of individuality. What is right for one person may not be so for another.

An overview of the way in which our minds become conditioned and our behaviour becomes predictable given a particular circumstance or situation might look something like this. As we journey through life we can categorise our experiences as follows:

1   Purely personal experiences.
     The result of isolated incidents; unique experiences, pieces of unchallenged information that become accepted 'truths'; perceptions of singular viewpoint; real and unreal.
2   Codes of conduct, morals, ideals and understandings held by many people in a group or social/economic class/strata; including religious groups, peer groups, clubs etc.
3   Deep rooted beliefs and prejudices common to the majority of people within a given national, cultural or large social or general religious group or society.

To each of these categories add the frequency by which an experience is reinforced. That is to say the number of times any particular 'truth' of accepted belief or behaviour is brought back into mind as being 'true'. For purposed of example the rate of frequency could be:

a)   Constantly
b)   Frequently
c)   Often
d)   Seldom
e)   Rarely
f)   Once (but deep).

This simplified illustration, revealing eighteen variable factors, representative of the complexity of inner conflict that results from trying to reconcile alternative and conflicting 'truths'.

Each one of the scenarios depicted above relates to the (at least seven) separately identifiable aspects of human behaviour which run from the needs of the Self alone to self-less humanitarianism, the ecological to the spiritual.

The accuracy with which human behaviour may be predicted can now be illustrated.

Most easily predictable is that of Category 3 [a]. Behaviour that is common to most people in most simple and direct situations. Alternatively, least predictable is behaviour resulting from Category 1 [e] or [f]. Unique, idiosyncratic behaviour observed rarely, if ever, publicly. It is important to remember that single, traumatic experiences can have deep and lasting effects.

Ways in which the content of the subconscious accumulates and is subsequently modified or fall into disuse can be seen in the following example. Here is a list of influences typifying development from birth to adulthood.

At birth: a basic inherited genetic memory plus pre-birth maternal emotional and physical influences (including drug, chemical, environmental), and direct and immediate physical impressions.

Add - initial family codes of conduct, essentially direct parental influence.

Add - broader family social and moral rules, contributed by parents and the wider family.

Add - social behaviour demanded by playgroup, school, parents of friends, etc..

Add - influences of religious teaching, Sunday-school, and knowledge of the law.

Add - imposed discipline of schools, clubs, associations and individuals.

Add - experiences of other people's interpretation and application of laws and social codes.

Add - an awareness of taking personal responsibility and the consequences of behaviour.

Add - the desire to satisfy personal needs and desires.

Add - an understanding of the need to work, to make money, to support one's self.

Add - experiences, some traumatic, concerning self-preservation, of being truly fearful.

Add - a desire to own property, to feel secure, and the need to protect self and property.

Add - an awareness of how moral and social codes change with the passage of time.

Add - an understanding of how values differ according to class, status, wealth and location.

Add - meeting financial needs within an adherence to business and social ethics.

Add - development of self-determination, a desire for self-sufficiency and to live one's truth.

Add - increasing awareness of the fragility of life and concern for one's health and safety.

Add - awareness concerning the sharing of common necessities and share for self.

Add - awareness of identity, uniqueness, while still belonging to humanity as a whole.

Add - an awareness of a need (to appear) to conform in order to belong, to get one's share.

Add - an awareness of individuality and the need or right not to conform.

Add - awareness of the many ways in which a single point of law can be interpreted.

Add - an awareness of injustices, maladministration of the law, misuse of power, etc..

Add – ad-infinitum....

Ultimately we all have a uniquely personal understanding of the world about us. This colours the conclusions we draw about other people. Remember that in addition to the foregoing our view also includes how people look, their physical characteristics, their mode of dress, the circumstances in which we observe them and a host of other factors. There is much room for misunderstanding. In our misreading or misunderstanding, and with the potential threat of the 'stranger' and the unacceptable, we fall back on our most basic and most powerful reactions. These are often those most commonly shared, giving us an added sense of security.

It is the wise person, and perhaps the brave, who holds back, who observes and who waits.

Try answering a simple YES or NO to the following questions.

Is it wrong to 'take', 'keep' or 'steal' -
Food to feed yourself?
Food to give to your starving family?
Something to give to those in need?
To compensate for being overcharged?
Apples that you find lying on the ground?
Stationary from work for personal use?
The company car and petrol for personal use?
Time off with pay for purely personal reasons?
Money you find in the street?
An inducement given as a reward to doing or saying something?
An inducement given to not do or say something, to be inactive?
Too much change/money given in error?
Goods that you know have be undercharged?
Take the law into your own hands because of an injustice?
Unrestrained action to defend yourself from attack?
Unrestrained action to protect property?
Action to prevent damage to yourself or your property?

According to the circumstances prevailing at the time, it could be argued that saying YES to any of the questions could be justified if doing so could be widely regarded as acceptable and because you genuinely feel that you have the right to take the action concerned. After all it is matter of conscience as much as it is a matter of law. But, and there is a but.

The need to justify one's actions points to a recognition that the act in question breaches one's personal sense of conscience, of what is right and what is wrong. The justification may be based on no more than an irrational fear, or that of simple greed looking for an excuse. We also know that while OUR special circumstances make it 'allowable', some people will draw their own conclusions and may see things very differently.

Justification indicates that a thought, word or deed has brought about some inner conflict. It is important to separate justification from acceptance and/or understanding. Justification seeks to find a reason by which a thought or action can be excused and placed into a context whereby the normally unacceptable becomes acceptable. Justification seeks to dispel doubt and guilt. Conversely acceptance and understanding are passive observations of behaviour, even one's own behaviour.

If you answered YES to any of the questions posed above, go through the list again but this time precede each question with the following:

a) *Is it acceptable to commit damage in order to take......*
b) *Is it acceptable to cause injury to another person in order to take....*
c) *Is it acceptable to take the life of another person in order to take....*

Where is the line between the acceptable and unacceptable to be drawn? Where there are differences of opinion, or more rightly, of conscience, who is right and who is wrong? Perhaps more importantly who is to decide which view is right and which is wrong? Are short term solutions that result in temporary transgressions of conscience ever justifiable? Can the taking of another person's life be justified? The law of the land, whichever land it be, can never reflect the opinions and consciences of all people within it: laws can only ever be broken. People who find themselves accused of being thieves, murderers or terrorists may feel they are marginalised by society, disenfranchised and otherwise powerless to avoid the suffering to which they have been subjected by what they see as an oppressive individual or regime.

We can also see how the justification of a minor

transgression can lead to greater and more complicated transgressions, justifications and conflicts. Telling a 'white lie' can lead to complications, giving rise to suppressed guilt and increasing anxiety and tensions.

Guilt is particularly interesting in that it appears to have no absolute scale of intensity or rationale. People can feel a sense of guilt subjectively that might be seen objectively as disproportionate to the scale of the transgression – but who is to judge? This is another pointer to the part played by the subconscious and its power of creating reactions disproportionate and inappropriate to the present time occasion. It also has to be remembered that the person displaying such disproportionate reaction may have been taught and come to believe that the even contemplating carrying out a 'forbidden' act, is a very serious matter.

Some people feel a disproportionate sense of guilt because they see also the possibility of greater transgressions following the lesser. Having transgressed in some small way, they are now afraid of being unable to trust themselves not to transgress again.

For some, their anxiety is made the greater because they lack the ability to discriminate between the lesser and the greater. People who regard ANY transgression is a failure to live up to their ideals, or live in accordance with what they believe to be 'right' or acceptable behaviour.

Suppressed, rationalised and secret, guilt commonly shapes human behaviour. Otherwise rational people carry hidden thoughts, fears and sense of guilt that result in patterns of behaviour other people find difficult to understand.

Two common sources of guilt that are carried silently, often 'to the grave', are those of theft or dishonesty, and sexual misconduct or deviancy. All judgement is completely subjective. Such secret guilt usually arises from relatively innocent and often isolated events in childhood. A time when Conscience was young and the urge to explore the boundaries of life was great.

Guilt that goes unresolved, grows with adult judgement of the behaviour in question. The fear of being found out remains, resulting in rigid, fearful and timid behaviour **relative to the subject in question.** Hard and inflexible opinions may have their roots in unresolved guilt.

This kind of extrapolation exists also where the thought of doing something 'wrong' or 'bad' is given equal weight to that of the act itself. The reasoning is this. Because most acts have their origins in thought, the act becomes possible *because* of the thought, therefore in order to avoid carrying out the act, the thought must also to be avoided. This is irrational but to the sufferer, a real and present threat or danger.

Another dimension to this aspect of guilt is revealed scientifically. Thoughts create energy, electrical, transmittable energy and a view held by some is that negative thoughts create negative or destructive energy. Also that this energy is capable of being transmitted from one person to another. Part of the way people interact is the subconscious ability 'read' other people, and to 'pick up' good or bad 'vibrations'. The suggestion is that the vibrations are brain wave transmissions. Extreme examples of brain power are those of telekinesis and telepathy, both of which are sufficiently proven to warrant widespread acceptance. Another face of this phenomena is 'crowd mentality'.

We come back then to guilt, our measure of right and wrong and a reflection of our spirituality and relationship with the ultimate power by which we feel we are, or shall be, judged. In this sense, for most people, the thought is as bad as the deed because the thought is known to 'God' from whom no thought can be held secret. We have devised ways of dealing this, the most simple being our request for forgiveness. The reason for our misbehaving is our weakness and while we aspire to perfection we know we are incapable of achieving it. Forgiveness allows us to live with our failures indefinitely.

States of anxiety and guilt arise typically following severe and restrictive influences in childhood. The developing mind is not yet capable of reasoned discrimination and readily accepts much to which it is exposed, even if unwillingly. A child subjected to harsh discipline, indoctrination into way of living, enforcing strict moral codes; accompanied by threats at disobedience, denial of affection and close physical contact are extreme examples.

Feelings of guilt, give rise to the prospect of discovery and the expectation of punishment. A reinforcement of the basic principle of action and reaction and the understanding that every act brings a consequential reaction. In this way everything is self-righting: guilt must be expunged in some way to redress the balance. Punishment fulfils the need to balance the wrong-doing. Without punishment or forgiveness the burden of guilt may become unbearable. This can result in subconsciously activated self-deprivation, self-denial, feelings of unworthiness, withdrawal from society and religious scourging. There are many variations of self debasement and behaviour designed to subject the individual to punishment, notably those found in certain forms of sexual behaviour and other forms of subservience.

*Nothing is without change.....*change is decay, destruction from which springs creation. Deep within the human mind is a sense of inevitability that tells us that somehow everything will balance out. We will get our just deserts. Within every problem lies the seed of its solution, and that each solution brings opportunity for another problem.

Problem is the word we use for a choice made difficult because of its potential outcome. Yet choices are with us constantly, in fact we resent not being offered choices and the opportunity to have a say in the way our lives run.

Should I or Could I?

There are times when making a decision, choosing an option, is difficult. Not just because of the obvious pressures of responsibility, risk, potential outcome and so on, but because of the conflicts arising within one's mind. Conflicts made apparent by our awareness of social, legal, emotional and moral obligations and the overall effects our decision will have on the lives of other people as well as on our own.

At such times we are drawn into balancing what we see as 'good' with the 'not good'. What benefits one person may be to the detriment of another. In our attempts to resolve the conundrum we pose the question, "Should I or shouldn't I?" This is no more than a way of focusing the mind on the question at hand but it makes the decision no easier. It is then but a short jump to "I give up, whatever I do I can't win!"

However, the problem will not go away, the pressure grows, a decision must be made. At which point there is a danger that the question "Should I?" becomes "Could I?", a very different matter. The question now posed is one of ability, not of conscience and the mind is happy to deal with matters of the real world. It is an opportunity for the ego to judge and be imaginative in its search for practical conclusions. Conclusions to what remains a moral issue of Conscience.

From "Could I?" the question inevitably becomes "Can I?" Bringing the question into the present tense. In the immediacy of hypothetical debate, the inner conflicts surrounding "Should I?" are submerged. The matter is now set out, a conclusion reached and a decision is made. This brings momentary relief but the original unanswered question inevitably returns, "Should I?"

The doubt and uncertainty surrounding "Should I?" can easily transfer to "Could I?" and "Can I?" with the unfortunate effect of a further loss of confidence. The doubt of "Should I?" spilling over into the realisation of potential action of "Can I?" The clarity of planned action is now obscured by the imaginary consequences that were temporarily set aside, and which now flood the mind once more.

The mind is now on a see-saw, going from yes to no and back again in agitation, minute by minute become more and more anxious; optimism giving way to pessimism and back again. A time of unstable moods, distanced preoccupation, self-doubt and indecision. There is a real danger that the right decision becomes ANY decision, just to get rid of the pressures of alternating anxiety and threatening depression.

The question of divorce is a good example of this process. Should an unhappy marriage be endured or should divorce be considered an option? The consequences of either choice will result in some unhappiness, trauma, criticism, legal and perhaps religious conflict. Once the question has been posed, the no-win see-saw is stepped upon. Representing a dilemma from which those in question will not be free until a decision is made, enacted and concluded, and even then, if ever.

What may happen is that the decision proves too difficult to contemplate and no action is taken. The 'decision' not to decide, to stick it out and make the best of things is mistaken for decision, action and conclusion. In the event, should circumstances go unchanged, the mental conflict remains, added to which is a sense of inadequacy at not having dealt with the problem previously. Mental conflict and dwindling self-worth results in unhappiness, declining health (a subconscious, protective opt-out mechanism making action, therefore decisions impossible) and increasing pressure on the other partner to 'take-over' the problem and the decision making.

At this point, it would be unfair of me to let the problems outlined in the situation I have just described go unanswered. An alternative approach to this kind of dilemma can be found in a change of standpoint. The restoration of a sense of entitlement, individuality and 'good conscience' from which springs the clarity necessary to confront difficult decisions with a sense of equanimity.

Decisions can only ever be made in the light of individual conscience and personal sense of right and wrong. There may well be argument about what is right and what is not right, legally, morally and in any sense, but the only measure of what is right for the individual is the 'right' by which he or she can live with in the future. One cannot do or allow to be done something one **knows** to be wrong without subsequently suffering the guilt associated with the setting aside of personal conscience enabling that 'something' to be done. Remember the rule of justification.

The picture or view of what has not yet happened can be changed simply by looking at it from an alternative standpoint. The future is not yet reality, we have power to create many aspects of the future and in particular those which affect us personally. We have no given right to change the future of others adversely and so must consider that fact when arriving at our conclusions. It is also right that we remember, the situation in which we are involved may have been brought about by another person, and so of necessity, that person, that causal factor, must equally be subjected to forces of change. We are entitled to extricate ourselves from situations that are not entirely of own making, in the knowledge our actions will bring change to others. That change is part of the redressing the balance, restoring harmony to both individuals.

A productive personal viewpoint that is one that sees with the eye of the observer, not that of victim or perpetrator. An observer who is clear in his or her conscience and who is able to see where breaches of conscience result in unhappiness. If those breaches are the result of the action of a partner, then there is an incompatibility to be addressed. If resolution is not possible, separation must be considered. Step by step differences can be addressed. Major stumbling blocks may be broken down into smaller, individual problems which then prove reconcilable.

Begin with optimism. There will be reluctance and disappointment at having to broach the subject of divorce and when the situation demands confrontation it is best approached sensitively and directly. If a sensitive approach is met with hostility try another approach before writing the situation off as irreconcilable. Step by step, a conclusion of certainty will be reached. Regardless of the outcome, a conclusion that can be 'lived with' in the knowledge that, in conscience, all that could be done has been done.

There will always be what we see as imperfections in life, but these imperfections are not failures. They simply the reveal our understanding of our situation in the world, our personal truths of all that is. We each attain our own 'understanding' a level of which is not comparable with any other. What is simple for one may be hard for another, there can be no true comparison.

To live as closely as we can to our ideals is objective enough. To know we have achieved all that we can achieve is a matter of fact for had we been able to achieve more, more would have been achieved. Laziness is not just an excuse, it is a reflection of who and what we are. If, what we call laziness is seen as the reason for underachievement then we have not understood 'laziness' –instead we have compared the inactivity of one with the activity of another, or we have assumed opportunity where none has been seen or taken, we have awareness of objectivity that is not shared with another; we have determined a need for action when another has not......

Conscience and conflict, guilt and accusation invariably hinge on what we think will be another person's point of view. That we will be judged and found wanting.

I repeat – to strive to live ever closer to one's ideals, to live in good conscience, to live happily with oneself, to be less critical and more forgiving of what we might see in other people as indiscretions or failures, to be optimistic in our belief that we all move forward, we all progress, we all achieve, and believe that in this positive approach to life, despite criticism, we make a positive contribution to the advancement of all.

8.   Creation and Destruction

Basic urges underlying neurosis

Two basic urges found in human beings are those of creation and destruction. From these two opposing and defining urges spring sources of anxiety, obsessional thoughts and compulsive behaviour and other functional disorders of neurosis.

From the earliest days of childhood, and perhaps even before, the subconscious is absorbing experiences that will provide the child and later the adult with a basis for individual behaviour. In particular those parts that come to characterize his or her reactive behaviour. The repetition, force and duration of those early impressions determining the likelihood and strength of subsequent reactions.

An adult's individual ability to control and overcome such reactions is itself partly determined by the innate characteristics established during foetal development (see separate notes on human body shape, etc.)

Throughout childhood basic urges of creation and destruction are enhanced or suppressed by environmental, social and educational circumstances. Ongoing development, combined with inherited genetic factors, result in the (observed) character, attitude and expression of the individual.

The CREATIVE urge can be loving and giving, constructive and pro-creative, and a natural and necessary sexual element – the "life-wish".

The DESTRUCTIVE urge can be hostile and with-holding, angry and destructive, showing cruelty and disregard – the "death-wish".

Moderating or balancing these extremes is another universal rule: an act of creation inevitably involves an element of destruction. For example the destruction of a tree to create wood in order to build a house. Any act of destruction is also an act of creation. From this simple example it can be seen that a balanced combination of these two urges can enhance and sustain human life in a symbiosis of human beings and their environment. Get it wrong and humankind as a whole suffers.

Either of these basic urges may be expressed or suppressed.

Expression of destructive tendencies can be inward, i.e. self-destructive or outward and may be physical, mental or both. Suppression may be inward, inhibiting free expression and spontaneity, or outward. When outward, destructive tendencies may be expressed by activities not necessarily regarded by others as being unnaturally destructive.

Expression of creative tendencies can result in self-absorbing or self-satisfying activities or pursuits not always demonstrating a caring or well-considered effect on other people. The artist or "serial lover" might be examples.

Virtually everyone shows creative and destructive urges at times, being revealed either when prompted by exceptional or specific circumstances, or frequently and habitually when they come to be seen as characteristic of a particular individual.

The most loving person is capable of an act of anger or destruction; the cruellest person capable of gentleness and love.

These urges are always present, awaiting opportunity to express themselves. One way in which they commonly do so is in the way we accept and reject other people. It is the individual's (higher) consciousness which determines controlled or desired behaviour, and his spiritual awareness which evokes or suppresses reactions in tune with his belief or faith.

When subconscious drives or urges are compatible with conscious desire and spiritual aspiration, mental harmony exists. Where subconscious drives are contrary to conscious desires the result is inner mental conflict; though the resultant anxiety may erroneously be attributed to a person who acts as a trigger for the reaction in question. For example, a desire to behave inappropriately may be attributed to the imagined or perceived opportunity to do so.

The manifestation of uncontrolled subconscious thoughts of a morally conflicting nature presents a seemingly insoluble inner mental conflict that can be of some magnitude. Should this persist a state of neurosis is said to exist though resulting behaviour may not be outside socially acceptable norms.

The root or cause of the neurosis is likely to be the result of an unsatisfied or unresolved childhood experience held within the subconscious and for whatever reason, now brought to prominence. Neurotic tendencies are common and may manifest themselves as depression, anxiety, obsessional/compulsive states or a specific phobia. (See sep. chapter)

An endeavour to satisfy the combined impulsions of both conscious and subconscious, can result in displaced opposing actions of loving creativity or cold destruction. The extremes of angels and executioners with a multitude of variations in between. No other person knows us as we know ourselves, and much knowledge is kept from us by our own mind.

Thus it is that obsessional thoughts become symbolized and the true source of the problems referred to only obliquely. These are circumstances in which analysis can be difficult and persistence is required. A case of where helping a client to understand the principle of why the problem exists is equally if not more important than knowing true source.

Self-knowledge of this kind is essential in bringing the patient to a state of stasis whereby he can both forgive himself for the way in which he has behaved and then begin to accept and ultimately control his reactions with patience and understanding.

A useful approach to helping patients who are in denial of their problem or who find themselves unable to deal with it effectively is to introduce the notion of there being more to life than is presently obvious. This kind of discussion is often acceptable because it makes no reference to their problem. When carefully managed the patient can be steered away from his worries and brought to think about happy matters. An imaginative approach reliant on the counsellor's ability to 'read' the client and expand his or her self view in relation to 'all-else'.

Essential to happiness is the observation and acceptance of both self and "all else" in the relative reality of the individual, in this case the patient. Expand the observation to include to notion that there is no absolute truth, only a collection of relative truths, validating the truth of the patient. Having tacitly agreed that all truth is relative and partial, it does no harm to introduce to the patient more "truths" for him to consider.

Slowly the client is brought to think about there being more to life than "his problem" and that within that greater picture could be a way in which his problem might be overcome, or at least managed more comfortably.

At this point it is impossible to direct or demonstrate precisely how this conversation may be developed beyond referring once again to the paramount importance of the practitioner/counsellor, having a very clear understanding of what he or she is doing. This can only be achieved by firstly having a clear understanding of your own faith and remembering that all truths are relative.

Every patient teaches!

Neurosis is a deep and complex subject which can be studied indefinitely and around which are many opinions and form of treatment. Clients can be helped in at what may at first glance appear to be a superficial and simplistic level but as with many things in life, much is to be said for simplicity. Helping a client manage his or her thoughts less fearfully and in doing so, opening a way to practical self-management and self-acceptance is no small achievement.

9.   Happiness and Fulfilment

understanding wants and needs

Happiness and joy are experienced when a *want* of some kind is satisfied, or when one or more of the senses are stimulated pleasurably.

Happiness can be a state of mind, permeating the whole being and lasting indefinitely, or it can be transitory and relative only to the moment of its being.

Happiness can be truly ecstatic or it can be something that simply brings light-hearted joy.

Happiness can be sought, or the circumstances in which it may be experienced, created but the state of happiness can also be elusive.

*"What difference does it make how much
you have,*

*when what you do not have amounts to
much more?"*

(Seneca 5-65 a.d.)

The drive behind our actions in the pursuit of happiness is the satisfaction of our *wants*.

A *want* expresses itself as a desire; desire motivates action; action is movement designed to bring about satisfaction; satisfaction of the *want* equals happiness.

Desire, motivation, movement and action result in behaviour designed to bring happiness. Simple, straightforward and direct. Shopping or sex, religion or politics, it makes no difference. We know what experiences make us feel happy or good and seek to experience them whenever possible. The pursuit of happiness may also be found in the avoidance of something that is known to produce unhappiness.

The drive to satisfy a *want of happiness* is at the heart of human behaviour.

What is a *'want'*?

Some Wants are common to most people and may be

termed Primary Wants.

Primary Wants account for commonly shared feelings and behaviour patterns. Primary Wants are so powerful that most could be described as *Needs*, and as such underpinning structured society. Failure of a society to provide or satisfy primary, basic individual needs of its people, leads to a breakdown of the social and legal structures of that society.

The satisfaction of a Primary Want results in pleasure.

The non-satisfaction of a Primary Want results in unrest and unhappiness.

The non-satisfaction of a single Primary Want can overshadow the pleasure derived from satisfying all other Primary Wants.

The origins of Primary Wants may be found in primitive, instinctive behaviour designed to ensure survival of the species. Wants/needs integrated in the processes of evolution, vital to the continuance of life, essential to survival of both individual and humanity or species as a whole.

In short, the satisfaction of Primary Wants could be regarded as essential to survival.

Primary Wants can be defined as follows:

Comfort – to feel well and be without pain.

Sustenance – to be adequately sustained by food and drink.

Shelter – to have means of protection from the elements.

Security – to feel safe.

With the growth of communities came the development of Secondary Wants. Secondary Wants are important because their satisfaction became the driving force responsible for the exploitation of planetary resources and the environment in which we now live.

Secondary-Social Wants much in evidence today include:

Bodily comfort – to achieve excellence as a means of pride and domination.

Sustenance – and the exploration of exotic foods.

Shelter – where the home becomes a means of artistic expression and status.

Security – and the need for exclusivity.

Acknowledgement – to be noticed, t0 belong to the world of other people.

Admiration – to be praised, reassured of personal correctness.

Status – to be held in esteem, envied.

Superiority – to have special skills or attributes.

Companionship – to be able to share and not be alone.

Acceptance – to fit in, be accepted by other people.

Attraction – to be found attractive, to mate, to fulfil gender role.

Strength – to be a protector, to aid those weaker or disadvantaged.

Exploration – to question and challenge, to break new ground, face the unknown.

In addition to the above Primary Wants or Needs, are those Wants which present themselves only under certain conditions. These are known as Reactive Wants; prompted by personal motives they produce individual patterns of behaviour.

To escape – to run away, disappear or hide

To hurt – to be angry, to injure, retaliate.

To pacify – to appease, especially one who is a position of power.

To overcome – to win, to achieve, to survive.

To hunt – to capture, to control and have power over, to kill.

To attract – to find and retain a mate.

To stabilize – to return to a state of familiarity and routine.

Reactive Wants, also satisfy one or more Primary or Secondary Wants. When a situation appears to threaten the satisfaction of a Primary Want, and one or more Secondary Wants, and one or more Reactive Wants, the resulting reaction may be extreme.

Reactive Wants may also be termed subconscious wants.

The subconscious is that deeper part of the Mind responsible for reactions, habits and other repetitive patterns of behaviour based on personal experience and indoctrination.

When motivated to act subconsciously, that is, to react automatically or habitually, we do not usually notice ourselves doing 'it', or if we do, do not necessarily know quite why we are doing 'it'. (See Chapter on The Conscious and Subconscious Mind.)

Reactive Wants can have their origins in early childhood experiences and become ingrained into the character of the individual. Reactive Wants are therefore more personal and individualistic than Primary Wants, though they may mirror or reinforce them. Behaviour resulting from efforts of an individual to satisfy his or her Reactive Wants, may be seen as personal traits or regarded as specially individualistic in some way. Greed, resulting from deprivation would be an example.

The 'special' behaviour resulting from the need to satisfy a Reactive Want can be an asset, or a disadvantage to worldly success; an obsession or a compulsion; a will to win or a need to lose.

Childhood deprivation, insecurity, rejection, ridicule, abuse or disadvantage may produce a subconscious or Reactive Want, or search for:-

that which has been denied,
retribution for that which has been inflicted,
compensation for that which has been withheld,
attraction where there was rejection,
advantage where there was disadvantage.
The bullied may become the bully, or the servile.
The ridiculed may become the taunter, or the shy.
The unloved may become the hurtful, or the fawning.
The deprived may become the mercenary, or the beggar.

These examples demonstrate extremes of reactive behaviour. People who exhibit such extreme behaviour may not be aware of either just how extreme their behaviour is, or that it is wrong (because to them it seems natural and just), or indeed why they behave the way they do. No matter how perverse the behaviour might seem to other people.

The only certainty is that the sense of satisfaction derived in satisfying a Reactive Want, is not only pleasurable, but is essential to personal happiness.

There are provisos. If behaviour resulting from the

satisfaction of Reactive and Secondary Wants is regarded as antisocial or in other way morally or legally problematic, any beneficial effect of its satisfaction is lost. The mental turmoil resulting from the need to satisfy the Want and satisfy the needs of society can be disastrous, producing repetitive antisocial behaviour in an individual.

There is a danger that when the pleasure derived from satisfying a single Want is achieved too easily, its satisfaction becomes habitual and addictive. Similarly if the satisfaction of a single Want is all that can be achieved, then the happiness so derived becomes the source of all pleasure in a state that is otherwise one of deprivation. 'I may be hungry and cold but I have a roof over my head.'

Akin to the world of the drug addict who sees nothing beyond the pleasure achieved by the next fix. Tobacco smokers notoriously and sadly refer to their addiction as 'my only pleasure'. People who, for their various reasons, come to accept that the achievement of that which is most easily achieved and which provides some personal 'happiness' is sufficient. People who settle for a low level of happiness, achieved through easily achieved pleasures.

Failure to satisfy a Want can result in exaggeration or over-compensation of happiness found in another, more easily attainable one. Treats and short periods of happiness are accepted as compensation for enduring other parts of life which are mundane, unattractive, abusive or worse. Working long hours in poor conditions entitles one to have a fling on Friday or Saturday night. Many people spend much of their lives doing things that provide neither happiness or satisfaction, their days relieved in the anticipation of such treats.

Over-compensation, that is, satisfying one Want at the expense of others, can produce exaggerated behaviour patterns. Especially so when the pleasure derived from satisfying a single want becomes habitual and or addictive.

Examples of Want-satisfaction over-compensation include:

A need for bodily comfort overcompensates into the need for:

excessive pampering; luxurious living; prescribed and illegal drugs; physical perfection;

rigid health and exercise routines; the absence of pain.

A need for a Sense of Security overcompensates into a need for:

wealth; possessions; home security and property defences;

insurance policies; aggressive behaviour; winning; possession of firearms and weapons; power over others.

The need to be acknowledged overcompensates into being:

a showman or entertainer; intrusive and imposing behaviour; being over-talkative;   excessive risk taking; wearing extreme fashions; defiance and intransigence.

The need to be praised overcompensates into acts of:

subservience; being a do-gooder; buying praise with gifts; over-generosity'; eliciting praise directly; boasting.

The need to feel superior overcompensates into being:

a snob; a power seeker; a Certificate collector; propagandist; dominant; the 'right address';   secretive; mysterious.

The need for companionship overcompensates into being:

overly gregarious; clinging; demanding; vulnerable to the wishes of other people.

The need to be accepting and like other people overcompensates into:

conformity through self-denial; becoming a door-mat; imitating other people; being over-sensitive to criticism; compliancy; susceptible to advertising.

The need to be found attractive overcompensates into being:

an exhibitionist; overtly sexually daring; excessively concerned with personal appearance;   seen to be wealthy and stylish; over-sensitive; vulnerable to ageist criticism.

The need to be a Protector overcompensates into being:

an over-protective parent; rigorous law enforcement; order-giving; dominant behaviour; the assumption of responsibility.

The need to explore overcompensates into being:

an adventurer; a risk-taker; a non-conformist; an anarchist; a record-breaking achiever; someone who does things that are pointless beyond self-satisfaction, i.e. walking round the world.

Primary Wants are common to all but the ways in which the

individual attempts to satisfy them will be unique to that person.

Wants are neither good or bad, nor right or wrong. They simply exist as a natural part of human development.

The ways in which Wants are satisfied may bring people into conflict. Different people with different needs and different priorities, all seeking to satisfy their various Wants at the same time. It is pointless the protector seeking to protect the vulnerable if the vulnerable seek only food.

The means by which a Want is satisfied is also an expression of individuality as the actions of one person are determined by his or her circumstances and experiences.

A single Want may not present itself as the obvious motivation for a particular action. We may not know precisely why we feel motivated to do something, only that doing that 'something' ultimately brings us pleasure; for example, visiting a bar for a drink. Is the motivation one of thirst? Perhaps but it may also be an opportunity to meet other people when the motivation might be seeking companionship, or to show-off some new clothes, or to boast about an accomplishment, or for some other reason.

Because we may not be aware of the true reason underlying our behaviour, it goes unchallenged. What purpose is there in seeking the true reason for our behaviour? Well, there are always alternative solutions, or different ways in which a Want may be satisfied. Without challenge, satisfaction becomes habitual and in fear of being denied that satisfaction, we become weakened and vulnerable. The visit to the pub is possible only as long as the pub exists, the other patrons exist, the money to pay for the drink exists....and so on.

In the pursuit of happiness or in the search for the causes of unhappiness we can look for the Primary or Secondary Wants that are unsatisfied. This is not always an easy task as a Want may have gone unsatisfied for many years. Lost in complex patterns of behaviour designed to compensate for non-satisfaction of a Want and obscured by the satisfaction of other Wants only a deep sense of being incomplete in some way, may remain.

Primary and many Secondary Wants are always positive in

74

their fulfilment. That is to say, their origins lie in the provision of basic human needs and those of simple betterment. Even though the efforts to satisfy a Primary Want may be exaggerated and perhaps cause some distress, the underlying motivation remains that of fulfilling a basic right of existence. Exaggerated behaviour may simply highlight a Want, the satisfaction of which has been neglected, denied or overlooked.

Reactive Wants are almost always negative in the appearance and in their effect. With its drive toward fulfilment centred upon the self, the motivation to satisfy a Reactive Want is uniquely personal. Being deeply personal, and indeed not even understood by the individual concerned, the motivational need to satisfy a Reactive Want may not be recognised or understood by other people. Any attempts to satisfy such a need may be seen by other people as simply manipulative, self-centred and selfish behaviour.

It is worth remembering that Reactive Wants include the passively negative traits of avoidance behaviour in its many forms. Destructive to the individual concerned but probably no more than frustrating or annoying for onlookers.

When all attempts to satisfy a Want prove futile, there is a desire to return to a state of familiarity. Return to a state of familiarity is the ultimate goal of the subconscious mind which regards all attempts at change as being potentially dangerous. (Refer to chapters on conscious/subconscious minds)

A form of contentment is to be found in being un-threatened by the uncertainty of change and the comfortably predictability of the status-quo. Justification and compensation for not searching or seeking to satisfy Wants to a greater degree than those presently existing is found in acceptance of even the most primitive and basic provision of essential needs. That is, having somewhere to live, enough money to get by on, an absence, or tolerable level of pain to endure. This is a state of mind adopted to many people in old age who live out their days in resignation of their plight.

Control by one person of another can be achieved through the denial of that person's ability to satisfy Primary Wants; by creating a state of deprivation and denial of human rights. Because the motivation to fulfil Primary Wants is so powerful, attempts at their denial is usually met with vigorous resistance. The ultimate fear of those denied human rights is that of imprisonment, the denial of freedom. A fear magnified when the prison regime is harsh and accompanied by additional threats of torture or other form of violation. All well known by dictators throughout history.

In everyday life, small deprivations and obstacles to the satisfaction of Wants, or which even threaten to do so, create anxiety and unrest. Unhappiness that is often disproportionate to the cause and an underlying cause of illness and premature death in society.

The threat may be specific, from one person to another, or vague and more generalised as when government policy flies in the face of democratic principles, freedom and a denial of human rights.

The power of Want deprivation, real, threatened or imaginary, should not be underestimated. Such threats and actions affect everyone, everyday in some way and are directly responsible for humankind's suffering and unhappiness worldwide.

Consider these effects.

The need for bodily comfort. Symptomatic of Want deprivation is the fear of:

illness; pain; poor access to or response by medical services; being cold; inadequate heating; losing one's personal belongings.

The need for a sense of security. Symptomatic of Want deprivation is the fear of or threat from:

theft; burglary; personal assault; vandalism; damage to home; boundary disputes; loss of mobility; reliance on others; loss of independence; old age.

A need to be acknowledged. Symptomatic of Want deprivation is the fear of or threat of:

being ignored; not being heard; of lack of response to complaint or request for help; isolation through illness, deafness or blindness; letters and other forms of communication going unanswered.

The need to be praised. Symptomatic of Want deprivation is fear or threat of:

criticism, especially unjust criticism' failure to achieve (almost anything); to be 'put-down', embarrassed or made fun of, especially publicly; feeling silly, ignorant and out of place.

The need to feel superior. Symptomatic of Want deprivation is the fear or threat of:

being usurped; being made redundant; having outdated skills; losing face or rank; becoming old or inadequate; a diminution of physical or mental abilities; loss of self-pride.

Need for companionship. Symptomatic of Want deprivation is a fear or threat of:

the death of a partner, divorce or separation; being denied access to a group; loss of mobility; isolation through location, illness.

The need to be like other people. Symptomatic of Want deprivation is a fear or threat of:

rejection by one's peers; the inability to dress to, or maintain other standards acceptable to peer group; being poor; not living to media imagery; unemployment.

The need to feel found to be attractive to other people. Symptomatic of Want deprivation is fear of:

disfigurement or self-perceived blemish; being under or over weight; being poor; embarrassed by some aspect of appearance; not having a (sexual) partner; being ugly.

The need to be a protector. Symptomatic of Want deprivation is fear or threat of:

being rendered powerless by any means – being old, being alone, state or police control, physical limitation, being poor, being bullied.

The need to explore. Symptomatic of Want deprivation is the fear or threat of:

any limitation of freedom – state control, law enforcement, exclusion by private ownership, confinement or imprisonment, being burdened by duties or responsibilities, being poor.

Happiness begins with Self and the ability to fulfil one's

dreams, desires and essential needs. In short, to satisfy one's Wants.

To achieve happiness, all Wants must appear satisfied and the satisfaction of one Want must not be at the cost of another Want.

As this principle is applied to the Self, so it applies to all. Helping others to achieve happiness is an essential part achieving happiness for oneself. The satisfaction of a personal Want to the detriment of the satisfaction of another person's Wants will be short lived and illusory. The Self cannot successfully act selfishly.

If you do not want another person to be happy, or willingly and knowingly deny another person happiness, then you will be unable to find lasting happiness for yourself.

Deprivation of Want satisfaction en-mass, that is throughout the populace, leads to the fragmentation of society as individuals exclude themselves from mainstream society. Such people, who may be termed 'drop-outs', seek alternative and possibly isolated lifestyles in their pursuit of happiness. However, unless these pursuits are mindful of and benefit all people, they will not prove successful.

The importance of a particular Want can be magnified, along with the happiness promised by its satisfaction. A luxurious Want can be skilfully presented as part of an Essential Want and the successful marketing of many trivial, inconsequential and wasteful products and services rely on this mental trickery.

Wants are common to everyone, though not everyone recognises them, and those who do, do not always discriminate between their relative values.

Wants are not weaknesses, though many exploit their use as such.

Wants are not negotiable but because individual needs differ, respect of those differences is essential.

The satisfaction of Wants is essential to human existence.

The happiness of individual and nation alike, demands the satisfaction of essential Wants and their satisfaction; their satisfaction must be seen as an achievable goal. Peaceful coexistence amongst people of the world cannot be achieved without respect for this common need.

The satisfaction of essential Wants is the achievement of universal liberty; respect for all people wherein lies the source of true freedom and happiness.

10.   Anxiety and Depression

Causal factors in society?

In understanding perhaps the most common single symptom presented by patients, anxiety and its associated condition, depression, it is important to consider the part sociological factors may play.

Once again we are moving into the area of commonalities; remembering that commonalities do not make for assumptions but rather an awareness of the underlying framework within which a patient's plight may be seen.

Anxiety and depression are perhaps the most widespread underlying causes of illness in mankind today. Almost without exception, people of most modern cultures appear affected by these two conditions to a greater or lesser degree.

The mildest presentation of these conditions can be seen as a disaffection with life in general, a lack of respect and an antagonistic attitude towards other people and property.

Secondary presentation is found in a superficial distancing from society, either by withdrawal into a solitary existence or in belonging to sub-groups themselves demonstrating any or all of the above characteristics.

What conditions present in contemporary life create such widespread and pervasive dispositions? What fuels this destructive predisposition in the face of the desire to create a fair and just society? Where does it go wrong?

Underlying causes of both anxiety and depression in can be found in the social and environmental conditions that have developed in a particular society. During the recent past, far-reaching effects of moral, legal and technical developments. Changes that have outstripped the abilities of many people to assimilate them or the changes brought about as a consequence. The creation of a strata of social structure occupied by those able to benefit from their exclusive access to a new technocracy able to perpetuate the need for change on such a vast scale, at such a rapid pace. A new version of an old problem. Farm verses factory via pen and paper verses typewriter to mechanical verses electronic, ad infinitum. An ever changing and seemingly inevitable, 'them and us' society.

The imposition of what is seen by many as excessive regulation and unfair or unfairly applied interference in the lives of the individual has created an almost universal resentment of "authority". Resentment for that which should command respect and which leads to disaffection and disrespect.

Whatever conditions we try to create in our domestic lives, encroachment by "The State" into the most inconspicuous corners of our lives becomes threateningly unavoidable. Personal choice of almost any kind becomes limited to options allowed by government control of one kind or another.

Examples of regulations restricting the personal freedom of the individual can be found everywhere. Restrictions on personal freedom include, in what numbers and for what reasons one is allowed to go, be or remain 'anywhere'. Also the limitations of private and public transport, public open spaces and recreational facilities, the use of the countryside and waterways and so on. When we move into fine detail the list seems endless.

Then people begin to FEAR the power of authority and in turn those empowered to administer it, people who live in fear of doing the wrong thing. Worse still, because it is sometimes impossible to know what is allowed and what is not allowed, there is the fear of unwittingly doing the wrong thing, and being subjected to the injustice of ignorance. The fear of suffering punishment carried out by people who have power over others, people who know the 'letter of the law' and who use that knowledge to their advantage, people who are themselves fearful of being seen not to fulfil the letter of the law, or who abuse their position; people who have the ability to disempower, people of whom we learn to be afraid.

Part of contemporary life is in knowing what is permitted, when, where and by whom. In simple, if harsh ways, the behaviour of the individual has become subjected to 'approval' of one kind or another but it is only in comparatively recent times such regulation has become so complex.

Over-regulation and regulation to the minutest detail has made the enforcement of ALL laws virtually impossible and the adherence to 'the law' by the individual equally so. Laws and regulations vary in their detail and application according to location, with much variation from place to place. We need only look to the times when one can shop, buy food, drink, or books (each being subject to different regulations), walk, cross the road, or stand still (loiter!), sit down (obstruction), or drink (drinking alcoholic beverages in certain public places now forbidden)to find examples.

To the' reasonable', normal thinking person all quite ludicrous but of course laws are made to protect the reasonable from the behaviour of the unreasonable but everyone suffers as everyone is prohibited from doing perfectly normal things.

Knowing what is permitted is now the province of the judiciary and the army of 'experts' plying their trade to those who fear transgression or who fall foul of legal obscurity and complexity. Too often Justice takes a back seat to bureaucracy with a result that the law, and those who devise and implement laws, fall into disrespect.

Fear is then accompanied by anger.

Domestic life has seen many changes but the pace of change has not always kept pace with that elsewhere. The protective barrier created by 'the family' and 'the family home' environment and rules, offers some protection from the pressures to change found in the outside world. The personal territory of the home enables the creation of a world reflective of the desires of the individual to the exclusion of the outside world. Privacy and some personal territory are essential to the stability and fulfilment of the individual to society as a whole.

Government departments, municipal bodies and business corporations and 'the few' have funds or enjoy positions of privilege by which they can create changes more or less at will The individual finds him or herself with very little power to either resist change or to institute major changes of their own.

The feeling of helplessness created by this differential, and particularly its maladministration is a source of much resentment, anger, frustration and public unrest.

One result is that people seek to separate themselves from the outside world, reliant on the sense of satisfaction derived from management of the personal territory over which they can exert control.

When taken to extremes this can result in excessively demonstrative behaviour centered around the home; excessive measures taken toward home security, closed circuit television, etc.; privacy by means of hedges, fences and walls; exaggerated expressions of individuality seen in home décor, artificially landscaped gardens; and the magpie syndrome creating a world of possessions. The list goes on in ways in which ordinary people seek to exercise, demonstrate and express their freedom and the (limited) power the enjoy over their personal domains. Behaviour extended to personal work space/office/desk, rooms in the home, bedroom, workshop, shed and in fact any way in which 'the self' can feel in control.

Regrettably even this security is limited, often by a lack of money, forcing most individuals back into the world they despise and resent. Property and territory is also threatened by those representative of 'authority' having legal right of entry.

Organizations whose representatives have legal rights by which they are entitled to enter your home, without your permission. These include: the police, television license authority, gas and electricity, water and telephone companies, court bailiffs, the fire service, Customs, Excise and Revenue, Local Authorities health and safety, planning and other departments; Social Services; The Armed Forces and Military Intelligence; and more...!

Not all people representing these bodies will be 'officials' in the sense of having been appointed to any office of responsibility; they will be ordinary men and women doing ordinary jobs who have access to your home and property. Not unnaturally this is in itself grounds for fears born of mistrust and suspicion of strangers endowed with such powers.

Some of the most damaging changes affecting physical and mental health have taken place in the workplace.

In modern society the greatest empowering element is money. Of prime importance is the means by which money is obtained, for most that is by way of employment of some kind. It is to be regretted that few people are fortunate enough to work in conditions conducive to their health and happiness. Fewer still carry our work that they find fulfilling or enjoyable.

The combined effects of the threats to a jealously guarded domestic life, unsatisfactory working conditions, and a sense of futility and injustice are sources of the negative malaise that pervades much of society. Living out an existence rather than enjoying a life of fulfilment is a reality that manifests in the minds of many people.

Even people who may not ordinarily succumb to these pressures may do so when faced with a personal trauma such as financial loss or health problem. Finding themselves robbed of their positive focus and who are unable to cope when confronted with the realities of underfunded public health care and the financial institutions and judiciary.

Employment, or work of some kind, is the means by which man traditionally survives – the way in which he acquires the basic necessities of life; food, clothing, shelter and warmth.

Until comparatively recent times mankind was tied closely to the land or sea, surviving on what he could produce directly from either or both. Drawing upon nature and the elements to harvest and create that necessary to support life.

Industry was 'craft' and diligence, centred on the provision of necessities. In the main, industry, including the farming industry, used natural materials occurring close to hand, frequently renewable and requiring minimal processing. There was a natural element of harmony between mankind and his place of dwelling and working. Food was taken according to season and locality. Overall mankind was closer to nature, in harmony with its cycles, and responsive to the environment responsible for and supportive of his creation.

Work and the production of goods, including food, is no longer a question of providing that necessary to ensure the continuance of life. Mankind has moved quickly from being a manager of resource to a creator of virtually anything that takes his fancy. Wilfulness that makes sympathetic use of the Earth's resources impossible and the destruction of his environment inevitable. Mankind now faces his biggest challenge, that of changing sufficiently in order to meet the challenges of a new and unpredictable future. Nothing creates fear more easily than uncertainty and unpredictability. Mankind has surpassed himself in creating his own source of depressing anxiety.

I may seem to have laboured some of the points made but the sense of frustration and anger towards those entrusted with 'our future' and who have now lost that trust, combined with feelings of helplessness and fear for the future seriously undermine the health and well-being of many people.

Money, in itself worthless, has become an object of possession in its own right, no longer simply representing worth or barter. The accumulation of money has become acceptable and is indeed encouraged as a means of provision for the future. The accumulation of money is felt by many to be an accumulation of power, the reverse is certainly true, the poor being regarded as powerless and subjected to treatment they would not otherwise suffer.

Why and how did we move from a socially domestic, communal way of life to one of isolation? Once again the answer is in part fear, the fear of being without, of disadvantage, indeed even of losing life itself. The fear is of being without (money) in a society reliant on the ability to buy/spend (consumerism).

A society equating freedom and respect to the possession of money and property is a vulnerable society, creating in its members a fear of being without money or the means by which it may be obtained.

Fear of being without or having insufficient money leads some people to criminal activity in a bid to gain power and respect. That such people may be regarded as anti-social is a misnomer, they are simple products of a single society. An example of the importance of the need for a sense of responsibility by those in authority comes from UK Prime Minister Thatcher, who once said that there was no such thing as 'society' . Then in the name of offering freedom to the individual, led her country into an arguably disastrously damaging race for personal wealth. 30 years later UK Prime minister Cameron stated his goal of creating a 'new society'.

The use of money is an essential ingredient of modern society but ceases to offer true benefit when held to have a value of its own. The demonstration of financial wealth has become a measure of success which has lead to the practice of making available highly priced, environmentally wasteful, 'fashion' goods, their high price making them a mark of exclusivity. Unlike those produced for economy, practicality, durability and appropriateness for use.

Nurturing the need to exhibit status are purveyors of haut couture fashion. Their clientele people who become an object of envy and emulation. The role of the 'exclusive' label has invaded virtually every aspect of daily life from clothes to cars, kitchens to coffee the means by which status may be preserved is guaranteed – at a price. The more ridiculously expensive the item the greater the status. Wastefulness perpetuated but wastefulness finding imitation in every strata of society.

The pressure to acquire ever more money by which status may continue to be demonstrated brings further problems both to those who have money and those who seek to emulate the wealthy.

Conflict between employers and employees and the fear shared by both at the prospect of losing their source of income is one effect. Positions of power demonstrated by the employer who threatens the employee with dismissal and the employee, essential to creating the employer's profits, threatening resignation.

Integral to the fear of losing status is the fear of rejection. The feeling that one's acceptance by other people is determined at least in part by one's ability to pay. The gulf between the haves and have not's perpetuated by those who find their need for security satisfied in 'having'.

Bridges may be built enabling those who prove themselves worthy to cross the social divide but this is subject to approval and many who succeed find their presence in the new strata uncomfortable or worse, unacceptable.

The have's create their own fear by having. The more you have the more you can lose and the more you spend protecting what you have. The more you earn, the more vulnerable you feel as you compete with other people also feeling pressured. Dog eat dog and the more you have the greater the fear. False comparisons and wasteful competition is the result.

The need for 'wealth' has led to the production of goods that have no purpose beyond their indulgence. The combined need for money and status has resulted in the over-production of goods and services that contribute nothing to the society supporting them.

We now have armies of people paid to administer the use of other people's money, from government staff collecting revenue and paying benefits, to the financial service industry, handling everything from credit card transactions to money lending. It is a business that does not produce anything beyond servicing its own ends and is another arm of a bureaucracy financed by the society is 'serves'.

Western Society is reliant on technology for the provision of essential and many non-essential products. Both come increasingly from 'new world' sources in India, China and South America. Herein lies the seed of a new future fear as the power to control almost every aspect of daily life is passed from the political and wealthy to the technically expert; more specifically the relatively few people controlling, programming and operating computer based technology.

Also, that these people are no longer 'us'.

Manipulation of every kind of information held in and transmitted between computers is possible in every field of usage . By manipulation I mean the way in which information is presented, misused, withheld, massaged and otherwise tampered with, as well as all manner of illegal, unethical and seriously questionable ways by which information is subjected to interference. Much interference is secret, that is, the undisclosed manipulation of information by state and other departments.

Some interference is no more than what might be described as imaginative public relations, the presentation of that which is sought. There is manipulation of financial affairs of all kinds, from government taxation and spending to company reports, share prices and dividends. Military control is exercised through covert surveillance, the creation of misinformation, including the manipulation of those to whom such agencies answer.

The modern world is run increasingly by remote control, through software programmers, IT operators and hackers. Even the wealthy and hitherto powerful have become vulnerable to the activities of the subversive who, without clear badge of identity, can wreak havoc on individual and society alike from the safe haven of anonymity.

Here we see the emergence or concealment of solitary individuals occupying positions of great power. People who are able to bring major changes to the world yet who go unrecognized and whose influence may be unrestrained. People answering no social responsibility beyond their own vision and agenda. From the perpetrators of identity theft who potentially threaten people individually to those involved in financial and industrial and commercial manipulation on grand scales. This invisible menace is set to become an increasing source of fear in modern society. While effected by individuals it is worth speculating on how much is sanctioned or instigated by state governments, commercial organizations or wealthy individuals.

Freedom, independence and personal survival are natural rights conferred on everyone as birthrights. The rights exist because the individual exists. These same rights, when expressed collectively or communally should therefore also preserve the freedom of the individual through a supportive social structure.

Social structures of this kind are usually thought of as democracies but most modern democracies can only ever offer an individual conditional freedom. Like conditional love, conditional freedom is not that to which most, if not all people would aspire.

A social society based upon the provision of mutual support demands an effective administrative body, a bureaucracy. Much of the work carried out by the members of the body, will be concerned with the provision of basic needs but many will be involved solely in the enforcement of regulations.

In any society there will be an element of dissent and so long as the aims and administration of that society are deemed on the whole to be fair, those in dissent will present no great problem. However, when there is injustice and mal-administration, those in dissent offer a voice to people who might otherwise remain silent. Any dissenting voice is seen as a threat to that administration. From Government ministers to Town Hall clerks. Fear at the top, fear at the bottom, unrest in the middle.

A huge over-simplification but this is the essence of my hypothesis.

In short, a politically socialist society tends to fail through:

a) Mistrust by those in positions of power and the subsequent creation of unwieldy legislation that is costly to implement and which stifles incentives.

b) The greed of a minority whose desire for superiority and power leads to a systematic abuse both within the administrative body and the public at large.

An alternative structure is one based on the right of the individual to self-determination as opposed to one of social conscience. Often misrepresented as offering the right to freedom of the individual, this is a society reliant on the survival of the fittest. The downfall of such a society is in the creation of 'winners' and 'losers'. Extremists of any kind present a threat to the legislation and to society as a whole.

Winners present a threat because wealth can take people beyond mainstream society *and* beyond the powers of its administration. Royalty, the aristocracy, industrial barons and land owners whose 'society' is exclusive of ordinary people. The power of great wealth is often combined with an hereditary entitlement.

Losers are seen as a threat when they drop out of mainstream society to form a subculture putting them too beyond administrative control. Also known as the 'black economy' a body of people who avoid the control of many branches of government. Individually their reasons for doing so include political disagreement, rebellion against unfair rules and regulations, social dissent and criminal activity. All live in fear of discovery by the administration, itself in fear of their presence.

Modern societies move from one governing experience to another. From the political extremes of both left and right, beneficial moderating influence is often spiritual in origin. Political influence is exerted on administrations by religious bodies, pacifist groups and humanitarian organizations, often aided by the occurrence of a severe threat to life or disaster.

While such spiritual influences should properly be regarded as relevant and moderating (if for no other reason than their passive and compassionate nature), their intervention is often resented by the political administration. Perhaps because they highlight its shortcomings but perhaps also because, by their very nature they are beyond political control, and so a potential threat to society.

Where two major religions exert political as well as spiritual power, society may find itself divided, a situation which, when conflated by the previously mentioned effects of winners and losers, fear is rife.

Societies' roots lie in the self-protective behaviour of spiritual, intellectual and cultural extremes whose ideals shape and reshape the world in which we live. A single emotion binds all people regardless of their economic, educational or social class, the emotion of fear.

Fear of 'others' should they be allowed positions of power, fear of being disadvantaged, fear of lawlessness, fear of injustice, fear of going unheard, fear of almost anything imaginable.

Fear, fear and more fear, sources of which are the tools of those manipulating society for their own ends. Who is there then to trust? Ask anyone and your reply will be likely be to "Trust no one."

Restricted, controlled, checked, directed, observed, monitored, cajoled, pushed, led, misled, encouraged and denied; everywhere people find themselves bound tighter, prisoners in their own prisons.

The minds of men and women become submerged in hopelessness, apathy, personal ineffectiveness removing from them any sense of responsibility. Disillusioned they look in vain for fairness and freedom. Religion promises divine intervention, a saviour, and a better tomorrow.

Chains that bind the guilty bind the innocent more so. Mistrust is widespread, the gulf between the haves and the have-nots grows, cultures within society separate and the greater the differences the greater are the fears.

The greater the suspicion, the greater control over society increases. Perceived freedom of speech and the freedom to enjoy thrill seeking activities and pastimes become tools of authority. Mass media gives unprecedented opportunities of criticism and ridicule. Rebellious voices may speak with a common voice but are reduced to a source of entertainment, rather than speaking to effect.

The growth of technology now provides many means of diversion and entertainment. Pleasure seeking becomes a means of channelling the excess energies of potential dissent into harmless activity of controllable cul-de-sacs where spontaneity and freedom of expression can be discharged in 'harmless' fun.

Enforcement agencies, known and covert are there to make sure any potentially dangerous overspill of dissent, objection and frustration is contained and eliminated.

The prisons bulge, the armies of law enforcement grow. With limited budgets the administration diverts resources away from social welfare needs in favour of wars and national security, further depriving the weakest and poorest members of society.

Thousands perish in innocent poverty and thousands suffer in the protection of the affluent creating even greater social differences. The gulf grows.

In growing strong, nations, societies, then too easily grow weak and vulnerable. Virtual reality is no substitute for effective dialogue and change. Throughout history suppression and diversion have shown themselves to be ticking bombs.

The anxiety and depression prevalent in the world have their roots in history and are perhaps inbred, making it difficult for mankind to break free from the cycles of the past. Frustrations and restrictions abound and feelings of personal ineffectiveness and resignation as well as those of rebellion are passed from one generation to another. Anger and apathy side by side in the hollow voice of protestation and fear that is itself feared.

On encountering a personal crisis it is understandable to look for causes beyond our control. It is not so much that we are loathe to accept responsibility for our actions but recognize that so much of what we are subjected to is the result of other people's careless, or cruel or unjust actions.

While it is true we suffer and benefit from the actions of other people, we cannot divorce ourselves from the society to which we also belong. The causes of many of today's problems are historical but we remain responsible in choosing to maintain, destroy or recreate the structure of our society.

The real problem lies in realizing that choice exists and not being frustrated by the legislature elected to act for us. Too often we are overwhelmed by feelings of hopelessness or anger. Finding those to whom we have delegated responsibility failing us and feeling helpless.

Seeing beyond this state may require us to elevate out thinking in order to find our own pathway to happiness. This is where counselling begins to bridge the void between earthly reality and that which is beyond. An interesting path offering another dimension to counselling and personal realisation.

11.   Anxiety, Stress and Fear.

Definitions, avoidance and management.

Anxiety is a state of fear created in the mind by one's imagination.

True fear is of the moment, anxiety is a fear of the moment to come: a state of anxiety may therefore seem to precede one of a state of true fear but it is important to separate the two. Imaginative fears fashion every aspect of our lives and are the result of the mind's efforts to restrain us from doing anything which might take us into a fearfully imagined future.

In simple physical terms, stress can be defined as strain or tension, indicating the presence of a force or power exerted upon a solid body which is then said to be 'stressed'.

In terms of human psychology, stress is usually taken to mean an influence disturbing or interfering with the natural harmony or equilibrium of a living body.

For human beings with the combined capabilities of memory and imagination, fearful real-life experiences, the anticipation of threats to life and personal freedoms are common place. For many human beings, stress induced by a fear of a real and present threat or an imagined or anticipated threat are a part of life.

Causes of stress in humans can result from physical injury or disease, exposure to harsh environments, deprivation of many kinds, and emotional disturbances: it is the latter with which we associate the term anxiety. It is sometimes difficult however to draw a line between the direct effects of injury, disease and deprivation and the mental anticipation of their recurrence which will now include memories of treatment, care or lack of it, etc., etc.. Hence a revival of the initial trauma is becomes a complex state of anxiety with many facets.

Causes included under the heading emotional disturbance' include: frustration, anger, injustice, fear of criticism, and the unrealistic demands of other people, or of one's self. The amount of stress or anxiety caused is determined by how much pressure an individual takes on board, and this is a reflection of how he sees himself relative to other people. (Does he see himself as being dominant, equal or subordinate to another person, or other people?).

The effects of anxiety, that is to say a sense of fear arising from the perception of an imaginary or anticipated threat, are the same as those caused by the presence of a real danger. In the biological sense, anxiety creates responses in the human body similar to those produced by fear.

The exposure to anything evoking a sense of danger, real or imaginary, triggers reflexes designed to protect and enhance an individual's prospects of survival. In order to survive, the 'body' concerned must either flee from or face and overcome, the threat. This is referred to as the **flight or fight** syndrome and the physical preparations necessary to accomplish either are the same.

The physical changes that take place in the body in times of stress are many and complex, beginning with a stimulation of the adrenal system. Increased action of the heart raises the pulse rate and blood pressure. Glucose levels in the blood stream rise. Blood supply to the muscles is increased whilst that too many other organs, including the stomach, is decreased. Muscles tense, breathing becomes more rapid and senses heightened and made more alert. Hearing is more acute and the eyes dilate to admit more light because of which people in stress often find their sensitivity to sound and light troublesome. A desire for solitude, to be alone in a darkened, quiet place is symptomatic.

Other reactions include an urge to empty the stomach, bowel and bladder. This may be no more than feeling mildly upset for a short while. Immediately after the initial reaction the entire digestive and excretory system is suppressed. People repeatedly stressed or persistently anxious are likely to suffer from constipation and digestive problems predisposing them to a variety of secondary symptoms.

Not all sources of stress are obvious because some arise from inappropriate subconscious reactions, however that fact that the reactions are inappropriate points to the anxiety originating in the subconscious.[see separate notes on conscious/subconscious mind]. Anxiety originating in the subconscious is commonly responsible for **panic attacks,** the complex symptom most feared by suffers.

In simple terms, a panic attack occurs when energy, created by anxiety/stress reactions, discharges spontaneously and vigorously. Symptomatically the sufferer may experience palpitations and tightness and constriction of the chest. Limbs tremble and shake, the skin feels cold and clammy. There may be visual disorientation, giddiness and feelings of unreality. All these symptoms are natural and will be counteracted by normal self-balancing mechanisms, though when a panic attack strikes it is difficult to remember or believe that this is so.

Symptomatically, in preparation for great muscular activity the blood has become loaded with oxygen and glucose. In the absence of activity and an accompanying depletion of oxygen and sugar levels, deep breathing is no longer necessary and muscles charged with fuel discharge energy by trembling while breathing becomes shallow.

The skin feels cold because of a restricted blood flow. Blood supply to the skin has been withdrawn to enhance supply to the muscles and minimize external bleeding in the event of being attacked and wounded. Part of the body's fear defence mechanism is the production of oil (sebum) and sweat which, when combined make the skin slippery and the body more difficult for an adversary to hold. Anxiety sufferers may also display a variety of skin conditions and problems caused or aggravated by their stress condition.

In addition to the primary reactions of fight or flight, the presence of anxiety may be revealed by the presence of any or all of three secondary or modified reactions, **avoidance, neglect and succumbing.** These variances are demonstrated by the sufferer avoiding a person, situation or subject; neglecting duties or responsibilities, even though their existence is acknowledged; or succumbing to a person or situation with resignation, though not without resentment and loss of self-respect.

Anxiety has a beneficial role to play in preparing us for

chosen or unavoidable situations. The nervousness felt before a contest or presentation, a touch of stage fright, butterflies in the tummy all increase strength and perception helping us meet the awaiting challenge.

The negative effects of stress arise when we find ourselves in situations to which we are unsuited, or that we feel unable to handle satisfactorily, or have been imposed upon us. It is a fine line between reactions which help and those which hinder. While some anxiety reflexes can act as useful spurs to performance, increasing alertness and speed of response, others, such as muscular tension, can deny fluidity, delicacy and free flowing responses.

Similarly in real situations the effects can seem at odds with the desired effect. Fear is a normal reaction to what appears to be a threat to life. The threat may be real in the sense of obvious and imminent danger, or implicit in warning of the consequences of a certain course of action. The effects on the body are intended to sharpen perception and release energy, however, when acute, fear can paralyze, produce confusion or incompetence – frightened rabbit, headless chicken.

Anxiety is a distressing and perhaps prolonged state of fear produced by the perception of a threat, well-founded or otherwise. In the form of worry it is probably one of the most commonly shared conditions of human life. The effects of anxiety overall are not helpful and if persistent can be damaging to health.

Anxiety could be thought of as frustrated fear. A sense of fear that cannot then let go of the physical and mental energy it has created. A state of frustration perpetuated by a mental preoccupation with the initial problem and worry about physical symptoms that are not readily explained to the satisfaction of the sufferer.

Much anxiety arises from feeling unloved to some degree: a lack of security or love, especially protective love, extending into all areas of life. Without a sense of being loved it is easy to lose the sense of self-value, symptomized by a lack of respect for one's existence or entitlement to exist as an entity of worth.

Regrettably bureaucratic and legislative injustices and the sense of personal disempowerment are rife in society. Modern work practices, short term employment contracts, bullying and many other factors create complex background levels of personal anxiousness to which many people have succumbed.

This is not only bad news as far as their health is concerned but for society as a whole, resulting in lawless and anti-social behaviour. The unloved, disrespected individual has less mental and emotional space with which to cope with life's threats and personal anxieties.

Everyday anxiety or stress produces mild, though noticeable effects. Typical symptoms include flatulence, nausea, aches, pains and a sense of unease, sleep disturbances, constipation, headaches, mood swings, lack of energy and the use of drugs ranging from caffeine, nicotine, alcohol, analgesics, antacids, etc., to prescribed medication and illegal substances.

If causes of anxiety persist the symptoms can worsen and may lead to more serious health problems which then cause additional stress. The presentation of secondary symptoms such as stomach ulcers, irritable bowel syndrome, haemorrhoids, hypertension and what may be called mysterious transitory pains and sensations can easily become a source of anxiety.

The anxiety sufferer may then enter a secondary stage where the original cause of the anxiety is replaced by the sufferer's focus on bodily and even mental symptoms. Attention is diverted to deal with physical health problems which, in their presentation, are real and obvious, not simply of emotional, mental circumstances. Additionally the sufferer also finds opportunity for symptomatic avoidance and neglect of work and responsibilities.

Visits to the doctor and hospital become an acceptable way of life. There is also the bonus found in the elation and temporary relief from worry as each diagnosis reveals an absence of abnormality or physical cause for concern. There is also the added attraction of the sympathy offered by family and friends. If the sufferer perceives that 'being ill' is the only way love and attention can be elicited from those from whom it is sought, (the absence of which is also most certainly contributory to the original state of anxiety), there is a danger that suffering will be found preferential to losing that love.

After many years of suffering a variety of primary and secondary symptoms, medication and the establishment of an illness focused personal regime, sight is lost of the simplicity and normality of life as it was intended. Tranquillizers and other medication interfere further with the body's mechanisms.

Based on a fear of the unknown and the prospect of an imagined negative outcome, potentially stress-inducing situations have existed since the dawn of human consciousness. This is the kind of stress that is typified by a question beginning, "What if"; hypothetical questions without meaning or answer beyond those to be found in the imagination.

Sources of stress may enter our lives when we find ourselves in situations to which we are not suited, or feel it so. Any situation not holding the prospect of a successful or happy outcome is stressful. This includes following a lifestyle which, were we to admit it, offends our deeper sense of moral values, our conscience.

This may include a lifestyle or association with someone denying us freedom of expression or inhibiting the development and fulfilment of our potential, to grow into entities of productive, loving and caring purpose. Identification of these sources of stress demands total honesty. Without honest self-admission and questioning we cannot hope to begin to address the causes of our unhappiness.

Avoidance and neglect are good indicators of stress and this includes those who choose not to confront the causes of their unhappiness. People who want to live happily and in good conscience but who find themselves unable to "walk their talk". Instead choosing either a life of parsimonious isolation and self-denial or to lose themselves in social excesses ranging from "retail therapy" to drug abuse. Helpful alternatives include Talking-Therapy/Counselling, Mindfulness or finding an absorbing interest.

Prolonged exposure to anxiety can underlie problems of

excessive weight and an inability to control the urge to eat and drink, even if the causes are now long in the past. From birth and throughout our early years, food, comfort and love become closely associated essentials, all involving touch and other expressions of loving care.

Parents unable to give their children sufficient emotional love or who feel it so, or who cannot spend as much time with their children as they would like may use food and drinks to compensate for their perceived shortcomings. Food and in later years money and gifts, become substitutes for more personal expressions of love.

People who feel deprived of emotional comfort, security and love, or who have been exposed to such feelings in their formative years, may turn to eating and drinking in an attempt to satisfy their emotional hunger. It must be remembered that much is in the mind of the beholder who may in fact be loved and cherished but not in the way that is felt or desired. Such erroneously perceived deprivation (in childhood) may have existed only in comparison with another child or children, siblings or beyond the family. Again honest self-appraisal is necessary.

The dietary picture is further complicated because some foods and drinks containing mood enhancing chemicals, some natural, others not so. Chocolate confectionery contains caffeine and sugars of various kinds elevating adrenaline and blood-glucose levels in the body, resulting in a mood/energy lift, however, after this initial lift the carbohydrate is converted into serotonin and phenyl ethylamine, affecting the brain and promoting feelings of sleepiness and tranquillity, and enhancing mood respectively. There are other benefits to eating pure chocolate in moderation but the use of confectionery chocolate with high sugar content to help achieve a more peaceful state of mind has serious negative implications.

Chocolate can be mildly physically addictive and powerfully emotionally so. When questioned more deeply, chocoholics may be found to be emotional people suffering a secret or un-admitted lack of emotional fulfilment or repressed sexual or emotional need. Or not!

The skin, being the largest single organ of the body is perhaps that most directly and obviously affected by the presence of stress, anxiety and fear. In the developing embryo, pre-birth, the skin and the nervous system evolve from the same cells and remain closely linked.

When a state of fear is experienced, a chain of reactions is set in place which directly and swiftly affect the skin. Blood supply is withdrawn from the skin, to be concentrated in the muscles, resulting in a visible pallor and loss of heat. Skin pores open dramatically increasing the release of sebum and perspiration. The result is cold, clammy greasy skin and when these reactions are repeated persistently, the combination of excess oils and diminished blood-flow inhibits the healing of pre-existing problems and gives rise to a variety of skin conditions.

The cycle of itching and scratching which accompanies these conditions also satisfies a psychological need associated with anxiety, that of the need to be touched. Self-touching, of which scratching is but one form, is an exaggerated form of holding and stroking (comforting actions); or actions of pleasurable intimacy (petting). Causes of itching may be purely psychological or a combination of emotional and physical circumstances but the fact that itching and scratching may be compensation for a lack of pleasurable and reassuring loving tactile pleasure should not be overlooked.

Lip chewing, eyebrow and hair pulling may be extreme examples of this same lack of much needed tactile pleasure and attention seeking self-reassurance.

The effects of stress on any one individual and the identification and removal of the causes of that stress are directly related to that individual's make-up. His or her willingness and ability to admit and confront the problem, to seek its origins and then take appropriate action is dependent on previously outlined factors of individuality.

All sufferers benefit from understanding something of the nature of their problem. While each patient will present a unique set of symptoms and circumstances resulting in the stress presented, certain factors will point toward the origins of stress.

Understanding that these common areas exist, that his/her problem is one that is perhaps shared by others, and that in this respect he is 'normal', is usually a good place from which to start. I have therefore put together some of the common factors of circumstance underlying human anxiety.

Anticipatory Stress

The point around which the stress factor appears to pivot is that of personal awareness, that is, the combination of individual perception and intimate and especially mental interpretation.

Potentially stressful situations have always existed and will no doubt continue to do so. It is the way in which these situations are viewed and interpreted which determines how an individual will relate to them and the subsequent effects they will then have.

Stress, in the context of the manifestation of certain physical and mental reactions, is taken to mean the creation of a state of anxiety, with symptoms paralleling those of fear.

Anxiety finds its primary manifestation in self-doubt, negative self-questioning and a loss of confidence, accompanied by a diminished sense of mental and physical control and ability. We do not feel afraid when victory is certain! Herein lies a clue to the successful treatment of anxiety states – the assurance of victory and removal of threat of failure (judgment) is a path to the restoration of confidence.

Usually, though not always, anxiety states arise from intimate mental reactions to particular stimuli. A point of clarity: sub-conscious **reactions** take place automatically, without conscious desire while **responses** are actions of conscious choice.

Individual perception is based firstly on what we see, hear, touch, taste and smell and secondly on how our minds interpret what we have sensed, (for the time being intuitive or sixth sense perception is set aside). We then endeavour to identify the nature and meaning of our sensations by comparing what we presently sense with previous similar experiences. This sub-conscious process is automatic and virtually instantaneous.

As brain cells are stimulated, each experience creates a

unique inter-cellular pathway, a network of nerve pathways, each representing a particular experience. The more often a pathway is used, that is, the more often a particular sensation is experienced, be it sound, smell, taste, touch or sight, the more pronounced that particular pathway becomes, making it easier and more likely the brain will use that route.

Any single specific sensory sensation can activate pathways of associated memories as well as those directly related to the obvious one presently experienced. Because this function is at a subconscious level the images or memories triggered may seem to come into the mind as random thoughts, unrelated to anything of which one is presently conscious.

When something sensed seems similar to one we are already familiar with, it is possible that the brain will tend to follow established brain cell pathways and integrate the new with the old. This is helpful to our faculties of evaluation and judgment, presenting us with a broad picture containing various elements of a subject or situation. However, this broad picture may also include irrelevances which cloud or prejudice judgment bringing us to see what we expect or want to see.

We tend to think and act in predictable patterns and make assumptions based on what we already understand, some of these assumptions are personal but many are common. A subconscious mind function that illusionists use to trick us and lead us away from simple logic.

In our earthly life we can never again start from scratch. It is impossible to have the freshness of an unwritten book. **We can only ever start from where we are but we can always try to look at life afresh and present ourselves with a blank page on which to write 'tomorrow'.**

Not all memories come from first hand experiences. Much of what we accept as 'true and real' is based upon the recollections of other people which may themselves have been retold many times. In this way fact and non-fact, possible and probable, real and imaginary become inextricably jumbled. Even when a factual account is passed from one person to another the account can never be complete or entirely true to fact because each will relate differently to the information.

As human beings we lack truly objective insight and are unable to question experiences from any position other than from our own peculiar and unique standpoint.

As we go through life we make generalized assumptions reflecting our personality, ability, desires and the circumstances in which we find ourselves. Our conclusions are prejudiced by previous experiences, our assumptions about the future and the assessment of our abilities similarly flawed. Driven by belief and desire we act with as much freedom as we can allow ourselves in the shadow of the presence of other people. Wrapped up in all this are the sources of our anxieties, worry-some assumptions and false drawn conclusions.

Stress enters our lives when we anticipate that the future will at some future time present us with a challenge we will be unable to avoid, the ultimate fear being that of our own death, or that of a loved one.

Reacting to the anticipated confrontation, the mind tries to provide us with as much information as possible, in the process presenting us with questions of "What if this or that?' In attempting to find answers to its hypothetical questions we find our thoughts flooded with "knowledge", first hand, second hand, accurate, inaccurate and in their sources, questionable. Our conclusions drawn from this mish-mash will be either comforting or frightening, reassuring or depressing according to our 'mood'.

"What ifs?" are unanswerable questions designed to stimulate and prepare us for fight or flight action. If the perceived threat is anything other than immediate, the resulting physical and mental changes taking place in the body leave us sensitively tense. When prolonged the worry becomes embedded in our thought patterns, our nerve pathways, resulting in persistent anxiousness and energy depletion.

Anticipatory stress begins the moment we realize we *may* be faced with something we cannot cope with or someone to whom we feel inferior and powerless.

Dealing with anticipatory stress.

In the avoidance of pessimistic anticipation, three specific facets or elements should be considered.

Firstly, the need to discriminate between fact and fiction, news and speculation, the possible and the probable and above all, discernment between personal reality and circumstances and those of other people.

Secondly, to accept personal responsibility *and* accept that one's abilities have not yet been fully tested. Only by stretching to meet new challenges do we grow.

Thirdly and perhaps most importantly is the ability to differentiate between the reality of **now** and the anticipated and imagined unreality of that which is not yet in form.

We may not be able to ignore or rationalize all our misinterpreted and inaccurate memories but we can try to stop taking more misinformation on board. In this respect it is important to be discerning in what we allow ourselves to accept or what become engaged, including: gossip, newspaper reports, news broadcasts, speculative debate, propaganda, sales hype and hot-air talk.

Focus! Your time is too valuable to waste on such things, control is self-control and you will go where your search for enlightened fulfilment takes you.

Objective Anxiety

The seeds of much anxiety experienced in adult life are sown in the early years. While the child accepts a great deal in happy ignorance of any potential danger, much in the world around him is new and can be found frightening.

These early feelings can be resurrected by similarities of association in later years and prove problematic because their true cause, that is the cause of fear perceived in childhood, is now a distant and subconscious memory. A situation further complicated by the fact that even though a state of anxiety is induced by the subconscious reaction, there may be no cause for concern now.

Common to this type of anxiety are reactions toward certain people, places and objects triggering negative feelings with which they were associated in the past. Usually only the feelings are experienced, not the memory of the earlier incident giving rise to them, thus leaving the true cause of present time anxiety a mystery. This can cause further concern and it is important to explain the structure of the mental processes behind their reactions.

The consciously remembered fears of childhood can remain while subconscious memories and the feelings associated with them, fade. Childhood fears arising through illness and misheard or poorly understood words associated with illness; family quarrels, especially those involving threats of desertion; repeated threats of "something awful" happening being used as a means of discipline or even as a joke can all lead to the child feeling insecure and fearful. Common triggers include facial characteristics, tones of voice, accents and times of day. Both consciously remembered and subconsciously activated memories combine in this process and present a challenge to the therapist. Beware the false trail of 'the obvious' answer that may be put forward by the patient.

The result can be a child who is anxious by nature and who grows up feeling apprehensive towards new and unknown situations. Nervous and hyper-sensitive to criticism, lacking confidence. Forever worrying about doing the right thing, of being found unacceptable and being unworthy of love.

To some degree we are all subjected to this kind of anxiousness and as we grow older find the power of old and unsubstantiated fears wanes. However, when younger, if subjected to particularly strong reactions, childhood experiences can be responsible for a truly debilitating level of anxiety.

Overcoming this type of anxiety can be achieved by firstly remembering that the cause of this type of anxiety is almost certainly an earlier experience. It is anxiety associated with the past, *not* the present. This means that the reactions presently experienced can be safely ignored. Building on this perspective, self-reassurance through positive, truthful affirmations can overcome the subconscious impulses that created the feelings in the first place quite quickly. Such self-reassurance also avoids the sufferer becoming even more anxious about his anxiety. By regaining control, confidence is restored making control of any future attacks easier.

Subjective Anxiety

I use this term to describe anxiety arising from sources entirely within the mind of the sufferer; that is to say where the presence of external stimulus is unnecessary.

Fears associated with thoughts of losing control, of one's self or a situation; fears of the consequences of one's actions, of behaving irrationally, of doing the wrong thing or of making a fool of one's self fall into this category.

Most people experience this kind of fear from time to time and such fears are normal. They arise from life circumstances, the effects are usually transient and therapeutic aid unnecessary for recovery. However, repetitive exposure to a particular person, situation or other stimulus may produce an habitually anxious state, the symptoms of which are at least inconvenient, at worst disabling.

Fears of this type may have a strong sexual connotations, for example, the fear of compulsively touching someone, even a stranger, intimately; of taking one's clothes of in public or of finding one's self unclothed in public; or of saying something, perhaps sexually inappropriate.

There are very strong grounds to believe that such fears are created by the subconscious in an attempt to ensure that we *do not* do the very things we fear we might do. It is likely that such fears are closely linked childhood experiences and discipline, especially where sexual behaviour was strongly associated with 'badness'.

Because most sexual urges and compulsions are instinctive rather than lascivious, thoughts and reactions of a sexual nature are a natural part of life. They may be more noticeable in the presence of sexually orientated stimuli and reinforced by individual personality and tendencies but never the less, all still quite natural.

In theory the risk is always there and behavioural outlets may be disguised in actions ranging from the friendly pat or hug to the barely concealed grope. Generally though the fear is a mental over reaction and on those occasions when perhaps we do go 'too far' we are likely to be quickly and sharply reminded of it, embarrassment acting as a further brake on future urges.

Focusing on the 'good', the best of our nature and living in good conscience is the best approach. Accepting also that 'bad' thoughts are not so much bad as unbridled or uninhibited, coming spontaneously into our minds can be dismissed with ease is the simplest way to approach this type of anxiety.

Suppressive Anxiety

Here we encounter anxiety arising from sources the true nature and origins of which are hidden within the mind and otherwise unknown. Because of their nature and the fact that their causes are located in and concealed by the subconscious mind, fears of this kind are the most difficult to deal with. The sufferer may sense a dark or secretive aspect to his problem but not show anything of this behaviourally.

Suppressed fear, and by this I refer to the cause of the anxiety not the anxiety itself, which is only too apparent, can be based on a sense of morality, frequently sexual. This type of anxiety is then accompanied by a sense of guilt the cause for which remains a mystery.

Throughout life but especially in the formative years, being told that certain thoughts, desires and actions are wrong when in fact they are perfectly normal, create feelings of guilt. When such thoughts, desires and actions are an inherent part of one's physical and mental make-up, they are difficult to avoid or deny, resulting in their secretive repetition, and of course, feelings of guilt.

In submitting to 'forbidden desires' the need for secrecy is paramount, the risk of discovery frightening and the shame of discovery abominable. Repeated submission creates repeated anxiousness, guilt and justification; the mind's solution? Bury the guilt far away from conscious thought in the sense that by avoiding the guilt the anxiety is also avoided.

Our secret now safe we continue pursuing our forbidden but private desires and practices, less guiltily but somehow remaining anxious in case we be discovered. Thoughts of the embarrassment that would be suffered should we be found out, induces a pattern of 'safe' behaviour concealing our secretive practices *and* thoughts and actions associated with that which is 'forbidden'. Hang ups about sexual practices, lovemaking, masturbation and all manner of variances fall into this category. Lovemaking in the dark avoids the body betraying 'forbidden' desire.

Underlying suppressive anxiety are the various indoctrinations and taboos to which we have been exposed. Family, friends, culture, church and society make suppressive anxiety very much of civilization's making.

Because the guilt remains secret, it is subject to remission and the sufferer to relief from its grip, by the sufferer's ability to either forgive himself or accept that his fear and his guilt are inappropriate. Forgiveness, essentially here self-forgiveness, is the ultimate answer and the resolution of such cases may well demand a spiritual or religious element be taken into account. Religious confession is one route but when the true cause of the guilt is unknown only the careful examination of present day behaviour, thoughts and desires may reveal the clues enabling the cause to be brought to light. Success demands counselling skills of the highest order.

Without admission or forgiveness, abhorrence of the forbidden acts leads to self-loathing and self-punishment. This may result in the denial of sexuality and its avoidance, for example feeling unworthy of being loved and remaining unattached; self-harm and mutilation having the effect of attracting sympathy and fulfilling the need for punishment; and sexual practices offering relief through expression yet which remain secretive or socially challenging and unacceptable, such as might be experienced in homosexual relationships.

All people have within their subconscious minds causes of feelings of guilt going beyond those of simple good conscience. Offering the patient a perspective that may be found helpful is to begin by reminding ourselves of our humanness *and* our spirituality. Here part of the technique is that the counsellor joins with the patient in adopting a shared view, hence a safe and respected view.

As sentient beings of evolving thought processes, we should see self-acceptance as an essential tool of progression; and that the transgression of historically based prejudices that have little to do with fact, goodness or simply human physicality is little cause for concern.

Obsessional States of Anxiety.

A suppressed anxiety may develop to the point where focus on the symptoms and conditioned behaviour patterns becomes an obsession. Typically the sufferer feels compelled, by fear and doubt, to adhere to certain routines, eat only certain foods, avoid certain places etc.. The sufferer may also be preoccupied with physical or mental routines such a counting or saying special words or prayers.

Overwhelming feelings of shame, shyness and inferiority can also fall into this category, along with blushing. There is no obvious reason for these feelings and symptoms which, should they persist, modify and limit behaviour further.

Here we witness the power of the subconscious mind as it uses fear as a means of preventing the sufferer from behaving in a way that would have given rise to feelings of guilt in the past.

Obsessional states can revolve around a religious belief that while superficially appearing to offer comfort and respite from anxiety, ultimately fails to offer relief. In this respect it should be remembered we remain mortal beings with minds capable of being subjected to severe and irrational indoctrination. The devotee whom becomes fearfully afraid of not keeping to a certain prayer patter or ritual.

Moral and cultural teachings, codes and ethics are seldom absolute or static. Attitudes and notions of correctness change

110

with the passage of time. It is important to remember that people of different ages inevitably have different notions of what is acceptable behaviour, a common cause of stress for all concerned. One effect is a natural segregation between disparate age groups, the aggressive the young and the defensive, critical old.

Obsessional behaviour is designed to protect the sufferer from that which he has become fearful. When established, obsessional behaviour creates additional fears such as the fear of change or of being asked to do something new. Implicit in change is a departure from the safe and predictable routine to which has become a way of life and to which the sufferer clings.

Of course it is perfectly natural to have an inbuilt reaction of resisting anything new. Resistance and hesitation is part of the mind's defence mechanism that encourages us to think carefully and avoid unnecessary risks. The beneficial effect of this protection is our adherence to that which has proved 'safe' and for everyday tasks to be routinely and habitually carried out.

Most people slip into quite rigid patterns of behaviour without giving it a second thought. This also reflects a specific mind function, that of subconscious automatic direction. Once we have learned to do a certain thing 'safely', in a way that suits us and has proved to work to our satisfaction, it becomes a subconscious act about which we need no longer think. Doing a job while putting our conscious thoughts elsewhere. Not all rigid behaviour patterns are either problematic or negative.

The physical, mental and emotional manifestations of anxiety and even the presence of anxiety itself are symptoms of an underlying cause, the continuance of which continues denies the attainment of true happiness.

Happiness is to be carefree, to be free from care, free from worrying thoughts and to know the lightness of the etheric, inner or 'higher' self. The attainment of such a state relies in part on a philosophical understanding that allows for part of us, which would otherwise appeared flawed, is perhaps simply not understood. 'The will of God' allows the believer to accept and forgive atrocities an unbeliever would find wholly unacceptable.

This maxim can be true of The Self. There appears also to be a state of mind or part of the mind to which we can retreat and from which we can look down, or at ourselves. For convenience alone I refer to this part as the 'higher' mind.

Beyond this, happiness is freedom from the past and in particular those traumatic experiences and restrictive practices which have lead to inhibition and anxiousness in later life.

Treating the symptoms, while helpful, is unlikely to bring lasting relief. A more productive approach is by helping the sufferer to understand the mechanisms of anxiousness and how normal it is to suffer in this way. Also helping establish a sense of self in which the expression of good conscience becomes both an objective and a means of control over negative reactions. Stop worrying about worry.

Living simply and gracefully in the goodness of one's conscience, showing kindness and forgiveness are stepping-stones to happiness. Living in good conscience and consciously doing no harm places one beyond harmful criticism and does not invite self-doubt.

Anxiety can reveal a further dimension to the Self. There is good reason to believe that through the experiences of our fears and anxieties we are spurred to seek and are then guided towards a realization of the spirit; the quest for the Self of inner truth.

Stress Management

The first thing to say is that stress is better avoided than managed. Having said that the next most important thing is to recognize when you are stressed. Because so much of what goes on in life is potentially stress-making, it is easy to accept excessive levels of stress without realizing what is happening.

We all suffer little anxieties, sometimes quite a lot of them, and deal with them but our capacity for stress is limited. We may reach a point when just one more problem is too much for us to handle. The burden of accumulated stress causes an overreaction, the proverbial 'straw' that breaks the camel's back.

Anxiety or stress reactions can be identified by feelings of: anger, frustration, exasperation, annoyance, being misunderstood, taken for granted, overworked, being unable to find peace and quiet and time for one's self. Feeling that you want to run away, withdraw, be silent, avoid someone, or everyone and everything. Neglect work, home even self – give up.

When we reflect on how our lives have changed, the causes of our stress may become obvious and appropriate action taken. There is often opportunity for a stressful situation to be better understood and managed even when it cannot be avoided. Beyond this we cannot always be certain where our anxiety reactions come from In which case, when we do get anxious we can challenge the validity of our reactions, ignore them and resist further negative thinking.

Sometimes we come across the phenomenon of 'knowing' with certainty about something or someone but about which we can offer no logical explanation. This we call intuition. Intuitive feelings may be distinguishable from subconscious reactions by an absence of uncertainty and inner conflict.

Intuition provides us with a sense of certainty that persists even though we cannot explain the reasoning behind our understanding or decision. Intuition is often felt to be the voice of conscience and of personal rightness, the truth by which we must live if we are to live happily. It is a way of saying who we are and what we stand for and because we are so certain of our feelings, we do not feel stressed or anxious.

Overcoming Anxiety

Anxiety can be overcome and future sources of anxiety avoided.

It is important to be able to identify obvious sources of anxiety but less so those of subconscious origins. With the latter it is more important to understand the principles underlying those concealed causes. Events bringing about subconscious causes of anxiety may in themselves be insignificant and the effort to identify them disproportionate to the benefit of their revelation. It would take a lifetime of counselling and analysis to reveal all the underlying causes of our anxieties, something the less scrupulous consultant uses to financial benefit.

There is nothing to fear in the events of yesterday, their power to change you lies within your mind. Tomorrow need hold no fear, the prospect of its form shaped only by your mind. Of what are you presently afraid? What is to be feared within this moment of your being that you are not enduring, overcoming and leaving behind you moment by moment? You ARE overcoming your fear NOW.

Avoid pessimistic anticipation. Live more in the world of NOW, not in the unreality of past hurts, grievances and injustices or in wild imaginings of tomorrow. If you need to forgive a person then do so, not to forgive condemns you to relive the pain of the past. An inability to forgive reveals a source of anxiety, the bitterness and anger of which remains active, colouring behaviour and destroying happiness.

Discriminate between fact and fiction, news and speculation, possible and probable, past, present and future.

Know the reality in which you live. Recognize your abilities, accept responsibility for what you do.

Stop assuming. If in doubt and you really need to know, then ASK.

Examine personal values, needs and beliefs. Feel useful as well as fulfilled, find purpose and reward in your life beyond the mundane, find satisfaction in everything that you do and know contentment.

Identify those people who make you feel uneasy, anxious or angry or whose effects take you away from your ideals. Know just how you would prefer to be. Are their words and actions really a threat to you do they merely create a sense of fear in your mind? Do they really confront you or can you simply step aside and let their energy dissipate elsewhere?

Find a balance in your thinking that lets other people exist and take responsibility for their own actions.

Feel equal among people because you are, not because you think you should be. Equality is respect for other people regardless of ability, seniority, social position or wealth. Respect other people and equally respect yourself

Be realistic is your expectations of other people and forgiving in your understanding of human frailties. We all make mistakes.

Compromise. Take pleasure in finding the path of greatest harmony, of making the best of a situation and bringing out the best in people. People who help other people feel good about themselves and reflect their happiness: everyone benefits. Nobody has the monopoly on being right.

If you need help ask for help.

Examine personal values, be certain in your own mind what you believe about the world around you. If you are uncertain about your own views your will be easy prey for the fears and fantasies of other people.

Anxiety can be beaten. Happiness does not have to be won

or fought for. Happiness is an entitlement, an endowment of birth. Dissatisfaction is human trait that is too often more destructive than its hoped for benefits. If life offers us a challenge it is to see past our preoccupation with fear and hardship and find joy in observing and experiencing that lying before and around about us.

Sometimes it is helpful to be able to talk freely about one's doubts and fears, when a new perspective may lead to greater enlightenment. Counselling and the opportunity to talk without embarrassment can speed the resolution of worrying problems.

Health concerns, worries about work or family, partnership dilemmas, and sensitive personal problems arise in the best ordered lives. Relationships can become strained, attitudes hardened and communication made problematic. For many reasons it may not be easy to find ways in which the trust, cooperation and understanding necessary for a speedy return to harmony and happiness are restored.

At such times skilful counselling can bring fresh insight and new perspectives in which solutions and the way ahead are to be found. Counselling can help people find within themselves the ability to deal confidently with difficult or confusing situation. Where relationships are involved one or both partners may be counselled independently. The focus of counselling can be a matter of pressing need; to clarify goals; to restore confidence and self-esteem; to overcome inhibiting reactions, guilt or embarrassment, always to look to a happier future. Solutions are there to be found.

Take time to relax in a controlled way, yoga and meditation can be very helpful. Hypnotherapy and the use of positive affirmations combining relaxation and objective thinking are also useful aids, especially in the management of subconscious reactions.

If you need help ask a friend, therapist, counsellor or guide. Be guided by your heart and your intuition as well as your intellect. Be grateful for that which you receive, even on those occasions when you choose not to agree with an alternative view, for even this has brought you closer to clarity.

Find yourself and find within yourself that which brings you happiness, joy and fulfilment.

12. Anxiety States, Agoraphobia And Panic Attacks.

Fear is one of life's inevitabilities. Human reactions to the presence of a threat to well- being or the fear of such a threat helps us avoid or overcome source of danger. However, as we now know there are certain types of fearful anticipation that produce effects that are counterproductive to well-being and survival. This type of fear we call anxiety – a state of mind producing feelings ranging from doubt, apprehension, and a sense of insecurity to sheer panic.

A simple fear is based upon our perception of reality and a threat to our well being that some aspect of that reality poses us.

The term phobia is used to describe a state of fear/anxiety producing reactions that disable rather than enhance the sufferer's abilities to survive.

The Fear may be real or imagined. The roots of many phobias are to be found in innate and instinctive fears of sources of danger occurring naturally in the world in which we live; snakes, spiders, wild animals, high places, deep water and so on.

Of the three hundred or more named phobias, Agoraphobia is one of the most commonly experienced and yet possibly least understood.

Any state of anxiety is a mixture of fears, symptoms and unanswerable questions and agoraphobia is no exception. Sufferers find themselves faced with any number of diagnoses for their condition, any or all of which may be accurate but incomplete.

A fear of being with or amongst other people, though not specifically of other people, is often mentioned as a symptom of agoraphobia. The circumstances described by sufferers in which encounters with other people are viewed fearfully reveal similarities.

A common factor is the sense of a loss of freedom, of not feeling in control of personal territory. Typically, Agoraphobics feel happiest in their own homes. Control is centered upon a concept of personal territory, a totally subjective concept based upon individual perception, This perception will be founded at least in part on personal experiences which need not necessarily be first hand. Misconceptions and learning about the experiences of others is sufficient; truth is a flexible and personal interpretation of reality.

Personal territory is portable and it can be very difficult for non-sufferers to understand the rules by which an agoraphobic lives.

Rules, and territory involve escape routes and means of escape. Means by which a sufferer is able to avoid people whose presence is regarded to be potentially threatening and by which their sense of personal territory is kept secure and intact. The perceived threat posed by the presence of other people may not be so much a threat to life but more likely a threat of personal failure or embarrassment.

Hence a sense of security may be gained from cycling instead of walking. When cycling it is easier to avoid being stopped and engaged in conversation and it is easier to make a rapid exit. Driving alone or perhaps with just one trusted friend offers similar safeguards. Travelling in unfamiliar places, where everyone is a stranger and where a sense of isolation comes easily may be similarly attractive. A certain sense of safety can be found in anonymity.

Travelling in any kind of enclosed and secured public transport; trains, buses even cars is almost certain to cause problems for the agoraphobic.

The need to be in control may lead the agoraphobic to use his or her condition as a means to manipulate other people in order to avoid feared situations. This is perfectly understandable and may not be too problematic for those in the sufferer's circle of friends or relatives who are 'in the know'; when the sufferer can balance his or her needs with those of other people more openly.

However, this opportunity may take on a very different complexion when unresolved difficulties exist in close personal relationships. Through the imposition of restrictions and demands, some agoraphobics may induce, encourage or emotionally blackmail partners or other people to forgo their own needs in favour of those of the sufferer. To a shy or sensitive sufferer who has a dominant insensitive partner, the limitations of the condition may seem a small price to pay for this opportunity to redress the balance of power; worse, it could be seen as payback time! Small price indeed to get the love and attention otherwise denied.

To other people, an agoraphobic may seem to be a different person while on holiday or away from home and on unfamiliar territory. This is probably because the fact that they are unfamiliar means that anxiousness is appropriate and possibly shared by companions. Additionally there are fewer reminders of normal routines and other people associated with agoraphobic fears and because of the predominance of strangers, less likelihood of being stopped, spoken to and of being TRAPPED.

Anonymity is to be sought at all times and on the whole it is easier not to be with other people, but importantly, not divorced from them either. The presence of other people provides the reassurance that help is at hand should it be needed.

The mobile phone has brought a sense of relief to many who can now avoid personal contact with people without suffering the perceived loss of safety isolation would otherwise bring.

In a general sense, agoraphobia is a fear of being trapped either because of the proximity of other people and the demands they might make, or of having been abandoned by other people. Fearful of suffering the embarrassment of having a panic attack in front of other people yet fearful also of the life threatening feelings associated with a panic attack and having no one on whom to call, a dilemma of anxieties.

Feelings or symptoms commonly described by sufferers of agoraphobia and associated anxiety states include:

the fear of crowded places,
the fear of travelling away from home,
the fear of fainting or collapsing,
the fear of feeling paralyzed,
the fear of becoming disorientated,
the fear of entering shops,

the fear of standing in a queue,
the fear of unfamiliar places,
the fear of being alone,
the fear of dying,
the fear of going mad,
the fear of the fearful feelings.

It will be apparent contradiction of many symptoms indicate something of the very complex nature of the condition. The sufferer can switch from one symptom to another with alarming and confusing speed.

While the history of every agoraphobe (and most sufferers' of acute anxiety states) is unique, two distinct characteristics may be observed.

Firstly, many sufferers have a history of anxious or nervous behaviour the origins of which can be traced to childhood. Characteristics which have resulted in the establishment of **safe behaviour and safe routines**, a marked fear of change and a pronounced (if disguised) lack of confidence.

Secondly, sufferers only become aware of their problem after suffering an unexpected **panic attack**.

Panic attacks, especially initial attacks, commonly occur in crowded or public places such as when queuing, when confined among people in a cinema of meeting, and when rushed, tired, over-worked, and when feeling under pressure. Further attacks follow resulting in the establishment of behavioural avoidance and limitation patterns.

These acute anxiety experiences may easily become chronic and are often suffered secretly. Too easily, a life based on safe places, safe routines and periodic escapes to 'foreign' areas becomes the 'norm'.

When the sufferer seeks medical help, the help offered may be medication, tranquillizers or anti-depressants, to help suppress or relieve the symptoms. Medication should be strictly limited to short term use and supported by additional help (counselling/befriending etc..).

Beyond these general observations there is a factor that appears **always present,** namely, that preceding and accompanying the agoraphobic state is the presence of **a sense of loss.** Typically such losses are those of bereavement, of status, of work, or of partner or children, as may occur from divorce. No objective measurement of the effects of any of these situations is possible but careful observation of the patient/sufferer may indicate areas of his or her life and circumstances which can be usefully examined more deeply.

It is important that **a sense of loss** is seen as a likely causal factor. The sufferer has found, and still finds the sense of loss deeply wounding at an intimate emotional psychological level. The identification and resolution of this loss is essential to full recovery.

In addition to what maybe called psychological or mentally related causes of panic or anxiety attacks, a number of physical, environmental and neurological conditions may be present and causal.

Many sufferers experiences dizziness and unsteadiness and this can arise from a condition known as **positional or spontaneous nystagmus.** Nystagmus is a reflex scanning movement made by the eyes in order to keep moving objects in view, as when looking out of the window of a moving car or train. This reflex is partly under the control of the balance organ in the middle ear.

If coordination between the middle ear and the eye is disturbed, for example by the use of alcohol or drugs, or working, sitting or standing in one position for an extended period of time and while cramped and tense, the nystagmus reflex can occur when the eyes should be still. The viewer then has the illusion that stationary objects are moving or the everything is spinning around. Unaware of the true cause of what is happening the viewer/sufferer becomes anxious; disorientation exacerbates these feelings resulting in extreme anxiety or panic.

Should the experience be repeated and the sufferer remain ignorant of the cause or have no otherwise satisfactory explanation of the problem, this disorientation can give rise to avoidance patterns. In short, the sufferer becomes unwilling to enter situations felt likely to produce the symptoms. If the sufferer was already in a stressful situation, especially one involving a loss factor, it is an event waiting to happen.

A common cause of this condition is spondylosis or other arthritic condition creating impaired mobility, especially of the upper body and neck.

Further psychological changes which can be causal to the establishment of agoraphobic like states include allergic reactions, dietary hypoglycaemia, caffeine and nicotine addiction/poisoning, hearing difficulties and poor left-right brain hemisphere coordination.

Allergic reactions are perhaps more common than is generally realised. In addition to directly producing anxiety-like symptoms, allergic reactions in general account for much anxiousness. Breathlessness, caused by allergic reaction and which may be diagnosed as asthma or hay-fever, can be disabling in the short term and can be a frightening life-threatening experience.

Other physiological and psychological symptoms of allergic reactions include: itching, sinusitis, cystitis, nausea, bloating, migraine, chest pain, muscle spasms, irritability, insomnia, anxiety, clumsiness, food addiction, and depression.

Diet is a not uncommon cause of anxiety-like symptoms, one of simplest and most common being that of **dietary hypoglycemia,** occurring when the amount of glucose in the blood falls to a very low level. The liver is responsible for maintaining a steady concentration of glucose in the blood. This condition can be caused by the combination of certain dietary imbalances and the use of caffeine and nicotine; causes which may also result in an over-stimulation of the adrenal system, seriously and perhaps dangerously stressing mind and body.

For the human body to function normally, an adequate amount of glucose(sugar) must be present in the bloodstream. The brain depends upon a constant supply of glucose (from the blood) in order to function and has no stored reserves of its own upon which to draw. If supplies diminish or are cut off the brain ceases to function normally. An immediate effect of glucose starvation is in nervous activity.

Symptoms associated with hypoglycaemia include: anxiety, depression, fatigue, irritability, forgetfulness, vertigo, panics, poor concentration, indigestion, headaches, smoking, food cravings, overweight, sweating, blurred vision, nightmares, allergies, restlessness, chest cramps, cold extremities, palpitations, numbness, stomach pain and loss of sex-drive.

It will be obvious that many of these symptoms can also be attributed to stress and anxiety, also allergic reactions!

An hypoglycaemic incident occurs when a diminishing level of blood sugar reaches a critically low level. Very high levels of blood sugar are induced by eating sugar rich, processed and refined foods. In addition both caffeine and nicotine stimulate the liver to release additional glucose into the bloodstream and a combination of these factors results in a dramatic rise in blood sugar level – part of the 'high' experienced from combining a Danish pastry, with a cup of coffee and a cigarette.

The body responds by producing insulin in sufficient quantity to lower the level of blood glucose and return the body to a more relaxed state.

Sensing a falling blood sugar level, the body/mind seeks to avoid blood sugar levels falling too low and the sufferer then experiences cravings for another cup of coffee, a cigarette or to eat something sweet. Cravings that are simply the result of a dramatic fall in blood sugar and not necessarily anything to do with true addiction.

Addiction is another facet of what can be a complicated problem.

If the sufferer does not have anything to eat or drink, or a cigarette the rapid decrease of blood sugar brings on an hypoglycaemic attack. An example being someone driving long distances, skips meals and whose intake of fluids is diminished, who then becomes unnaturally tired, loses concentration but remains unaware of what is happening. An accident waiting to happen.

Physiological changes brought about by a combination of low blood-sugar levels and lowered amounts of oxygen in the blood, plus the hormonal and adrenal changes already mentioned can bring about altered states of mental function, anxiety and depression.

Primary dietary sources of hypoglycaemia include a diet high in sugar content, refined starches and carbohydrates. Habitual snack eating of these foods, frequent drinking tea, coffee, colas and other sweet and alcoholic drinks, chocolate addiction and sweet binging. Add nicotine and the effect is almost inevitable.

I repeat - falling blood sugar levels trigger cravings for more caffeine, sugar, nicotine, alcohol, chocolate.....encouraging and quickly establishing a cycle of dietary indiscretions that border on dependency.

At this point please be aware that I have not wandered away from the main subject, but brought to the reader's attention the importance of establishing the sufferer's Life Style, as this may have a direct impact on the problem: either as a cause or hindrance to recovery.

High caffeine intake is responsible for much edginess and hyperactivity, including sleeplessness and, conversely lethargy. Caffeine increases alertness for a time but not if the user is already alert. Caffeine stimulates heart action and its over-use can produce palpitation-like heart beats. Caffeine also increases urine output and the effects of a single cup can be present after six hours.

Smoking nicotine/tobacco increases blood pressure, constricts arteries and initially increases the amount of sugar in the bloodstream – part of the (misleading) 'lift' effect smoking gives. However, the effect of increased insulin output combined with the decrease in oxygen produced by inhaling carbon monoxide, results in pallor, trembling, weakness, light-headedness, breathing difficulties and in extreme cases a loss of consciousness.

Once again, if the sufferer is also stressed, tired or pressured, circumstances which themselves encourage the use of caffeine, nicotine and alcohol, attributing causal factors may not be easy.

When faced with a situation of this kind it is most important for a practitioner to say that that while the underlying causes are not yet obvious, by introducing small changes, say in diet or in dealing with an unwanted habit, piece by piece the picture will become clear.

While there is always the possibility of a physical or environmental cause for the presentation of anxiety symptoms, and such factors may indeed underpin psychological causes, where the condition persists the pursuit of psychological and behavioural causes will likely prove fruitful.

Underlying fears of all sufferers include those of losing control, of fainting, or of doing something embarrassing; also of feeling trapped and unable to extricate themselves from a situation in which they feel any of the things they fear may happen.

Needing to be in control can be an indication of agoraphobia.

In their desire to control 'everything', sufferers try to control their anxiety by controlling their reactions and emotions. Because by nature human emotions tend to reveal themselves forcefully and spontaneously, agoraphobics may consider their own feelings to be a potential a source of danger. The result, with the exception of a few trusted family members or special friends, is to distance themselves from other people who in turn find a rather cold and unfeeling person who never the less remains kind and otherwise considerate and loving.

An inevitable result of the need for control is the creation of a self-protective barrier between an agoraphobic and his or her family. The frustration and unhappiness thus caused creating further anxiety.

An additional complication when endeavouring to suppress feelings is the suppression or loss of sexual response and denial of desire. While there are many agoraphobics whose lack of sexual fulfilment had actually led to their condition, there are many whose anxiety has led to problems in their sexual relationships. Whichever the case the tensions created make management of the problem more difficult.

The final phase, if there can ever really be one, is the development of a **fear of the fear.** The sufferer becomes aware constantly, of the possibility of having a panic attack. Every aspect of life is dominated by meticulous planning in order to avoid feared people or situations.

Loss as a Common factor.

I have observed a number of factors preceding the onset of agoraphobic-like states, all of which involve a sense of loss.

The loss itself may not always be obvious, indeed it may be a sense of loss, rather than an actual loss, which triggers the onset of anxiety; or that a sense of loss in some way creates a predisposition to anxiety. Whichever be the case such a connection can invariably be found.

A significant loss is that of bereavement, especially where the opportunity to express grief fully and freely has been denied. The denial may be purely the result of an inability or embarrassment at such a display of 'private' feelings. Or it may arise from a lack of privacy or circumstance of relationship. Freedom to express grief is inhibited in many ways – explore!

Another common loss-trigger is an enforced stay in hospital, particularly where surgical treatment requires a general anaesthetic. Here the potential sufferer experiences a loss of freedom, loss of conscious control, loss of family presence, loss of being listened to, a loss of identity, loss of privacy, loss of respect, even a loss of a piece of oneself.

A burglary, robbery or loss through theft may be the distressing start of agoraphobia. The sense of a loss of privacy on having personal belongings taken, the surrender of personal territory to an uninvited stranger, the inability to prevent assault on person or property, the ensuing sense of vulnerability and fear of repetition all contribute to helplessness, turning to easily into hopelessness and loss of 'everything'.

A fear of the future must not be overlooked. In its simplest and most direct sense this is the **fear of dying,** though not necessarily a fear of death, comes uppermost in this category. The fear may not be of one's own death but that of a partner on whom one relies, or from whom separation cannot be faced.

Before leaving the subject of loss, one more very important situation must be mentioned and that is the sense of a **loss of love.** For various reasons already mentioned, isolation may bring the sufferer to feel unloved as well as unloving.

The expression of love may be denied the sufferer through bereavement or other circumstance of physical separation; or through relationship problems that have resulted in a withdrawal of love by someone previously close. The sense of loss may be intensified by a lack of sexual fulfilment associated with the loss of a loving relationship.

The practitioner's identification of this kind of loss is very important, for his or her own safety! An awareness that to the patient/sufferer, someone who appears caring and 'loving', and who makes him or her feel safe, may also be worthy of their love; a love that has for so long denied.

Any sufferer can benefit from honest self-appraisal and an admittance of a personal and perhaps unspoken sense of loss. The sense of loss may be buried in the subconscious and unrealized. Professional help maybe necessary here, though no sufferer should feel that he or she is abnormal, mentally ill or beyond hope.

Everything that happens, happens according to certain principles, including those of cause and effect. Understanding causes can help us understand effects, effects to which we are all subjected. Overcoming personal limitations, no matter what their nature, is no more than this. Whether the understanding is of a principal or of a specific event the opportunity to overcome and resolve is there.

There is no right way or wrong way to deal with an anxiety problem; only ways that are appropriate or inappropriate, fruitful or otherwise and sometimes a process of elimination is the only way of determining which paths prove most productive.

It must always be remembered that YES and NO are of equal value in the search for personal truth.

Nervous Hypersensitivity

Symptomatic of agoraphobia is a physical state in which nervous responses and reactions are greatly intensified; rapid if not instantaneous in their presentation. Typically a panic attack thus arrives swiftly and potently.

It is important to recognize that acute anxiety (panic) attacks may occur as an expression of exaggerated stress symptoms in someone whose nervous system had become oversensitive or **sensitized** to them.

Panic attacks do not come from too much worry alone. An anxious person may worry constantly yet despite obvious signs of stress, continue to function normally and not suffer panic attacks.

Panic attacks begin when continuous and extreme stress reactions overwhelm the nervous system and produce a kind of nervous hypersensitivity. A sufferer then experiences normal anxiety symptoms to an abnormally high degree of intensity. This may be in addition to the condition of adrenal stress and constant nerve-muscle hyperactivity.

There is no great mystery about **sensitization** and most people experience it in a mild form at some time or other. For example, when, at the end of a day of tension we are become upset by some trifling matter and over-react, the over-reaction is a reflection of our temporary nervous hypersensitivity. All we want to do is unwind and relax and when unable to do so find some trivial problem pushes us too far and we 'snap'.

An agoraphobe experiences a similar kind of uncontrollable nervousness but without warning or obvious reason and with an important difference. Instead of the power of the stress being released in an emotional outburst, it is directed inwards, the energy dissipating through the nervous/muscular system resulting in an anxiety or 'panic' attack.

It is perhaps worth mentioning at this point that any form of safe physical activity will provide an alternative channel by which this unwanted energy may be released. One client's answer to being struck with panic attacks at home was, at their onset, to run up and down stairs and literally run the energy out of them. Note: This kind of approach is only for the fit and healthy.

To understand agoraphobia one must appreciate the truly alarming swiftness and the severity of the feelings of panic which come with sensitization. Powerful reactions originating deep within a mind fearful of the circumstances in which it finds itself.

Even more alarming is the fact that one attack can follow another, and another, each flash mounting in intensity until a point of nervous, physical and mental exhaustion makes further reactions impossible.

Sensitization seems to occur when certain parts of the autonomic nervous system are persistently and/or so seriously alerted that they remain in a constant state of readiness.

The autonomic nervous system regulates essential body functions through the sympathetic and parasympathetic nervous systems. Body organs connected to both these systems are then regulated by their opposing actions. This is achieved without need of any conscious control.

Sympathetic nerves release adrenaline, stimulate the heart, suppress digestive activity and generally enhance physical activity. Parasympathetic nerves release acetyl choline and have the opposite effect. In short, the former winds you up, the latter relaxes you.

In a panic attack, the initial part of the reactive process of 'winding up' may be virtually instantaneous while the relaxing or 'winding down' response may be prolonged. When the initial phase is severe the ensuing relaxation may result in several hours exhausted resting.

Panic Attacks

The causes of panic attacks often, if not always, lie in the past; in stressful or fearful events that have taken place long before the present day situation with which the attack is immediately associated.

A panic attack occurs with the resurrection of a subconscious 'memory' of a previously anxious situation and the associated historic reaction. The sufferer remains unaware of this historical cause because the memory in question is rarely lifted into consciousness at this time.

The subconscious mind produces 'fear' reactions as it mistakes present time events with those of the past, so preparing the body to fight or flee.

Although conscious thoughts can sometimes trigger an attack there need be no conscious awareness of what the subconscious mind is doing. Panic attacks can happen when life appears to be going very well, the sufferer being happy and relaxed when the attack strikes.

The subconscious mind can be triggered to react by circumstances that are in themselves entirely devoid of any real threat or danger but which, because of their similarity to a previous occasion which *was* found fearful, rings alarm bells. The hapless sufferer suddenly experiences a panic attack which appears to come out of the blue and for no reason.

Not unnaturally the sufferer is afraid of the sensations to which he or she has been subjected and is fearful of their recurrence. This gives rise to a **fear of the fear** syndrome which then plays a part in perpetuating panics. Reversal of this process, by explaining what is happening, is an important part of initial treatment.

If the subconscious trigger is repeatedly activated, relief from the stream of impulses to which the nervous system is subjected, comes only when anxiety has reached its zenith. When the mind and body can no longer accommodate stimulus to further nervous excitement, extreme fatigue makes further physical exertion impossible. Proper recovery requires a prolonged period of complete rest.

Panic attacks and agoraphobic states generally develop in three stages.

1 The Causal or Trigger event.

An initial physical and/or mental trauma inducing a state of fear. This may have occurred in childhood or at least many years prior to the onset of agoraphobia or anxiety/panic attacks.

2 The Revival Event.

A second trauma or circumstances similar enough to the Causal Event to prompt subconscious cross identification. By mimicking the earlier trauma, the subconscious is triggered into

131

producing a state of high alert, or anxiousness, by the Revival Event.

The Revival Event, when the first panic attack occurs, is often regarded, incorrectly, as the start or cause of the problem. While there may be real-time circumstances which do produce panic attacks, when the arrival of the first panic attack is unexpected and unwarranted, it should be regarded as have been caused by a Revival Event.

3   The Fear of the Fear.

Safe patterns of behaviour, that is to say controlled behaviour designed to avoid circumstances associated with the Revival Event or previous panic attacks can be established surprisingly quickly.

When the fear of suffering a panic attack becomes a major focal point in life, patterns of behaviour can become ritualistic and obsessional.

This kind of obsessional behaviour is **symptomatic** and should not be regarded as a separate or additional problem.

Many people who suffer from agoraphobia do not understand what is happening to them, or why it is happening. Sufferers may become even more fearful when lead to believe they have psychological problems requiring psychiatric help or medication.

Vulnerable to suggestions of treatment, the agoraphobic or anxious patient's situation may be complicated even further by the use of prescribed drugs. Without early, knowledgeable help, restrictive patterns of behaviour, secondary symptoms and drug dependency become an established way of life from which release can be difficult.

Sufferer's fears and changes in behaviour bring additional problems when they effect relationships, especially within families. Counselling has to be far ranging and informative and must create a platform on which a recovery program can be constructed. It is a platform built by the patient and the patient's family and friends and which provides a safe haven of basic understanding. This is essential lest it is the practitioner becomes that platform and on whom unnecessary demands may then be made.

It is essential that these secondary peripheral problems be addressed: not to do so creates additional pressures on the sufferer. In turn this may lead to a greater sense of isolation. It is also important to look for other causes of anxiety present in the sufferer's life. These may not be directly related to the Causal Event but will probably be associated with the Revival Event, even if only historically.

Underlying causes can carry powerful emotions and for this reason their existence may be denied or un-admitted; even when there is clear self-knowledge of their existence they remain unspoken. Examples include unresolved injustices of all kinds, strongly held resentments involving close relationships, sexual repression, lack of sexual or emotional fulfilment and guilt arising from unspoken and/or unfulfilled sexual desire.

Such factors may not be causal but unless resolved will prove barriers to recovery. A task demanding masterly and sensitive counselling in circumstances of complete confidentiality. In this respect simple honesty between counsellor and patient is paramount. A direct, patient approach allowing spontaneous, open responses is the key; nothing must impede the flow between conversants; taking notes in the presence of the patient should be regarded as inappropriate.

Skilful, therapeutic counselling is essential in revealing, evaluating and neutralizing the **loss factor** present in most cases of agoraphobia and which is likely also to underlie other acute anxiety states.

A Therapeutic Approach to Agoraphobia.

To overcome the condition it is helpful to look at the three separate stages or parts of agoraphobia detailed above in reverse order.

Firstly to control The Fear of The Fear and begin to rebuild self-confidence.

Establish a new way of life by gradually altering habit patterns in a relaxed and controlled way. Initial changes need be only very small and relatively undemanding; things which, with encouragement, the sufferer feels are achievable. **Gentle persistence** brings the subconscious mind to accept the changes that are desired which, once established, enhance the ability to go forward.

This process of change must be personal and relate directly to the choices and abilities of the patient. Small changes, such as changes in the times of daily activities helps modify entrenched routines and open the way to greater and more significant adjustments. Hypnotherapy self-help/use recordings reflecting personal goals can be helpful here.

Secondly, confronting the Revival Event.

By openly discussing the incident and how it came to be repeated and/or avoided, combined with the sense of control building from the previous stage, examination of the problem becomes easier.

Review what changes have taken place, especially in the presentation of symptoms since onset of the condition. Introduce the thought that further changes can be made and bring the patient to look at his or her life and circumstances objectively and optimistically. Bring the patient to talk freely about the condition and the symptoms without feeling afraid of either.

Talk about what symptoms are most troublesome, those that can now be tolerated, and those which can be fairly easily ignored.

Introduce to the patient the idea that as progress is made, week by week confidence will grow; further changes and ultimately freedom from the grip of the condition is a reality.

Thirdly, dealing with the Causal Event.

As a natural progression from stage two, explain clearly (again) how and why these anxiety states arise. Emphasize how natural they are and that while it can be helpful to identify the original causal event, it is not essential to do so.

I believe it is unnecessary to identify the original trauma or incident precisely in order to make progress. It is more important to understand the principle behind the manifestation of the condition and that by being without fear of the condition, the subconscious mind is encouraged to release into consciousness the memory it has withheld.

More important than identifying the original source is being able to lose the fear of the symptoms and gain the confidence necessary to handle panic attacks effectively. More of this later but it is a realistic and achievable goal for the most serious and chronic cases. Achieving this is enormously strengthening to the individual who is then more capable of confronting other sources of fear.

I have observed that when the fear of a panic attacks or anxiety state is removed and when confidence is rebuilt, the subconscious mind reveals the cause. It is as if the sufferer has to prove to his or her own subconscious mind that this fear is no longer to be regarded as a threat. That the only way of doing this is to stop being afraid of 'it'; the 'it' being nothing more than a bad memory that should properly be left in the past.

I realize this explanation is something of a psychological simplification but knowledge of the principles by which a problem or condition arises can be significantly instrumental is achieving recovery.

Cornerstones of Success

Underpinning the three stages detailed above, introducing to the patient the following four steps, will go a long way towards ensuring speedy and lasting success.

1   **Face The Condition.** Do not try to run away from it.

Face up to what has happened and accept that what is happening is natural. It may be unpleasant and frightening but that does not make in unnatural or that you are in any way abnormal, You are not being punished for something. Anxiety and panic attacks are a part of life to be understood and overcome.

Your feelings are personal to you. Other people may be unable to understand exactly how you feel – don't blame them for that, accept it as a fact of life. There is much about other people that you do not understand. You do not need to rely on their sympathy and goodwill to get you through. It is nice when you do get help and encouragement but if it is not forthcoming you can do this for yourself. In fact no one else can do it for you

The really good thing is to know that recovery is on the cards; you can and will get stronger and as a result be more confident, self-determined and understanding person than hitherto. As you are taking control of your condition you are taking control of your life.

The part you play is up to you. The danger for anyone in this situation is to begin to adopt an illness as an alternative way of life, succumbing to long-term medication, becoming institutionalized and reliant on on-going 'therapy'; or just using the condition as a means of getting your own way.

You may think I paint a harshly judged picture but I do so only because there are people who become life-long patients, who wear their badge of suffering proudly. I leave that thought with you.

2   **Accept Anxiety.** Accept the responses and how you feel.

When you feel an attack approaching, try not to fight what you feel, instead, accept what is happening. You have had these feelings before and know what they are. You know that there is no need to be afraid of them.

Each day, take time to relax. Use some positive affirmations to remind yourself of the reality of your situation. You are in control. Focus on how you are – sitting down relaxing. Focus on how you want to be. Relaxing in this way is good practice for relaxing when a panic attack strikes, letting the attack pass quickly and without resistance. This avoids the energy of the attack building and allows it to dissipate easily. Panic attacks need last only a minute or two and once limited to this brevity, un-sustained by your fear of them, they soon cease.

3   **Relax, Float, do not tense.**

Any tension you create when trying to control your reactions is fighting force with force. The more energy you put into fighting to stay in control, the more energy your subconscious creates to ensure your reactions dominate. By relaxing and not tensing you effectively fight you subconscious reaction to prepare you for action. By passively relaxing you demonstrate how you are looking ahead and in denying the reaction to tense, that you are in control. You are preparing for the future and in doing so, exercising both control and understanding.

Instead of multiple waves of anxiety lasting for hours, attacks are limited to one-offs of lessening duration. Aim to bring your body and mind to be harmoniously relaxed and see your anxiety attacks as a means of helping you focus on this objective. Through your anxiety you are building a means of self-control that will then stay with you.

4   Let time pass – be patient.

Stop worrying about time, stop thinking about how long you have been suffering, stop being afraid of be incapacitated. After steps 1,2 and 3 you will have got used to the idea that you are in control of your mind and body and your life to a far greater degree that you realized. Concentrate on how you **want** to feel, not on how your subconscious anxiety tries to make you feel.

Prescribed Medication

Some anxiety sufferers will be prescribed medication to help induce muscle relaxation, mental quiet and assist sleep. While the use of tranquilizers, antidepressants and hypnotics **may** be of help in the early stages, their prolonged use (more than two weeks) carries serious risk of psychological and physical dependency.

The question of cessation of their use then arises. If the patient has been subjected to this type of prescribed medication for more than a few months the implementation of a dose-reducing program will almost certainly be necessary to avoid the presentation of withdrawal symptoms.

Drug withdrawal after long term use should be under supervision plus appropriate support and counselling. This may not necessarily be offered by or available through, the prescribing practitioner, with whom the patient should still discuss his or her cessation of use.

Psychotropic (mind affecting) drugs inhibit normal mental processes by blocking certain brain activity. In many instances even the producer (drug company) does not know precisely how the medication it produces affects the brain.

Inevitably drug use inhibits clear objective thinking. With the additional risk of dependency there is a clear risk that drug use hinders recovery. Effects that can linger weeks or months after cessation of use.

Use and withdrawal symptoms following cessation of us of prescribed medication can interfere with memory recall, distort thought patterns, disturb and distort feelings and emotions and even remover the desire to 'think' very much at all. Any of these effects may be regarded as welcome relief by the sufferer, at least in the early stages, but counselling and other supportive help is **must** but administered concurrently to avoid complications.

Tranquillizers and antidepressants do not remove the causes of either anxiety or depression. Without significant additional and preferably alternative methods of help, the use of drug therapy with its accompanying risks **must be questioned and if possible avoided**.

With continued use, body tolerance to drugs increases and the drugs become less effective. Prolonged use of prescribed medication leads to an increase in the strength and frequency of dose administration. After several months continuous use cessation will almost certainly produce **withdrawal symptoms.**

Withdrawal symptoms may be psychological and/or physical in origin. Whichever, and it is most likely to be a combination of both, withdrawal symptoms can mimic the very symptoms they were intended to relieve. In combination with the continued presence of the original problem the result can be a worsening and declining situation. **This must be recognized and explained to the patient.**

On cessation of drug use, the artificial blocks put on the mind in order inhibit anxiety are removed haphazardly. A result of this is that thoughts and memories, feeling and fears which may not have been experienced for a long time, or if ever, start to occur, also haphazardly, that is, unpredictably. This can be **very** disturbing for the patient who is left in mental turmoil.

Physical symptoms of drug withdrawal include many

anxiety-like sensations of greater intensity than those previously experienced. Draw your own conclusions.

Because withdrawal symptoms are chemically induced, combating them with relaxation routines and other mind techniques, including hypnosis, may be less effective than usual. A patient may find relaxation therapy and other alternatives that proved helpful previously, are now less so. In counselling a patient in this situation may be experiencing symptoms far worse than before **in addition** to those for which help was originally sought, and for which medication was prescribed, but which still remain untreated or unresolved.

The cessation of drug use and the presence of drug withdrawal symptoms should be regarded as a transitional stage and as such, a separate part of the recovery program. Drug use prolongs recovery. Specialist or experienced help is appropriate when dealing with drug withdrawal symptoms.

Symptoms commonly mentioned include a fear of being with other people, fear of feeling trapped, fear of a loss of control, giddiness, palpitations, difficulty in breathing, choking feelings, sweating, headaches, stomach churning, vomiting, nausea, exhaustion, panic, fear of dying, tensions, loneliness. Obsessional thoughts, fear of fainting, feelings of unreality, afraid to go out.

Associated Symptoms

Those of general anxiousness, tight chest, chest pain, tight throat, dry mouth, muscle tension, especially in neck and shoulders, headaches, tender spot on head, heartburn, indigestion, gut pain, irritable bowel syndrome, spasms, chilling and cold skin, pallor, skin irritations.

Feared Situations.

Streets, shops, church services (or of taking communion), cinemas and theatres (especially if unable to have an aisle seat), travelling in trains, buses, airplanes or any kind of transport where free exit is restricted or denied. Supermarkets, queues of any kind, lifts, tunnels, hairdressers (common), open spaces and parties.

General outlook.

A successful approach to overcoming the multitude of problems presented by the agoraphobic or acutely/chronically anxious patient may include a number of different therapies.

Treatment should take into account personal, physical, mental and spiritual needs and abilities; also family and working circumstances and the patient's usual or preferred lifestyle.

Therapy must be practical and supportive; drug use minimal and patient's questions answered as fully as possible.

A full understanding of the condition and the patient's background must be established. Thorough evaluation should reveal any stressful situations present in the patient's life and ways in which such situations may be resolved discussed. The effects of relationships, past and present should be discussed, understood and constructively managed.

Patience is essential. Patience on the part of the sufferer, who may have taken years to arrive at this point of therapy; patience from the sufferer's family and friends who may be at a loss to know what to do to help. Patience from doctors and therapists.

Spectacular recoveries do happen, this much I have witnessed, but more often recovery is a step by step process, the rate of progress being determined by the patient's circumstances.

There is no 'norm'. It is reasonable to set achievement targets, if that is what the patient wants, especially when a drug 'run-down' schedule in involved, but rigid timetables are inappropriate and to be avoided, **especially** if requested by the patient.

Overall and given the foregoing, the outlook for full recovery is excellent.

Reminders to the Patient - Getting Back In Control

Remember, the major role the subconscious mind plays in causing and maintaining the problem. Certain circumstances in which you have found yourself has unfortunately resurrected some old reactions your subconscious has associated with the present. What you have suffered is are reactions to an old memory, not your present day experiences.

Remember, Your subconscious mind remembers things in far greater detail than you are consciously able to recall and you are probably unaware of the incident that is responsible for triggering your attacks and the memory of what happened at that time. This is normal.

Remember, although an anxiety attack makes you *feel* as if you are disabled, you remain the capable, intelligent person you were prior to their onset. You can still make decisions. You are still in control. You may feel like an unintelligible wreck, unable to comprehend the simplest thing, and that you are gasping your last breath, but that is the reality of a panic attack, not the reality of YOU.

Stop being afraid of feeling afraid. Stop feeling afraid of how your body feels. You may be wound-up but your body is designed to wind-down automatically. You have experienced the feelings that go with a panic attack often enough to have become familiar with them. You don't have to like them but you don't have to be afraid of them.

Stop being afraid of yourself. Think of your **Self** as a rational, conscience intelligence who stands alone. Think of your panic attack as the irrational by-product of a subconscious mind that is reacting to something that happened in the past, something irrelevant to your life in present time. Irrelevant to your life in the present; irrelevant to YOU.

Recovery is not reliant on remembering something that happened to you years ago. You know how and why the problem began. At some future time you may indeed come to know the original source of the problem but for the time being, just concentrate on getting on with life.

If you feel anxious but see nothing in your life to make you feel anxious, you can attribute your feelings to a subconscious reaction. Your subconscious trying to assist and protect you by helping you react swiftly and automatically, taking action without 'thinking'. Sometimes it misreads the situation at hand and urges you to prepare for 'flight or fight' action unnecessarily.

When you demonstrate to yourself – and your subconscious – that these kinds of reactions are disadvantaging you instead of helping you, you will find that gaining control of irrational thoughts and feelings is more easy than you imagined.

Remember:

    face your condition, know it for what it is.
    Accept what you feel, let the feelings come and go.
    Relax float, try not to tense, let things happen.
    Let time pass, be patient, all is well.

You may find it hard to ignore your next panic attack but once you have let it come and go without unnecessary fluster and upset you will feel something of the power you are able to exert over yourself. Soon you will almost look forward to an attack so that you can practice and reassure yourself of the control you have. Then the attacks become less frequent.

You will find it easier to relax and let an attack pass quickly if you spend time relaxing each day. Relax to a pattern so that you build up an habitual subconscious reaction with which you can countermand your anxiety reactions at will. If you combine your relaxation with positive affirmations or suitable hypnotherapy this control process will be speedier.

Take each day as it comes. Don't waste time regretting the time you have spent suffering. Instead regard what has happened as an opportunity to find yourself anew and to take control of your life in a new way. Build the future you want for yourself.

Yesterday has gone, its fears and threats are no more. Today is with you, in your sight and in your hands. Tomorrow and its unseen opportunities await you.

What you **can do** is more important than what you cannot do.

You **can do all that you need to do** to achieve fulfilment and find happiness in your life, this choice destiny places before all people.

13.   Phobias and Obsessional States

A phobia is a dread or uncontrollable fear, generally of a morbid nature, of an object, person or situation, on which the sufferer's attention becomes focused.

A phobia may lead to obsessional behaviour.

Obsessional behaviour is typified by a persistent, recurrent compulsion, to act in a particular way. The sufferer usually knows that the performance of these actions or routines is illogical but is unable to overcome the state of fear induced by not carrying them out.

Phobic fear is based upon a real fear associated with the situation or subject in question. This 'grain of truth' is supporting the phobia and gives rise to an irrational fear whereby the sufferer's fear is wholly disproportionate to the perceived risk or potential threat in question. It could be said the sufferer lacks the ability to distinguish the possible from the probable.

For the sufferer, if the possibility of a certain thing happening cannot be ruled out, then there is something to fear. Because the imagined threat cannot be quantified, neither can the amount of anxiety or fear necessary to prepare for its eventuality. Fear therefore must be total!

The sufferer's recognition that his actions are excessive, disproportionate and unnecessary points to a powerful subconscious reaction being responsible for his or her irrational behaviour. Impulses to act having been triggered by some thought, word, place, person or situation. The triggered fear becomes anticipated. Anxiety is increased by the prospect of confronting something known to produce a severe reaction.

There is also the possibility that an earlier subconscious memory has been triggered by a present or recent time experience.

Compulsive hand washing is a fairly common phobic/obsessional problem. While it is wise to wash one's hands at certain times, it is unnecessary to wash them after coming into contact with any or every possible source of contamination. The 'grain of truth' is that germs, bacteria, toxins and potentially injurious substances exist virtually everywhere and precautions should be taken to avoid risks to health, especially those including intestinal bacteria and other sources of food contamination.

The reality of this grain of truth is that there are 'germs' everywhere, and the body's natural defences can combat many, **but not all** of them. Usually the sufferer knows this, and witnesses, yet remains unable to control, his or her illogical behaviour.

Treatment to help cope with phobias and obsessional states will firstly usually involve counselling and some basic analysis aimed at finding the cause. Then appropriate supportive therapy to control and overcome the bothersome patterns of behaviour.

The object of therapy is to find a middle path, a way of moderation and compromise. Human make-up gives us the capacity for exaggerated and excessive behaviour that disturbs the natural harmony of body, mind and spirit in which we feel at our best. It is also therefore natural for the body, and mind, to seek the restoration of that harmony, one in which safe proportionate and helpful behaviour still exists. The road to successful therapy must offer this understanding, without which *any* change of 'safe' but phobic behaviour will be resisted.

Depression, especially if long-standing, can encourage the onset of obsessional behaviour and a lack of objectivity leading to morbid dread. Limited activity and a lack of desire to see other people or leave the home may lead to the development of an agoraphobic state.

Symptomatic of a depressed state of mind is an inability to rationalize, together with limited motivation and general apathy. Resulting in the development of restrictive habit patterns in which the adoption safe or basic and undemanding routines is increasingly demonstrated.

In such cases it is important to treat the depression. If possible also to finding the cause before confronting any obsessional behaviour directly. It may be helpful to control the obsessional behaviour therapeutically in which case it must be made clear that such control is treatment of a symptom and that finding and treating the cause of the depression remains paramount.

An obsessional tendency can be regarded as an attempt to achieve security and someone with this trait may also place disproportionate emphasis on the need for order and personal control. Any intervention in the life of someone with this tendency, even that is ostensibly helpful and obviously beneficial, will be resisted, perhaps vigorously.

Confusion and disorder are anathema to this person. That part of the world under the sufferer's control might appear disordered, inefficient, untidy and confused to the observer, and it perhaps is, but to the sufferer it is an orderly, controlled and 'safe' state.

Obstinacy and inflexibility are also characteristic, plans must be carried out and routines adhered to. A third element of control is that of 'thrift', the withholding of money. Giving away 'anything', especially money, is giving away power and the ability to control.

Therapy can be difficult. Without his/her complete cooperation and trust, the compulsive, obsessional patient will remain withdrawn and uncommunicative.

Simple obsessional/compulsive behaviour is common in children where it manifests as superstition. Avoiding standing on cracks in the pavement, intricate ceremonies before going upstairs or getting into bed, touching wood for luck and so on. Development into adult life sees the demise of most, though perhaps not all such superstitions.

In early years a predisposition to obsessional behaviour may be created by the imposition of high moral standards and strict discipline associated with codes of conduct and behaviour considered safe and necessary for social acceptance. The highly anxious child may react by setting himself high moral aspirations to win parental (and other) love and support, developing a very strong need to be 'correct'.

The development of obsessional characteristics may be selective and related to specific areas to which (an early) guilt is attached, for example tidiness, sexual taboos, punctuality, cleanliness, etc., and only become problematic in the area of life concerned.

Any additional source of anxiety or guilt can produce exaggerated attention-seeking symptoms resulting in fixed patterns of behaviour accompanied by a phobic dread of deviation from routine. This happens when a latent obsessional behaviour pattern is triggered by a recent event; i.e. an incident in adulthood not necessarily having any obvious or direct connection with the original childhood cause and associated reactions. These initially mystifying cases can be tricky as the absence of obvious cause often proves worrying for the sufferer. Another case where an explanation of the mechanics of the problem comes first, control of the symptoms second and looking for the precise cause third.

A dominant parent, or one with unrealistically high expectations of his or her child can be responsible for the child lacking confidence, feeling insecure and forever trying to prove worthy of being loved; someone who is also open to abuse and manipulation. A lonely, unhappy victim living in a state of mild anxiety; who wants to change but feels unable to make a go of things alone. A person seemingly unable to establish relationships on any basis beyond that of parent-child.

Here the original role of parent, mother or father, is transferred to a new friend or partner, i.e. husband or wife. The 'child' then proceeds to punish the 'parent' for past domination, even though it may not presently exist, and accept punishment for imagined failure, leaving the door open for bullying and other forms of partner abuse.

One possible result of parental behaviour perceived by the child as being loved conditionally is the manifestation of Anorexia Nervosa. Sufferers of this condition may be found to be people who feel unable to leave the parental care on which they have become dependent. A love-seeking dependency from which, in their sense of failure and unworthiness, they feel unable to release themselves.

In an over-simplistic sense, the anorexic is a child not yet able to accept personal responsibility and who has not yet been given the confidence and permission to leave the nest.   When the sufferer has been abused by one parent and fails to find comfort and support from the other, is unable to escape into independence, the acceptance of a kind of no-win situation is almost inevitable. As an adult, later in life this person may suffer severe anxiety, bouts of depression and possibly self-harming.

This is particularly challenging for the counsellor who will almost certainly be seen by the patient to be in a (pseudo) parental role at some stage. Indeed, because only a loving parent can restore confidence and give permission to 'leave home' the counsellor's **very careful** assumption of such a role may be essential in bringing the patient to independence.

If the anorexic/obsessional person marries, their husband or wife may (in some aspects of their relationship), take the place of the hitherto problematic parent. The pseudo-parent may then suffer his or her partner's displaced resentment and anger. Punishment of this kind can take on almost any form and is often the underlying reason for marital difficulties, wrongly attributed to what may be loosely termed incompatibility. Careful examination and counselling is called for.

At this point I would highlight my preference in seeing married-couples/partners seeking counselling separately. Each is then able to speak openly, without fear of their partner knowing matters best kept private or thought silly or irrational. Respect between partners is maintained, or if not present, must be established.

Trust is essential to privacy; trust is essential to a successful partnership. Privacy is essential both to the individual and to the partnership.

Returning to the subject of marital problems arising from misplaced parent-child roles. If a husband is not the strong person his wife seeks, he may be seen to be too weak to satisfy her need for a dominant 'father'. The result is that he, a considerate husband, is frustrated by his wife's unresponsiveness to his advances. She, on the other hand, enjoys his respectful loving attention but at the same time remains expectant of his domination and in this respect, unfulfilled. Clues to this may be found in partner's sexual preferences, which may go unfulfilled. Not the recipe for a happy or lasting relationship.

Guilt is usually associated with a phobia and together with the general state of anxiety (which as we have seen is present *before* the development of subsequent relationship problems) makes the sufferer vulnerable to self-punishment, forgiveness seeking and perhaps revenge directed toward the parent/pseudo-parent reactively felt to be responsible for his/her position.

Self-punishment -

Arising from feelings of personal failure associated with the expectation of punishment which fails to materialize. Frustrated at wanting to be different yet at the same time feeling unable to change, the sufferer turns anger inwards, rather than towards an undeserving partner. Any resulting self-punishment creates a win-win situation for the sufferer whose actions encourage, if not actually elicit a loving, sympathetic partner response. Self-punishment includes not eating, deliberate carelessness and clumsiness (inviting accidents), self-damage (accidental or intentional), suicide attempts, and 'failing' (which can include *any* kind of failure or non-achievement).

Forgiveness-seeking -

Forgiveness is an acceptable alternative to punishment. It is the helpless child seeking sympathy, typically forever saying, 'I'm sorry', often where there is no call for apology, in order to be told, reassured, that "It is alright, there is no need to worry'.

Revenge-taking –

In the realization that if I am different from other people someone must have made me like this – it is not my fault. This kind of thinking is supportive of the sufferer wishing to avoid taking responsibility. Revenge is by dominating the partner, family and friends whose lives are manipulated, subconsciously and consciously until their lives become centred around the narrow and often bitter world of the sufferer's phobic, obsessional needs. This is the classic situation of the invalid sufferer who, unable to go out or meet her needs herself, makes demands of other people.

Punishment – forgiveness – revenge -

Three faces of the same person, one caught up in a spiral of thoughts, fears and reactions, seemingly beyond reason control. Blaming self and other people for a life seeming at best second rate, at worst almost intolerable. Anger, frustration, forgiveness, revenge, despair; as the sufferer takes a roller-coaster ride of emotions in a never-ending struggle for reality, security, comfort, happiness and most of all, love.

Above all else embrace and love this person to release the butterfly.

To leave such fear and guilt behind can take a lifetime. The longer the phobia has existed, the longer it usually takes to leave it behind. There are no hard and fast rules but as a rough guide I suggest thinking in terms of months and years of gradual and progressive improvement to bring a long-term sufferer to feel happier and in control of his or her life once more. Then to look to ongoing infrequent support to ensure independence and confidently making life-path decisions.

It is very important to take matters slowly at first and let improvements come naturally. The mind then opens gradually, allowing the patient to examine the underlying causes of his or her condition.

Insight into the reactions presently taking place in relationships, evaluation of behaviour, control of reactions and the construction of controlled interaction and communication with other people can be considered essentials of therapy.

Failure to identify the true cause of the problem may result in only partial recovery and/or subsequent regression and for this reason some form of analytical approach is desirable.

Drug therapy may be already established and while this could be regarded as undesirable by a counsellor coming late to such a case, it is unwise to stop usage or change dosage before therapy is well under way. This is to avoid the unwanted complication of having to deal simultaneously with the problem and any psychological and/or physical dependency on prescribed medication. Withdrawal symptoms are best handled after symptoms and causes of the presented problem have been identified and isolated, when the patient can know precisely what symptoms are caused by what.

Finally, it is important to remember that a phobia is no more than an exaggerated, very powerful habitual action or reaction. We ALL live lives of habit. Almost every minute of every day habitual reactions tell us what to do and how to do it; because habits are (usually) helpful -we just take them for granted. We also know how hard it can be to change even the smallest habit and how unsettling the prospect of change can be. All this is equally true for the already anxious patient.

It is true that old habits can be hard to drop but the mind is capable of learning new routines, especially when there is no option but to do so. As we grow older we leave many childhood habits behind. Old habits become submerged as new ones take their earlier prominence but again it is important to remember that old habits remain dormant and 'live' to the right stimulus. I stress here that the patient must be told that in reacting inappropriately in an old way is not taking a step backwards or returning to 'square one'; it is simply being human. It does not mean that the old reaction is back to stay.

Life is a process of learning, we overcome obstacles are the greater for it

Overcoming a phobia is no exception – it is a hurdle to overcome, a habit to be left behind and in understanding we conquer!

14.   Phobic Reactions

A phobic reaction is one typified by an automatic, uncontrollable fearful reaction to the presence or thought of a given and predictable stimulus. Following an initial reaction to the stimulus and prompted by the thought of confronting the stimulus, repeated exposure leads to anticipatory stress and development of the characteristic 'fear of *the* fear'.

This is not to be confused with a fear of fear which is usually taken to mean a fear of suffering the symptoms of fear.

Phobic reactions can usually be attributed to one of two basic origins, though there may be other sources which are masked or not yet understood.

Firstly there are instinctive or innate fears and the triggering mechanism responsible for these fears is present at birth. The source of origin is genetic and likely the result of evolving development producing physical and therefore also mental changes likely to enhance survival.

Not all such reactions are immediately apparent, revealing themselves at such time as is appropriate. In human infants the fear of strangers normally occurs between the ages of six and twelve months. There follows a period of personal development and exposure to a widening variety of circumstances and hazards and it is during this period of development the individual will learn what is 'safe', by example or experience. Parental example is important in reinforcing or modifying innate reactions. Common examples are fears associated with spiders, 'wriggling things', cats and dogs, which to some provoke phobic fear but to others only mild anxiety.

Not all creatures show fear to the same degree. A baby bird will panic at seeing the shape or shadow of a bird of prey and there are other examples throughout the living world indicating a genetic patterning of innate fear responses.

Immediately after birth, it appears that almost any species is capable of adopting 'imprinted' reactions on exposure to example behaviour. This phenomenon is observed when one species acts as foster parent to another and this perhaps indicates an extension of the innate fear survival mechanism.

Another element of innate reaction is seen in behavioural interaction where the severity of fear is related to and determined by behaviour. For example, to confront an obviously aggressive dog will provoke a greater level of fear than when approaching one that is passive. However, in the presence of someone fearful of any dog, then even a passive dog will sense the opportunity for dominance and act accordingly. Body language cannot easily be disguised. Much of our relationships, with animals and humans, are determined by the unspoken signals we give before close encounter or opportunity of verbal communication.

Secondly there are conditioned or 'learned' fears. The mind has the ability to remember experiences and the capacity to store and recall by association everything that has happened to us, together with how we felt and reacted at the time.

Physical changes take place in the body automatically according to where one's attention is focused. When something is sensed that triggers a memory associated with a potential source of danger, appropriate physical changes then take place automatically.

There are occasions when despite having no conscious awareness of any danger, subconscious perception and memory associations result in fear reactions being triggered.

Traumatic experiences, serious and especially unexpected threats to life, leave very strong impressions on the subconscious as well as the conscious parts of the mind. Subsequent exposure to anything even remotely associated with the circumstances of the traumatic event result in the creation of automatic, powerful and perhaps disabling fearful reactions. Stray thoughts, dreams, sounds and all manner of insignificant things can trigger this kind of attack, which may also bring back memories of the original incident. This is typical of trauma 'flash back', an horrific and disabling fearful panic.

In ordinary circumstances, i.e. outside those of fear and anxiety, this simple reactive process is responsible for the adoption and development of habitual behaviour. Habitual behaviour is automatic behaviour governed by circumstance allowing us to 'think' about one thing while 'doing' something else automatically, This mental ability of running on auto pilot is of enormous benefit allowing multi-tasking of familiar everyday jobs.

Instances may arise where an innate reaction becomes associated or combined with a learned reaction, each reinforcing the other. When this happens control of the over-reaction can be difficult because it involves the suppression of a natural survival mechanism at a basic level.

Over-eating while not in itself a phobia illustrates a shared innate/learned reaction, the fear of hunger. An innate response to hunger or the thought of going hungry is to 'want to eat'. The presence or thought of food produces automatic responses of salivation and production of pre-digestive secretions. Learned reactions of eating at certain times, on certain occasions and at certain opportunities similarly triggers 'want to eat' preparation' reactions. Add to this the automatic reactions to the sight or smell of favourite food. A combination of reactions can make dietary control very difficult indeed, especially for the individual who eats when alone, bored, unhappy or for any of a variety of what are loosely termed 'psychological, reasons.

A phobia almost always contains an element of innate survival reaction, often the foundation on which the phobia is based. When something occurs mimicking a naturally helpful innate fear the combined effect of reactions to the 'event' and those of 'the innate fear' produces an experience sufficiently powerful to become the source of a phobia. A simple example might be a child who opens a door to what is thought to be an empty room only to be surprised by someone saying 'Boo', turning on the lights and throwing a trick snake. The child may then develop a phobia about closed doors, dark or empty rooms/houses and any one of a dozen permutations.

Three elements can may be found to influence the behaviour of the chronic sufferer.

1   An experience from which a 'learned' fear is created.

2   An innate or instinctive reaction closely associated with

the learned fear.

3   Avoidance-pattern behaviour focussed around the phobia.

Four separate defining stages of a phobic reaction may be seen.

1   The reaction persists.
2   The sufferer avoids anything that is likely to trigger a reaction.
3   The sufferer sees and knows his or her reaction is unreasonable.
4   The reaction itself is disabling, restricting or life limiting in some way.

The degree to which each of these elements is present varies from person to person and may also be partly determined by the nature of the phobia.

Phobias fall loosely into three categories: simple phobias, social phobias and agoraphobia.

Simple Phobias

A simple phobia is one where the fear is of a single object or situation, subsequently avoided. The reactions suffered are irrationally excessive though not usually disabling. People can become phobic about almost anything. Most people have a phobia of some kind though for most, the reactions are mild to moderate.

The roots of a simple phobia may be wholly learned or partly learned, partly innate.

Social Phobias.

A social phobia is basically one of self-consciousness; a fear of being seen, heard, smelled, etc., in certain circumstances. This kind of fear is probably at least partly innate, reflecting primitive life where concealment and/or acceptance was often essential to survival.

In early infancy a child automatically reacts to the sight of eyes, even a disc on which circles representing eyes have been drawn will elicit a smile response/reaction. Later there appears to be a reversal of this response/reaction and the child automatically withdraws fearfully from the close presence of a pair of eyes.

Fear is closely associated with staring eyes in the animal kingdom, including the human animal. Humans and animals adopting a defiant or threatening position will often indicate and support their stance with a wide-eyed stare. Some butterflies and birds not having this ability or sufficiently large eyes to deter predators use eye-like markings on their wings to deter predators.

Being stared at produces a feeling of unease in most people and actions attracting attention are frequently avoided: most people just like to 'fit-in', urban camouflage is the art of disappearing into the crowd.

This basic innate fear is exaggerated or modified in the presence of a communal structure when it becomes linked to learned fears associated with social etiquette. Common examples of phobic social self-consciousness include being afraid of saying or doing the 'wrong thing' when in company of people with whom one does not usually associate, taking too many manoeuvres parking a car, breaking wind in public, or just being laughed at.

The learned aspect of a social phobia is usually the result of childhood experiences involving discipline, emotional ties and threats of being thought of 'badly' by other people. Such threats may bring the child to a state of dread resulting in a lack of confidence in later life. The combining of an instinctive fear and learned self-consciousness can produce a disabling phobic reaction. The result is someone who feels insecure, shy, withdrawn and fearful of being laughed at, found wanting or being rejected by other people. A social failure.

The phobia or fear of doing the wrong thing can become closely linked with just 'doing wrong', when it becomes a more powerful fear carrying with it conscience created feeling of guilt and the prospect of punishment if found out. If the underlying cause of the phobia is supported by religious indoctrination and fears of even greater retribution, the effect can be devastating.

The approach to resolving such a case should include time spent in examining social structure as a whole; religious beliefs; parental/teacher expectations and the reason for any feelings of guilt. Time is necessary to establish a happier, freer, forgiving outlook.

Agoraphobia.

Agoraphobia is a term often mistakenly used to describe a fear of open spaces or of people but this description is too narrow. In broad terms an agoraphobic person will feel that he or she is, or will be, trapped in some way.

Agoraphobic fears include those of travelling in *any* vehicle not driven by the sufferer and from which the sufferer cannot 'escape' at will. Indeed feeling unable to move freely and unhindered are at the heart of this phobia'; tunnels, and the dentist's or hairdresser's chair are common sources of anxiety. Being in a public place where one might be stopped by 'anyone', friend, stranger, policeman, robber, it doesn't matter. It is the thought of being stopped and unable to proceed freely, of being trapped, that triggers the fear reaction.

Typically the sufferer is unable to explain *why* he or she feels afraid, knowing deep down that their fear is groundless but nevertheless feeling afraid and seeking reassurance and refuge in a 'safe place', which in extreme cases limit them to their home.

In addition to the primary source of fear is the secondary fear of fainting, dying, having a heart attack, losing control, screaming out loud, or appearing odd in some way; all related to the symptoms of anxiety produced by the initial reaction. We will look at this in greater depth in a special section on agoraphobia.

As this is an area of multiple phobias, the cessation of reacting to one may result in the appearance of another. Agoraphobics may be found sexually inhibited in some way, or in a sexually incompatible relationship: in both instances guilt is a factor.

This has given rise to some therapists approaching the problem through sexually orientated analysis and awareness therapy. While this aspect must not be ignored there is a danger it is seen as causative and over emphasized. Sexual frustration/incompatibility is responsible for a variety of anxiety related symptoms and behaviour.

The suppression of sexual practices, desires and deviations can be an underlying cause of severe phobic behaviour but it would be wrong to generalize as most relationships with a sexual element will almost certainly contain elements of frustration and suppressed desires.

Anxiety sufferers may find their built up tension can be dissipated by sexual activity. Masturbation is a convenient and pleasurable way of finding temporary relief from such tension, especially to aid the onset of sleep. Viewed as therapeutically symptomatic rather than indicative of a sexual problem this is particularly helpful to women, though equally so for men.

When an agoraphobic state has existed, perhaps unrecognized and untreated, for some time, many sufferers experience bouts of depression. Any recurrent or persistent state of anxiety can lead to depression as hope of recovery or relief fades. The danger here is that when the sufferer eventually consults a doctor, the doctor may treat the patient's depression. The results can be disastrous. Without effective relief from the underlying phobia the prospect is long term, ineffective drug therapy creating more problems and making future therapy more complicated.

Overcoming entrenched habitual phobic reactions can take a long time and for some sufferers compromise and partial recovery or control must be considered an acceptable outcome. The phobia may still exist but with reactions no longer disabling, a pattern of living that is relatively free from restrictions can offer happiness, security and fulfilment.

The process can be summarized to the client very simply.

Once an action or experience has taken place there exists the possibility of re-action.

Anything learned can be un-learned providing there is the willingness and opportunity to do so.

The control of and recovery from phobic reactions can be achieved in several ways and the following therapeutic combination has proved successful.

1 Reduce and then eliminate the fear of the fear.
   It is essential the sufferer accepts that his or her reactions are understandable and natural and; that such irrational behaviour is in no way abnormal, simply unfortunate. There is no mystery.

2 Promote the adoption of new, positive, counter balancing reactions through affirmation and visualization techniques and the therapeutic use of hypnosis. This will include a built-in relaxation response trigger the sufferer can use to combat anxiety attacks.

3 Encourage the acceptance of reality through gradual

exposure to the source of the phobia. Build self-confidence through visualization and new experiences which prove that which is feared need be of no threat. There is no substitute for experience though I consider the technique known as 'flooding', where the sufferer is exposed harshly and totally to the phobic target, to be risky.

4   The use of positive self-statement reflecting present time reality and a desire to change. Affirmations replacing negative fears and imagined unreality.

A gentle, patient approach encouraging self-help and self-management will bring results. All fears can be overcome.

Medical names for common phobias.

Phobia	A fear of
Acro-	heights
Aichmo-	sharp objects
Ailuro-	cats
Algo-	pain
Andro-	men
Bacterio-	Germs
Ballisto-	Missiles
Belone-	Needles & pins
Claustro-	Confined spaces
Cyno-	Dogs
Eyrthro-	blushing
Geno-	sex
Gymmo-	Nakedness
Haemo-	blood
Hypno-	Falling asleep
Lalo-	Talking
Lysso-	Becoming insane
Melisso-	Bees
Myso-	Contamination
Ochlo	Crowds
Osmo-	Odours
Paedo-	Children
Photo-	Light
Pryo-	Fire
Siderodromo-	Railways
Sito-	Eating
Toco-	Childbirth
Triskaideka-	The number 13
Xena	Strangers

15.   Aspects of Agoraphobia

A phobia is an unnatural fear and of all the phobias specifically identified by name, and there are more than 300, Agoraphobia is probably the one most commonly shared in the true phobic sense.

Everyone experiences a sense of fear at apposite moments, providing appropriate reactions that potentially enhance the prospects of survival. In contrast, the heightened anxiety created by a phobic fear can result in disabling over-reactions and panic.

Any state of anxiety is a mixture of fears and conflicts and agoraphobia is no exception. In the early stages this can lead to an over simplified diagnosis, which may be correct in the narrow view but which overlooks the larger picture presented by apparent disparate symptoms.

The single most typical symptomatic fear in agoraphobia is that of being with other people, though not actually *of* other people. In effect, a fear of being anywhere, or specifically, somewhere where other people may be, which is why many agoraphobics feel happiest in the comparative safety of their own homes, and in extreme cases, their own room.

At the centre of this most typical symptom is the fear of becoming a centre of attraction. The dread of being asked a question and finding all eyes turning awaiting a reply. It is a such times of high anxiety the agoraphobe dreads: when the brain seems to stop working, the voice vanishes, the legs turn to jelly and there is nowhere to hide. The agoraphobic prefers to be 'invisible' and attract as little attention as possible.

While on holiday or away from familiar people and surroundings an agoraphobic person becomes a different person, for despite the anxiousness of encountering the new, the agoraphobe *is* invisible in the sense that he or she encounters only complete strangers, encounters are likely to be brief and inconsequential, and ultimately, should there be any embarrassment it too will be short lived and quickly left behind.

Many agoraphobics can 'go out' but feel uncomfortable if forced to deviate from their normal routine. Surprises and sudden changes of any kind are anathema to the agoraphobe who associates the possibility with the presence of other people, hence their avoidance.

While a unique history underlies the experiences of every sufferer there appear to be two distinct paths leading to the presentation of this condition.

Many sufferers have a history of anxious behaviour going back to childhood. For these men and women, feelings of anxiousness and the restrictions they impose have become a way of life, though not always without resentment. For others, the first hint that anything is amiss comes with experiencing their first panic attack. Perhaps occurring when rushed or tired or in a crowded store or busy street. This was followed by further panic attacks and the sufferers avoidance of places where these attacks occurred. Safe routes were established but ultimately the only *safe* place is home.

For the agoraphobic's family and friends, the whole thing is usually a bit of a mystery. Not unnaturally it is virtually impossible for anyone who has not experienced a panic attack to know the feelings of terror they bring: the sense of isolation and extreme fear the disabled sufferer experiences. The resulting barrier further isolating the sufferer and creating yet more anxiousness and frustration. It is worth mentioning that one of the simplest and most under-rated 'therapies' needed at such a time is supportive, safe, physical contact and reassurance – an embrace or cuddle!

The single fear common to all sufferers is that of losing control. A fear of fainting, especially while away from the home, of doing something embarrassing, of being trapped and so placed in a position where this feared loss of control might happen – a nightmare of possibilities.

In a desperate effort to retain control, sufferers begin to suppress *all* reactions, making them tense, nervous people who, in demonstrating their attempts of self-reassurance, are likely to refuse help settling instead for isolation.

A complication arising from the suppression of all reactions is the suppression of emotional reactions, including those of sexual desire and response. While there are those agoraphobes whose lack of sexual fulfilment has been a factor leading to the condition arising, there are also many whose anxiousness has led to problems in their sexual relationships. Whichever the case, the additional tensions worsen the problem and increase the difficulties to be encountered in unravelling the causes.

The final phase, if there can really ever be such a thing, is the development of a fear of the fear, whereby the sufferer is aware constantly of the possibility of encountering a feared situation or of experiencing a panic attack. A fear from which respite comes only with sleep or medication. It is not a question of having good and bad days but bad days and worse days.

The causes of agoraphobia may not be entirely limited to those of mental and emotional states of mind. The potentially detrimental effect on the embryo brought about through maternal stress and trauma, especially during the second and third trimesters could be a factor affecting the child in years to come. This is perhaps too speculative to be taken seriously as a therapeutic approach and if explored could potentially open the floodgates on myriad problems that would perhaps be BEST LEFT ALONE .

Some physical influences may account for the difficulties some sufferers experience in functioning in vestibular* and perception areas of the brain and it is their efforts to compensate for this which leads to their agoraphobia. Only a small minority of sufferers is likely to be affected in this way but it is a cause practitioners must be aware of if they are to avoid wrongly focussed clinical care.

*Sensory receptors necessary for equilibrium adjustment, orientation and balance.

There is one more element common to most, if not all, agoraphobics and that is a sense of loss, though this is not always obvious. A sense of loss can trigger the onset of agoraphobia but even when the loss of apparent the connection may not be obvious.

An example is that of bereavement, especially where there

was little opportunity to express grief or where pressures of time and daily routine were particularly demanding or exacting. Another trigger situation is a stay in hospital, especially when accompanied by the emotional and physical trauma invasive surgery. This situation involves a loss of freedom, loss of family, even the loss of a piece of oneself!

A burglary or theft may be distressing start of agoraphobia but beyond these more notable examples there are many less obvious, perhaps because they are intensely personal and to which other are not privy. Deeply sympathetic, patient counselling can help release the emotional barriers to recovery.

The fear of future loss must not be overlooked. In its simplest and most direct form, the fear of death is uppermost in this category. A personal fear fuelled by repetitious thoughts and symptoms drawing the sufferer's attention to his or her personal physicality and the threats posed by particular pains and sensations. A fear not always focussed upon the self, but of being left alone following the death of a partner.

Before leaving the subject of loss, one loss commonly experienced must be mentioned, and that is a loss of love. Feeling unloved, rejected or feeling unable to love, is totally subjective, but without the experience of abandoning oneself to love, a dimension essential to life is missing.

16.   Agoraphobia – (self) Counselling Notes

1. Look for a sense of loss. Commonly following a bereavement, the discovery of a partner's infidelity; a redundancy, especially if after a singular, long-standing employment; or the enforced move of dwelling place and loss of friends.

    Examine and 'talk-out' all points carefully. It is important to both rationalise and bring back to the client an awareness of the control he or she has. Not an particular outcome but 'control'.

2. Examine aspects of relationships carefully and exhaustively. Agoraphobic symptoms can develop concurrently with feelings of wanting to break an existing partnership, including one of marriage; or of wanting to be unfaithful. This may manifest as regret and dwelling on an enjoyable past relationship. Look for feelings of guilt, repressed sexual problem and effect of a dominant and partner who's effects are negative.

3. Look for aspects of the client's life that are being avoided. Agoraphobia makes a perfect trap into which the sufferer may fall, thus preventing he or she from confronting a feared subject or situation. The restrictions imposed by the condition take this dilemma out of the client's hands, he or she being incapable of taking the feared action, the question of its confrontation being rendered pointless. Recovery is hindered without such a situation being resolved.

    Ask what it is the sufferer will have to face or do when recovery takes place. Conversational clues include phrases such as "It's not fair on my wife/husband as it stops him/us doing 'X'"

    Also look for the condition being used as a means of self-punishment to appease guilt; and as punishment to partner who may or may not know what it is she/he has done.

4. Is there an obvious lack of love from someone attached to the client, or fear a relationship will end?

    Illness of any kind but especially one that is selective in its manifestation allows the suffer to exert control over those with whom he or she is associated – partner, family, friends, employer, etc..

Unless the patient feels confident in achieving a balanced and fruitful relationship with those he/she feels at present inadequate or disadvantaged in some way, recovery can be protracted, difficult and incomplete. In the process of restoring confidence the patient may over-compensate and become very demanding of other people. This stage is not unnatural and must be managed in therapy to avoid greater disharmony – though some temporary disharmony may be helpful where a partner has been dominant and lacking in understanding.

5. A proportion of wives (and perhaps, though not so commonly, husbands) will not relinquish their symptoms until their partner has also received 'therapy' or counselling or is included in the patient's treatment in some way. This may be to afford the patient an opportunity to bring out into the open a matter he/she has found difficult to broach. It may equally be a way of punishing the partner for some as yet undisclosed action.

    Apportioning blame is to be avoided and can be by presenting counselling in the guise of an analytical examination of the relationship in question. Along the way pointing out how the actions of one person may be misinterpreted by another and how grievances, although small in themselves, if unresolved may sour an otherwise happy union.

6. To help overcome the patient's fear of panic attacks and their symptoms, bring him or her to confront those feelings gently and explain what is happening. If not already undertaken, ensure the patient is medically well, suggesting a visit to the GP if necessary.

    When assured of his or her fitness suggest the patient creates a state of breathlessness deliberately by running, skipping or doing any exercise that is not strength demanding or damaging in any way and which the patient feels is appropriate. The object is to get the patient used to having a rapid heartbeat and breathing heavily AND THEN resting and recovering. From this kind of experience much reassurance can be gained when experiencing and recovering from a panic attack. An aid to self-control and management.

7. Follow all the points outlined in the notes on agoraphobia.
8. To increase the patient's confidence and ability to relax, use two or three progressive hypnotherapy sessions (pre-recorded is fine) for the patient to use at home daily, for four to eight weeks. One session is seldom enough as most sufferers are unable to accept the very positive suggestions necessary immediately. Sessions must begin gently and as the patient becomes more used to them and is able to relax more easily, more definite suggestions are then introduced. Ready-made recordings will be available from professional hypnotherapists or through your doctor.
9. Make sure the patient knows what you have in mind. Avoid too much mystery but do not overload your patient with too much information too quickly. The patient seeks reassurance that you are able to help, if you think you can't, for ANY reason, say so.

   You need not reveal that you intend to discuss 'X' or 'Y' if you think this might frighten-off a patient who is not yet ready to confront such matters. Pace is all important. To the patient, any form of self-control of his or her symptoms will be regarded as progress. Establish a string of little what may seem little successes before introducing a subject you think may be challenging.
10. Be patient with the patient. Lead but do not push. Keep it simple and direct.

17.   Communication – Friendliness S.A.I.D.

In this chapter we look at the spoken word and some of the ways in which speech can be used. We consider what a conversation is, its purpose and steps we can take to ensure what we say is what other people hear.

The first requirement of verbal communication is that there be a *speaker* and a *listener.* For effective communication to take place, only one *speaker* and one *listener* is required. One person speaks while another listens. When addressing an audience the relationship between speaker and listener is the same, though the *speaker* may be ignorant of any feed-back and unable to ascertain the true effectiveness of his communication.

When communication involves two people who are both speakers and listeners, then a *conversation* is deemed to take place. Feedback is instantaneous making it easier for the parties to ensure mutual understanding.

Whichever the situation, the objective of the speaker is to impart knowledge or convey understanding, to the *listener.* If the listener does not understand, the communication has been ineffective in achieving its objective; if misunderstood, the demands on the speaker are increased. Not only does the speaker have to achieve his original objective but in order to do so, must first dispel the effect of the misunderstand.

Some people say, of themselves, that they never know what to say when in the company of other people. Socially or at work they feel at a loss for words and unable to join in conversations. They may ascribe their feelings to a lack of confidence but it is equally true that often those lacking confidence speak most, and probably loudest.

There are many reasons why 'not joining in', is a perfectly natural thing to do. Individual interests, knowledge and experiences vary greatly; any conversation is likely to be narrowly focussed on a particular subject, person or event of especial interest to the speaker who hopes his interest is shared by members of the audience. Listeners falling outside this catchment of interest may find listening is boring, only politeness preventing them from walking away.

Someone unable to establish friendships may attribute their inability to shyness and poor social skills, which may be true. However it is important to acknowledge other causes rather than to focus simply on communication skills.

If you have something to say, and opportunity to say it, then do so.

If you have nothing to say, or no wish to say anything, say nothing.

If, in your silence, you feel socially uncomfortable, ask a question and pass the burden of speech to someone else. Many people are happy to have the opportunity to talk about themselves or a pet subject and the skilful enquiry can bring a useful, if mainly one-sided, conversation. By appearing to take an interest in people you may even be complemented on your social skills.

Don't feel pressured by silences. Silences are natural breaks occurring at opportune moments. If, at such a moment, you feel no reason to remain in that company's presence, leave: your departure will be taken as part of the moment. If you are content to stay, be silent in your contentment until there is a reason to speak.

Four elements are essential to effective verbal communication: subject, attention, intention, duplication. S.A.I.D.

Subject.

Before you speak you should first have a subject in mind, around which your words can form, leading to your natural ability to communicate simply and effectively whatever it is that you have in your mind.

The objective of one person communicating with another is to impart, share or give an understanding. Without a subject there is no view, opinion or value and so logically, there is nothing to share or say. To try to make a conversation without having something about which to speak, is clearly difficult. Without clear intent, the speaker is unable to convey anything relevant or meaningful to the listener, who may then become suspicious of the speaker's reason for talking.

To enter into conversation on purely social grounds can be difficult. Inconsequential small-talk is easily seen for what it is – trivial and usually time wasting. An alternative to meeting a social challenge is to show interest in what somebody else has to say. Ask questions and listen to what is said. If you have the time and really do feel that you want to be at whatever gathering you have attended, become a good listener. With a little imagination on your part, joining in is then easy and calls for only the minimum of effort. Don't blame other people for wasting your time if you choose to put yourself in that situation.

Attention.

It is the responsibility of the speaker to wait for, or create conditions that are conducive to effective communication.

Having decided that there is something about which to speak, the speaker must firstly attract the attention of his intended audience <u>before</u> beginning to speak.

If what you have to say is important then it demands your listener's undivided attention.

Too often we address someone who is not facing us; or who is preoccupied or listening to someone else or who is in the next room! Then, having said he has not heard what you said, blame *you intended listener* for not listening.

172

Intention.

There may be a delay in getting your intended listener's attention, or losing the attention of the person to whom you are speaking. When this happens, **Stop talking!** Your presence alone should command attention, silently! Patience is called for and your intention to speak, to communicate a particular matter, must meanwhile be maintained.

It is easy to lose the thread of a conversation, or become disinterested, or feel the moment has passed. At such times effective communication is very difficult. Rather than persist with the attempt, either abandon it, or arrange a more suitable time for it to take place. If your subject demands urgency, take control of the situation and create the right conditions. If you are at first thought rude or intrusive, the content of your effective communication will hopefully dispel such feelings.

Duplication.

In your, (the speaker's,) mind thoughts begin as mental pictures, images bringing clarity to your thoughts. These thoughts and pictures must then be transformed into words, expressions, inflections and emotions that recreate similar mental images in the mind of the listener.

The images you create in your listener's mind may not be identical to those in your mind but what you say must convey your thoughts in a way that brings your listener to understand what you intend.

The listener may repeat your communication to you in a slightly different way in order to gain clarity and ensure he has interpreted what you have said correctly. This response is usually prefaced by questioning phrases: "What you mean is..." and "Are you saying that..."

The speaker should accept responsibility for the effectiveness of his or her communication.

The teacher has not taught if the pupil has not learnt and the way in which a subject is presented is a important as the subject itself.

Equally important is the fact that just as the speaker must be motivated to speak, so too must the one to whom he speaks be motivated to listen. It is wrong to suppose that other people want our opinion or will be interested in what we might have to say.

While I have the right to speak, you have the right to ignore.

The ability to communicate effectively is affected by mood. When someone is feeling 'low', and 'under-the-weather', motivation to do anything is also low and the ability to communicate is diminished. In this case attempts to communicate may lead to exaggerated forms of behaviour being substituted for words These attempts often fail because the effect is to appear either aggressive or indifferent, sullen or uncaring, so discouraging others from enquiring.

Someone whose mood is depressed needs comforting but the very condition that demands sympathetic understanding is the cause of its denial. Unless the cycle is broken, the depressed state must run its course, which may end up with long periods of silence and withdrawal. It may even become habitual or cyclic resulting in misunderstandings and broken relationships, leaving the sufferer in even greater isolation.

Unresolved, this kind of situation, which may begin simply through some transient circumstance, can lead to family break-ups, long term depression and anti-social behaviour.

If you feel off-colour, fed up or miserable, then say how you feel. It is better to be thought a grump than leave other people wondering what they have done to upset you. If you are concerned about something, say so. If you feel frustrated, taken for granted, ignored or powerless, say so. Let other people know, don't leave them guessing.

Don't expect other people to solve your problems and don't expect them to be mind readers.

Friendliness.

Another element of effective communication is friendliness. Attraction between two people.

The degree of attraction shown towards and shared with other people is directly related to the ability to exchange views.

It is usually pointless to even try to discuss or reason with someone who appears hostile, even when you are not the cause or the object of that hostility.

Hostility is associated with anger and feeling threatened, both of which induce a sense of isolation – a barrier to reasoned communication. This is dramatically demonstrated in hostage and siege situations where sympathetic efforts designed to remove any sense of isolation and to engage those concerned in some form of communication are more likely to succeed that overtly aggressive approaches.

At the other end of the scale, those people enjoying spiritual, emotional and pleasurable physical closeness need but the briefest glance, word or gesture to convey 'everything'.

Successful public speakers, entertainers and advocates often smile and encourage warmth in their relationship with an audience, and this is the case even when serious matters are to be discussed. The warmth must be sincere; if it is not a sense of manipulation and dishonesty will quickly undermine all other best endeavours.

To smile inappropriately can appear condescending, reveal lack of understanding or otherwise destroy the credibility of the speaker. Structure is important and there are occasions when an audience, or the person to whom you are speaking, needs preparing for the communication about to follow. Following which, transition from preparation to matter in question must be seamless if, subsequently, the listener's resentment is to be avoided.

Genuine friendliness and friendship can overcome obstacles that communicating disagreeable, controversial and unpleasant subjects can bring. Presenting a topic in an open, unassertive and compassionate way can also gain the listener's acceptance more easily; removing any sense of hidden agenda or ulterior motive.

In conversational exchange, statements made by other people that are contrary to one's own can be accepted, rejected or ignored.

Acceptance does not mean agreement. Acceptance of another person's view or opinion is no more than that, unless that person presses for a response. If invited to respond, state your own view or opinion, prefacing your opinion by saying that you accept that the other person makes a valid point. This is no more than stating the obvious as his view could not exist if it were not a valid point, at least to him. His opinion may be based on a lack insight or information but that does not invalidate it, only opens the way for your input and elaboration.

Acceptance means that you do not set yourself in a position of opposition, thus maintaining ease of communication. Nor do you deny modification of your own view should you wish to adopt or include some part of what has been said, and expand your own understanding.

Always leave the way open for development, expansion and greater shared understanding.

When your opinion is not expressly called for, or you do not offer it, acceptance can be no more than your lack of opposition.

Silent acceptance may lead someone to believe that you are in agreement, when you are not. This is relatively unimportant, especially when you are in the role of counsellor and when the flow of communication is more important than precise or otherwise pedantic accuracy.

Rejection of another's view or opinion is aggressive and final, conveying an inflexibility that may be attributed to your attitude rather than a point of firmly held principle or factual knowledge. It may also covey your disregard for something of genuine importance to another, and thus your disregard of him also.

Ignoring another person's view may appear as passive acceptance and prove no impedance to the conversation. On the other hand, boredom or a superior attitude might be showing.

Self-Image

Self-image is yet another aspect of communication that may determine the outcome of an encounter.

Your manner, appearance and attitude are important to your ability to communicate effectively as they underpin your acceptability, by other people, and in turn, what element of friendliness may be achieved. All are derived from your sense of self-image.

Self-image is not necessarily the presentation of who you think you are or how you know yourself to be. Self image can be constructed for a particular purpose, to achieve a certain objective. In other words, self-image can be whatever you want it to be, though there are constraints of ability and natural culture. It is not possible to always disguise the fact that one is a fish-out-of-water, never the less, we all present ourselves in ways which either suit us personally or in ways we think make us more acceptable to other people.

To a large degree self-image is based on how we believe other people see us. For example, we may say we dress to suit ourselves and do so in order to feel comfortable but that 'comfortable' is in part a reflection of how we want to blend in with, stand out from, or in some other way affect the way the outside world will view and treat us. Characteristically the introvert and shy will 'dress down', the socialite will dress 'suitably', the extrovert will dress 'up'.

When we look in the mirror it is usually to check the image we present to other people, even if it is only to be sure it is the image that represents us truly. However, all this is in the eye of the beholder and we can never look through another's eyes, see with another's bias and desires. We never really know how others see us, even when we think they have told us.

Generally we dress and behave in ways we think appropriate to an occasion and that are most likely to be found acceptable by other people. On approaching someone, we are aware of who and or what that person *appears* to be; and who that person may *assume* us to be. There may be elements of role play, reflecting social structure, financial status or other factor.

For example, the way we react on being stopped by a police officer will be in part determined by the circumstances, then by the police officer's attitude or manner (here the friendliness factor comes into play – or not!). We may act submissively, cooperatively, aggressively, dismissively or in another way reflecting how we see the situation and our prejudices towards the intrusion into our life of someone who has power over us.

Fear is a factor!

In all our encounters we actively encourage the other person to see us in the way we think he or she should, or will, if we cannot disguise an emotional reaction. That person then draws a conclusion about who and what we are, perhaps concluding also that initial impressions were the correct one's. So it is that we all show public and private faces to the world at large, the world within, exclusively our own.

Self-image – created, accepted, reflected, reinforced.

Anticipate aggression or rejection in your encounter and your behaviour and image will convey as much. Likely you will be met with caution and suspicion, even aggression, and you will conclude that you were correct in your expectations.

You then believe, wrongly, that you can 'read' people, knowing how they will react towards you, when all the time you are setting them up to fulfil your own self-prophecy.

You can change another person's view of who and what you are, and as they reflect that image you become that person, changing your view of yourself.

Someone who feels dowdy and uninteresting and impoverished tends to dress, stand, walk and express himself in ways conveying that state of mind. Other people see only that picture and react accordingly, not necessarily unkindly but reflecting who and what they see. The circle is completed as the role is created, accepted, reflected and reinforced.

Dress up instead of down and smile instead of frown. Look up and shine. Project and bask in the sunshine of your self-image.

Accept or decline invitations according to how you truly feel and remember to keep a place for kindness and compassion and that old friend duty. Live with yourself and make it easier for others to live with you.

Accept that other people may be taken up with their own preoccupations and opinions, some will be discourteous or cruel but go beyond role playing and come to be the person you know yourself to be, who you truly want to be.

18.   Communication – Beyond the obvious

In the course of a conversation, a commonly occurring situation is one of a sudden and unexpected change of mood or attitude, for which there is no obvious reason. One moment everything is fine, conversation in full flow, the next, clear signs of disinterest, withdrawal or even hostility are detected, and the conversation collapses.

An unexplained distancing between conversants has occurred, perhaps followed by a period of silence, or an escalation of assertive or aggressive reactions.

When there is no obvious cause for the breakdown, the true reason can remain a mystery. However, the mind does not like 'mystery' and so an element within what had been said becomes the attributable, if ambiguous cause. The parties concerned are left to recover what can be salvaged from both conversation and relationship and, if possible, make sense of what has happened.

Obviously there is a reason why this sudden change of mood has taken place. The two most common or causes, and ways in which they can be managed, is the subject of these notes.

Firstly, a WORD has triggered a sub-conscious reaction. That is to say, a word used in the present conversation has been subconsciously associated with a past incident or conversation, and the emotions associated with *that* time are now reactivated.

Secondly, a WORD has been misunderstood, either in its precise meaning or in the context in which it has been used.

Trigger words.

In most family, social and working circles there is someone who can be relied upon to react predictably to the mention of a particular subject. Just one word is enough to get him or her 'going'.

Individually this is true for virtually everybody. We all have, within our minds, sensitive subjects we prefer not to think about, perhaps associated with an embarrassing moment or something about which we feel a sense of guilt. Most of these remain private but when such a trigger is exposed, we may then become vulnerable to innocent, or not so innocent taunts and manipulation.

Many of the subtle changes that are brought about by subconscious reactions to trigger words, go unnoticed or unrecognised for what they really are.

As we go through life we experience many people, places and situations, pleasant and unpleasant, that leave their marks on us, or, more precisely, on our subconscious minds. The use of words, either our own, or someone else's become integrated into these experiences. Words that now highlight the event or incident which can invoke an emotionally charged defensive reaction.

Childhood experiences should be considered to be of particular importance. The immature mind of the child is open and eager to learn; it is also unprotected by the caution of reason and experience and so vulnerable to emotional hurt. So much is new and lessons learned in childhood are the foundation of our survival abilities.

Not unnaturally, childhood experiences carry strong reactive associations and although childhood memories may fade, the reactions associated with them do not. Much adult behaviour is determined by the influences of those early years.

Sometimes a single word is sufficient to trigger a reaction powerful enough to change mood and physical state almost in an instant. Changes which may then be attributed incorrectly to present circumstances.

At this point it is worth noting that many common anxiety states, including that of Agoraphobia, have their roots in unremembered childhood experiences. The occasion of the first revival of those early memories, for example the first panic attack, is mistakenly thought to be the beginning of the problem. It is not! Understanding the principle of subconscious reactions producing reactions, including panic attacks, that come out of the blue, for no apparent reason, is of paramount importance to the sufferer's ability to break free from what may otherwise become a downward spiral of failed therapies, medications and other treatment.

To return to my main theme.

Take for example a child who is called a 'Mother's boy", perhaps innocently by another child, light-heartedly by a relative, or disparagingly by a teacher. Use of the term might coincide with the child in question feeling alone and isolated, vulnerable and anxious, as might be the case on the first day at a new school, or being separated from his family in some way, such as, being hospitalised. The child is going through a traumatic experience, the focal point of which may become the word, or label, Mother's boy.

The child is now sensitive to the use of the phrase because of the emotional associations he now subconsciously (and also perhaps consciously) holds. Associations of insecurity, ridicule, weakness and anxiety. However, school turns out to be exciting, the world turns out to be not such a bad place and the memories of childhood are forgotten as the child grows to manhood.

The boy, now a man, is married with a family of his own. As is the way of things, family squabbles and arguments arise and during one such, this man's wife happens to say, "I expect you will take your mother's side, you're her blue eyed boy."

Within the context of the argument she may well be right, as might he be also in taking his mother's view. His wife may only have used the words because she has no real argument of her own and is looking for a way out, or resents her mother-in-law. No matter what her motive is, her use of the words 'Mother' closely linked to (blue-eyed) 'boy' is enough to trigger a subconscious reaction associated with those words, in her husband. The result is that he feels threatened, becomes defensive of his mother and, losing all sight of the subject in question, the conversation descends into an emotionally charged row. The wife doesn't know what she has said to warrant it, the husband doesn't really know why he feels so defensive and so attributes it to something his wife has said, or implied, about him and his mother.

There is now a rift between husband and wife, neither really understand why and how things have gone so wrong. He knows he is acting uncharacteristically and irrationally but being overwhelmed by his own feelings, finds he can do little about it. She is confused and feels misjudged yet also guilty feeling that she is in some way responsible for what has happened.

We all have a store of subconscious trigger words, just waiting for someone to literally, pull the trigger! Each carrying their associated moods and feelings. Not all associations are bad, some words bring us to feel warm, happy, melancholy or even loving – every emotion, mood and state of mind can be catered for. Some are highly reactive, others less so, but all are capable of producing an almost instantaneous change, the effects of which can mystify and confuse. Sadly, many such words and their associated reactions, the products of experiences that happened long ago, form barriers that have the potential to affect us throughout our lives.

Such is the power of words.

Overcoming the effects of subconscious trigger words.

What can be done to avoid the potentially unhappy outcomes of such reactive behaviour? In conversation, when you become aware of an otherwise unexplainable change of mood taking place, ask yourself," Is this real? Is this a genuine response to present circumstances or is it reactionary and inappropriate?"

(Précis: A reaction is automatic, is usually inappropriate to present circumstances, and is usually excessively forceful in its presentation or expression. A response is action chosen for its suitability to present circumstances, undertaken consciously and conscientiously. See chapter on conscious/subconscious minds)

The change of mood could be in you or the other person but once recognised, the situation may be managed constructively and more easily.

The following procedure can be used to control subconscious reactions arising within a conversation and help maintain communication.

Firstly, it is important to recognise when a reaction is taking place. It may be in yourself or someone to whom you are speaking. The means being observant: suppressing the display of your own reactions and not *counter-reacting* to those exhibited by the other person.

Secondly, if the person to whom you are speaking shows signs of reacting, take control of the conversation and introduce a communication break. This can be done quite easily and without drawing attention to any change of atmosphere. Make an excuse and leave the room, or at least the presence of the other person, for a few minutes. Get a drink, go to the toilet, do something unconnected to either you or your conversation. In doing so, you remove yourself, and any association he may attribute to you with his change of mood, from his sight, depriving his subconscious from further reaction due to your continued presence.

On your return, ask the other person a question, preferably about a subject you know is of interest to him and definitely unconnected to the subject previously under discussion. Smile as you do this and look expectantly for an answer, appear interested and comfortable.

As you do these things you tell him that the change of mood he experienced has not broken the bond of conversation. You also show:

    A.   You were unaware of his reaction, or, if you were, you have no bad feelings about it.

    B.   You value his opinion, demonstrate an interest in him and even imply a shared interest.

    C.   You look to him to respond, to answer your question, resulting his mind being placed on that subject, in consequence of which you are changing his mood.

After a little time has been spent on this diverting tactic there can be a return to the original subject and conversation.

This procedure can be used effectively to resolve communication breaks due to 'unknown' reactions but is less likely to succeed where the cause is related directly to the subject under discussion. In this case, it is the nature and character of the individual and his passion or sensitivity toward the subject in question that is responsible for the breakdown. Criticism of 'the cause' may be taken as criticism for the person, who feels then feels under attack. With a loss of friendliness, the ability to communicate effectively is diminished.

Here the way ahead is to back off, ask questions, appear and be interested, open up to explanation, show passivity, accept without agreement, and be patient.

Misunderstood words.

Many words have alternative meanings, some are archaic and whose meanings are open to interpretation, some words will hold personal attachments to unrelated subjects, others sound similar but are spelled differently and have alternative meanings, and different words may hold or convey the same meaning.

We also rely on the context in which words are used to understand their meaning.

Constructing sentences correctly is as essential as ensuring that the person to whom you are speaking is listening, is free to listen and is able to hear what you say. (See chapter

Communication S.A.I.D.)

"Golden beeches" or "Golden beaches"? "Yew wood" or You would"?

What comes to mind when you read (hear) the following?

"I wonder if he will be all right at the bar?"

This is an example of a sentence that cannot stand alone. That is to say, a sentence that is incomplete and which, in order to be understood fully, must be taken within a greater context than it alone presents.

Without knowing who *he* is, why there is cause for concern, the nature of *the bar,* and whatever is he is at *the bar* for, the sentence makes no sense.

Because a question is implied, though not actually posed, the listener's attention is divided. Who is the subject, what is the problem, how important is the problem, what might the answers to these questions be?

Also, the listener might wonder if he should enquire on these points but hesitates in case he has heard only part of the conversation, or whether the question is purely rhetorical.

The result – confusion, and a listener lost in his own thoughts.

As for the real meaning – what did you make of it? Do we have a yachtsman having to negotiate a difficult sand-bar; a barrister going into court; a ballet dancer facing a new exercise; a new and inexperienced member of staff in an hotel; a gymnast entering a competition; a man going for drinks in a crowded pub; or something else?

Equally important is that the listener examines carefully precisely what he has heard. The way in which words are used and the care with which sentences are constructed, likely reveal the true purpose of the speaker trying to attract your attention. It might be at work, in the street or at home but all may not be what it at first appears to be. There are times when it is necessary to see beyond the logic of the words to find the real objective of the person talking to you, or at least trying to attract your attention.

Take the following statement as an example, one which

might be used by someone trying to engage your interest and open a conversation.

"I have a real problem with my radiator."

An apparently ordinary sentence but, like the previous example, one that is incomplete. A sentence that cannot stand alone but unlike the former example, deliberately, rather than carelessly so.

This kind of spoken statement is commonly used as a way of introducing a new subject or, more often, to fulfil another purpose altogether – meeting a need that will never be mentioned.

Re-examining the sentence, note that it begins with "I". This is a good indication that it is the speaker who is the true subject and to whom your attention being directed: not to the *problem*, or to the *radiator*.

The speaker says *I have a problem* but does not tell you what the problem is. Unless you intend ignoring the speaker, you have been invited to enquire as to the nature of the problem. This is a commonly encountered situation and superficially insignificant: a safe question that does not (yet) directly involve a request for your help.

In responding and enquiring of the problem you demonstrate to your listener that you are sympathetically interested in him, and that you are acting in a friendly manner towards him. Only by ignoring him completely will you appear none of these things.

You have enquired and are now engaged in a conversation with someone to whom you might otherwise not have spoken. What does this person really want – comfort, attention, support, a friendly ear, an opportunity to moan?

Look closely at the opening sentence. The fact that there is insufficient detail for you to respond meaningfully should tell you something about the person, who you might know; and this is an early opportunity for *you* to take control of any subsequent conversation. For example, you could respond by acknowledging the speaker by saying *"Oh really,"* without making further comment.

Returning to first principles. There is insufficient detail. There is no mention of what the *problem* might be; the word *radiator* has several different meanings and a variety of applications. So what is the true objective of this person?

Perhaps just to reassure himself that someone cares about him, but risking annoying people by speaking so ambiguously. He may feel a need to be noticed and attract attention to himself, using sympathy as a ploy. Both opening gambits of which people soon tire if repeated often.

There is also a risk of introducing an additional disruptive element or barrier to any subsequent conversation. The words *problem* and *radiator*, both of which are unknowns, invite the listener's personal reaction and inner speculation. As the listener's mind hunts for possible explanations, word association may easily throw up memories, or memory reactions and mood changes related to past experiences in the listener's life. It is now the listener's reactions, and possible preoccupations, may now take precedence.

While the object of the speaker was to engage sympathetic attention, the effect his words have on his listener – confusion, annoyance and preoccupation - is to the contrary.

Without underlying motive, the same subject could have been phrased differently.

"One of my central heating radiators has developed a leak that is proving to be something of a problem."

Or.

"I have a problem with my central heating system: a leaking radiator. I don't want to drain the system down, do you have any ideas ?"

A descriptive, clear expression that leaves little in doubt, most aptly invites a positive, sympathetic response.

An incomplete statement that invites you to question, can be a means by which you are drawn into conversation, for an as yet undisclosed purpose: or it may be the manner in which someone habitually speaks, again with a less than obvious motive. Listen carefully, respond and control the conversation to the degree necessary for you to avoid manipulation and retain independence.

A word is a symbol used to express a concept or a thought picture held in the mind of the speaker. When used effectively, words create a similar image or understanding in the mind of the listener. The picture created in the listener's mind will be based on the listener's experiences and so differ in some detail from that of the speaker, leaving the possibility of misunderstanding. To help avoid this, a picture that contains more detail and that is more specific need to be created. Alternatively the speaker can rely on the listeners own imagination to provide an picture and understanding and leave it at that.

For example, I might ask you to picture in your mind, an autumn afternoon. My words will bring into your mind a picture representative of the subject I have suggested, but it is *your* representation, not mine. A picture based on *your* experiences, a picture that is familiar to *you*; one that, for *you*, has a particular or special association. Your picture has great detail, in fact far more detail than I or anyone could put into words. My words have been instrumental in the recreation of an experience, part of which is the mood associated with that experience.

Truth is in the saying, "A picture is worth a thousand words", the knack of effective communication is in creating the right picture. Picture in your mind an autumn afternoon; the air is still, the sun a glowing red ball sinking gently behind trees now silhouetted against a gold-pink sky, the first traces of evening mist rise across the fields, the first star twinkles... The differences between our pictures may be great, but how different would yours be, and your mood, if I had preceded my initial suggestion with this fuller description?

In attempting to describe the indescribable the speaker is reliant on his or her listener or audience having experienced something similar; in fact not just the experience but also the mood with which it might be commonly associated.

The importance of firstly listening carefully to what is said and then understanding the words and their meaning is emphasised. Also looking beyond the logic of the words and the technicality of language, in search of the speakers true objective.

Is your mood being deliberately changed? Are you being softened up or being made artfully fearful?

The importance of the imagination cannot be overstated. How do you explain the colour red to someone who has never had sight, or the sound of a bell to one who has been profoundly deaf all his or her life?

Words can carry information, be logical in their meaning and create or reveal purpose.

Words are physical objects in their own right. Each word a collection of characters conveying specific literal meaning; or specific vibrations representing those characters, created orally and aurally and carried on the air. The creation of words follows the laws of elemental physics. Energy, of the Mind, is transformed into Mass, the solid matter of words. This mass is then carried to a recipient whose mind transforms the mass of the words into energy. Mind energy, the energy of emotions, enthusiasm, or fear, all of which hold the potential of greater action.

In addition, the way in which words are used and projected reflect the mood, character and intent of the speaker. The *manner* in which words are used is an important part of the conversational picture. The tone or weight of a word or collection of words (sentence), might be *heavy, light, short, colourful, drab, high, flowery,* regardless of their precise, literal meaning.

The manner and way in which words are used, the tone of voice, the accompanying facial expressions, the speakers stance, the structure of the sentence, the circumstances under which the sentence is used, all affect the way in which words are 'heard' and understood. The listener, taking all these factors into account, must then interpret and determine meaning,.

The listener must also deal with any feelings aroused within him or herself, reactions subconscious reactions as well as conscious memories recalled by the words just heard. He or she must know whether to set aside his reactions, or heed feelings that make him wary of what he has heard and from whence they came.

The ways in which language is used allows both the spoken and written word to be presented in ways that create an impression contradicting the logic of the words used. In every day terms this is the ability to 'yes' in a manner which leaves the listener in little doubt that the speaker really means 'no'.

Words create moods. (see chapter on this subject)

In addition to conveying meaning and logic, words are capable of changing the mental and physical state of a listener. Perhaps more than anything else, it is this feature of modern language that is responsible for the anxiousness underlying and pervading modern society.

The accurate and perceptive dissemination of what one reads and hears is of paramount importance to self-determination and freedom from shackles forged by other people's words.

Humankind is unique on Earth in having the ability to communicate imaginatively with others of his species. This ability, combined with the ability to communicate symbolically, that is, with words has created a weapon by which humans may subjugate one another. Words are the ammunition of people who then wield weapons more powerful than any physical force. Whether presented directly, as in media newscasts, disguised, subtly or otherwise, in 'entertainment' of almost any kind, or in the printing of a simple leaflet, information and misinformation creates and influences the nature of the world in which we live.

Words can build, destroy, encourage, inhibit, release, undermine, create, subvert, enhance, colour, quieten, annoy and many, many more things.

Desire and fear create thoughts. Thoughts are brought to life with words, words initiate action, action brings effect.

Self-control is in remaining free from the control of others, and their words.

Self-control begins with the dissemination of what has been heard; understanding what has been said for what it is and for what it may be; understanding what has been said in the context of place and time, of speaker and circumstance. All to be constructed into a sensible and intuitive overview before offering any response.

Be aware of how other people use words to influence you. Listen carefully to what is being said and understand it for what it is, not for what you might be led to believe it is. Be aware how your own desires may lead you to believe other than what the content of what you have heard actually means.

To illustrate this point I use an example of a television commercial advertising a pension fund. The question posed to the viewer is this:

"How do you choose a company to provide a pension scheme?"

The advertiser then goes on to supply, what it suggests should be your answer.

"There are some companies with below average performance, some with average performance – and then there is Prodirect Penco Inc"

From this, one could be led to believe that P.P.Inc is the best, which is clearly the advertiser's intention. From the facts contained within the sentence we can see that what is claimed is that P.P.Inc is not below average, nor is it average, with the implication that it is above average. As a stand-alone sentence, the implied comparison has little if any virtue.

On what basis is 'average performance, based? Over what time-period have comparisons been made? What geographic area does the comparative study cover. Is the comparison based or investment returns or subscription returns? What is the basis of the term average, mean, median etc.? There are many further questions than could be legitimately inserted here but the point is made.

While the statement and claim made in the advertisement may be true, it means no more than what it says. That is, the performance Prodirect Penco Inc., places that company in the band of companies with performances that are above average in some way. Of a hundred companies, fifty might be shown to have performances that are above average. Prodirect Penco Inc. might be bottom of that list of fifty, performing less well than forty-nine other companies, but the claim is still legitimate.

The craft of the advertiser is to get you interested, allay your fears and encourage you to invest in a particular product. In reality, from this advertisement, you are little wiser than you were before hearing about P.P.Inc., but if you happened to be thinking about your future and your pension needs, you could be hooked into enquiring further.

Being television, there is the added visual element. A mood manipulating medium used by advertisers to enhance susceptibility to their product, to stop you thinking too rationally. Eye-catching pictures, emotive scenes, reassuring voice-overs and suitably suggestive music create an ambiance in which you may view products favourably. Your response is more likely to be reactive rather than responsive, your judgement based more on emotion than logic.

Across the media, any form of news reporting, including 'live' interviews, contain bias, assumption, projection, anticipation, supposition, and speculation which supposedly relates to and reflects the subject under discussion. This is far from a that comprises a combination of personal opinion and (hidden) agenda; the true objective being personal to the reporter, director, interviewer, interviewee, film company, or media owner, who in turn may represent a political, economic, religious or corporate body.

NB

A this point I should explain how relevant and important this is to you, the counselor and your client. Part of your objective is to build your client's confidence, and self belief. Guiding him or her to think questioningly, about anything or everything offers a pathway to independent thinking where decisions can be made more confidently. Self-determination!

Returning to the subject of information dissemination.

Presentation of an item of news becomes a manipulation of facts designed to sway public/audience opinion and reaction. This common practice is responsible for much unrest. Viewers, listeners and readers are subjected to headline grabbing clips, partial explanations, examples of misdoings and accusations of incompetence and guile in rapid succession. Nothing is ever explained fully enough to be worthy of sensible conclusion, nothing is ever as it seems. The news reporting media as a whole leaves in its wake, a trail of anger and frustration.

Much news reporting, especially that from overseas, is derived from 'official sources'. These may be government departments or press offices, presented through news gathering agencies such as A.P. and U.P.I.. When you see the same clips being used by a number of t.v. channels or the same photographs shown in different journals it has likely come from a press office somewhere, or a reporter or *paparazzi* with his or her own agenda. Editing is then used to create the desired impression, photos cropped and films cut to exclude anything that might place what is presented in true context.

Much news presented as being factual is just not factual. A single piece of information, which itself may not be wholly factual or taken out of context, is used as a basis on which to build a grand and convincing picture. If some details are missing, no matter. If some opinions are a bit wild, no matter. If an idea cannot be disproved it must be considered a possibility. When a subject of fearful interest is presented with fervour and enthusiasm, in an emotionally charged way, the possible can become the probable. The consequences are taken as factual, inevitable and acceptable because the initial premise was based on 'fact'. Well actually no, it wasn't.

Described as *experts*, people are paid to give their professional opinions because there is benefit in expert opinion supporting a particular view or helping achieve a particular objective. A common media objective is a presentation that has impact. Headlines are a quick and easy way in which this is achieved, a partial headline being a ploy often used in television presentation, for example. 'There was a serious fire in a Midlands warehouse earlier today, a woman was attacked in her local supermarket and a dog caused a serious road accident during the school rush hour'. Any the wiser? Of course not, there is no mention of where any of these incidents took place – keep watching for that, it may be in your town, OR NOT.

Whatever the underlying motives of companies and presenters are, the effects brought about by their intervention into the lives of people at large are enormous. Effects brought about by changing the mood of the listener, viewer or reader, frequently by the introduction of some worry , fear or sense of hopelessness. There is little profit in good news!

Unnecessarily sensational, graphic details create distorted and unjustifiable changes in the everyday lives of millions of people. A common argument justifying this kind of presentation is a need to present people with the truth, a need to create public concern. It is more likely to be a way of keeping thousands of men and women working in the world of journalism, earning a living in a fiercely competitive world with ever greater dramatisations of the world in which we all live.

An unfortunate effect is to saturate us all with such a huge volume of news, that any sense of reality is lost, everything becomes remote, impossible for us to comprehend or change and so relatively meaningless. The result is momentary anger, pity, anxiety or shame, a view of diminishing values and a world of diminished value. Depression and apathy.

The viewer, reader, listener is manipulated to achieve an objective, perhaps nothing more than to hold his attention and so improve viewing figures, essential to maintain advertising revenue, or buy a newspaper, or sway opinion. The staff presenting the news is reliant on your compliant support – keep watching, keep buying the newspaper, keep phoning in, keep writing, your actions justify our existence. Now there is a powerful thought. Stop reacting, stop getting angry, start getting happy!

The use of words as a means by which people can be manipulated is not restricted to the media, there is much in everyday conversational encounters about which one should be wary.

Be aware of instances when the person to whom you are listening uses words and phrases to 'paint a picture' in your mind: the effect will be a change of mood. Such occasion might be to build up to a joke or funny story, following which your mood will be lightened. Equally it could be painting a picture of something you will find revolting or depressing, or that distresses you in some way.

Ask yourself, "Why is this person doing this to me, what is his objective, what does he want and, most importantly, do I want to be changed?

Some examples of picture-painting speech is obvious. The insurance salesman who's carefully chosen words are designed to make you feel anxious or fearful, and who then offers to protect you from the consequences of the perils he has introduced to your mind. Or the financial consultant who seeks only to help you weather the storm, protect you from potentially risky investments and who appeals to your desire for security, or greed, with promises of wealth. Or the politician who encourages you to vote for him as he alone can avert the tragedy that awaits you should his opponent be successful.

Less obvious is the unassuming kind of person we might meet in the course of our day. A person who, almost without our realising what is happening, changes our outlook in some way. On whose departure we feel aware that somehow we have changed, or the day is not what is was. We might be uplifted, downcast, worried, enthused, even grateful, but in whatever way, another person's words have brought about a change of state in and therefore, around us.

Recognising what is happening *before* another person's words have had time to take effect is an acceptance of one's ability, and duty of responsibility, to remain in control of one's life. There is always choice. Choose what you expose yourself to, choose how you want to change or be changed.

With a little effort it is possible to put a smile on the most miserable face.

This brings us to the importance of clear speech and of the need to take care with the words and phrases we use when speaking to other people.

It is important to recognise other peoples' reactions to what we say, the words we use, and the way in which we use them. There are two main objectives on which to focus. Firstly, the careful use of words to ensure clarity and avoid misunderstanding, with the objective of a smooth flow of communication and mutuality in conclusion. Secondly, the deliberate use of words to convey meaning beyond words, with the objective of controlling both the conversation and the person to whom you are speaking.

This is the power of words.

How often are we truly aware of the effect we have as we speak?

There are occasions when words are inadequate or inappropriate: when a demonstration of emotions is a more effective way of communicating our sympathy, love and understanding, and equally our disgust. Without words we can we can accept or dismiss, demonstrate our love or our loathing, embrace or send away.

Understanding what other people say and mean demands our understanding of their words and their use of words and our acceptance of their communicative abilities, poor spelling, grammar, syntax and so on. More important is the other person's ability to convey what he or she wants you to understand and share. The spelling may be poor, the accent and grammar atrociously foreign to you but if you understand the meaning of what is being said, communication has been effective. The objective has been achieved. Criticising the way in which something is communicated creates an almost impenetrable barrier to true understanding, an essential part of which is a trusting, open receptivity on the part of the listener.

When something you hear upsets you, remember the upset may be unintentional or deliberate. How you feel about what has been said will reflect you relationship with the person who has said it, as well as you ability to distinguish innocence from contrivance. The upset may be yours alone, but even this may be planned if the speaker knows you to be reactive to certain words or subjects. Here the speaker's need to influence you reveals the value he places on your opinion or ability and the status you hold in his eyes. Recognise this also, use this acknowledged status to gain a better stance in your conversation. Control your reactions, respect your right to self-determination.

We are all entitled to our points of view. No one person can ever know absolute truth, all truths are relative to their time and place.

Absolute truth is beyond human comprehension. Only in our collection of smaller, relative truths, can we approach sensible understanding and shared inclusion. Inclusion is at the heart of communication, dogmatic exclusion, denies the beating of that heart.

19.   Communication – Reasons Why

Why do people say and do the things they do?

Some of the reasons why people say and do the things they do.
Because it gave him pleasure....
Because she saw it as the solution to a problem...
Because he felt it was expected of him....
Because she felt compelled to reply.....
Because he felt he had been asked to do it......
Because he wanted to avoid unwanted consequences...
Because she felt she was fulfilling someone else's wishes....
Because he felt obliged to act in the circumstances....
Because she felt to do otherwise would have been wrong....
Because he was acting out of habit, unaware of the effect he would have...
Because she thought that saying or doing what she did, would help...
Because his words satisfied an irresistible desire for expression...
Because he felt immediate action was called for....
Because action was demanded and she saw no alternative..
Because she needed to demonstrate her ability...
Because he wanted to assert his authority...
Because she wanted to draw attention to the matter...
Because he needed to draw attention away from something else...
Because she wanted to an opportunity to explain something...
Because in doing this he avoided doing *that* (whatever *that* might be)...
Because this was an opportunity to express her feelings..
Because he feel trapped and so forced into action...
Because she wanted to encourage someone else to speak or act...
Because he felt that a simple acknowledgement would give a false impression...

Because she finds saying nothing very difficult...

Because taking control offered an opportunity for gain...

Because she thought that in demonstrating her insight she would gain status or approval..

Because he felt threatened he reacted defensively....

Because she feared criticism if she did not offer an opinion...

Because in speaking first, others, with contrary opinions might not speak...

So often we are left wondering what on earth motivated someone to behave in a particular way, or say something seemingly out of character. We worry and question ourselves to what part we might have played in provoking someone's unexpected response.

Our conclusions are coloured by our expectations of what we expect to see and hear 'next' - normal and usually helpful response to any given situation. What we actually see and hear might be somewhat different and what we then *allow* ourselves to see and hear is a compromise. All our experiences and the conclusions we draw are seen from our own unique, personal perspective.

Sometimes we hit lucky and really do understand the other person's deeper motives, fears and feelings but more often we do no more than arrive at conclusions that serve our own purpose and support our own prejudices and point of view.

Admitting that we do not understand another person's point of view or belief can seem a hard thing to do but in doing so we can open a dialogue from which genuine understand can flow. Not to do so can lead to a breakdown in communication, bad feeling and disharmony, based on unchallenged assumptions.

Provocative words and actions are often used as a means of demonstrating dissatisfaction or frustration following an inability, or lack of opportunity, to communicate effectively whatever it is that has given rise to these feelings.

Provocative words and actions are ways of drawing another person's attention and prompting a reaction, in so doing opening a dialogue in which the true subject can be broached or discussed.

Provocative outbursts may point to personal and emotional problems but are not necessarily indicative of difficulties within a relationship. There is likely to be an underlying personal problem which is not being brought to the surface; a subject that is being avoided, perhaps because of a fear of the consequences of doing so.

There could be a longing to confront the subject in question and an inability to do results in provocative action designed to force the forbidden subject into the light. Heated and emotional discussion remove the inhibitions that have prevented a less dramatic exchange.

Because *any* reaction is emotional in nature it is difficult for it not to be felt as some kind of personal attack. This does not bode well for the happy outcome of the desired communication. The outburst is to do with a need to expression feelings of some kind. Feelings are not well expressed in words and so the combination of words and actions does fulfil its purpose, albeit painfully.

Watching and listening is more important than talking.

Both demand time and patience and allow understanding to form while at the same time, demonstrate interest, an effective precursor to conversation.

When we cease to assume and set aside our prejudices we may instead, question.

When we have listened carefully and understand the views of another person we may have no need to question.

20.   The Domination Effect

Dominant, Negative and Jealous People.

Most of us sense when we come into contact with someone whose objective is to influence us, our opinions, thoughts or behaviour; whose intention is our *domination*, if only on a purely personal level. Most obvious are people who act arrogantly, even aggressively to achieve a particular objective but there are others who exert their influence in subtle and controlling ways and it is they are the subject of this chapter.

Dominate: *'to exercise control over, to enforce one's will upon, to influence.'*

However, in order to *dominate* one does not have to be *domineering*.

Domineer: *to exercise authority and influence in a harsh or arrogant manner.*

The circumstances of being subjected to dominating influences may be unavoidable, such as those occurring in family relationships; or through a working relationship – supervisor, employer, workmate; or in other parts of life – police officer, judge or magistrate, neighbour, bank manager, revenue inspector, doctor and so on. All perfectly natural occurrences but perhaps the saddest and most damaging cases are those existing between partners, tied into intimate relationships from which escape is very difficult. When one partner lives in fear of upsetting or disobeying the other.

Because of the circumstances by which the domination comes about, it may be necessary for the person 'dominated' to accept a subordinate role in order to gain a personal objective, avoid punishment or other unwanted consequences of confrontation.

When such dominating effects are prolonged and endured; or when the domination is particularly harsh, aggressive or humiliating, the sufferer undergoes a major change in his or her subconscious reactive behaviour. In effect almost undergoing a personality change.

Initial Conscious resistance by the sufferer gives way to a typical form of survival behaviour: his or her reluctant acceptance (accompanied by justification for this submission) which, if perpetuated, becomes a pattern of reactive, automatic submission which persists in spite of the increasing resentment that usually accompanies repeated submission.

If extreme and humiliating, such persistent domination may bring the unfortunate victim to the limit of endurance and beyond. This results in explosive behaviour and extreme reactions including suicide, attacking the dominating person, running away, suffering acute and chronic anxiety, sinking into deep depression or having a constant fear of losing control.

With the exception of physically attacking the **Dominating Personality**, or D.P., other behaviour patterns reflect the suppression of the sufferer's desire to act against the D.P. because of a love tie. The resentment becomes internalised. Without an outpouring of the emotional stress that has been created, self-critical mental turmoil leads to a loss of self-esteem and confidence.

Underlying these complex emotion states is a desire to escape, to run away, to hide, to make a new start elsewhere. The sufferer may find relief in quiet moments of withdrawal from contact with the D.P.; or undertaking something in which he or she feels free from interference and criticism. This activity may be kept secret and the fact that it is kept secret may induce a sense of guilt; of being 'found-out'.

Prolonged mental pressure created by attachment to a D.P., may be indicated by signs of physical distress. Tenseness, internal bodily disorders, digestive problems, irritable bowel syndrome, skin problems, headaches and a variety of uncomfortable or painful symptoms of vague or unclear origins come and go. Recurrent infections, colds, etc., occur as a result of immune system suppression resulting from the effects of prolonged anxiety.

Ultimately, because illness in any form gains sympathetic attention, illness becomes an escape from some of the effects of the dominating person. Illness then becomes an acceptable part of life, allowing for the developing of more serious conditions. Once such a downward spiral is embraced, diminishing mental and physical resistance can have a fatal effect.

Such a bleak picture is not inevitable. By understanding what is happening and developing a stronger sense of 'Self' and rebuilding confidence, the grip of the most persistent D.P. can be broken. The key is to recognise what is happening, especially in the early stages of attachment.

Therapeutically it is equally important to identify both D.P.'s to whom one is currently attached AND those who have been influences in the past.

Controlling the effects of a dominant person – counselling advice to patients

A very important aspect that is easily overlooked and misunderstood is that the dominant personality who is the cause of the problem, does not act in an aggressive or even assertive way. Some of the most disabling and damaging effects are caused by people who seem caring, obliging and inoffensive on the surface. How then, can these D.P.'s in disguise be recognised.

Here the patient/sufferer holds the key.

The key is self-observation. Noting how and when one's mood or outlook is changed. As an example let us say that you are feeling pretty good, you are happy enough and feel that things could run along quite nicely – at which point you might add 'if only...' - in which case you have just identified the presence of a person bringing an influence of domination into your life.

It is important to separate the situation containing this influence from the situation itself. Work/school/whatever, would be fine if it wasn't for the influence of a particular person, maybe friend, maybe teacher, maybe boss: whoever it is, it is someone who spoils the event FOR YOU in some way.

The person in question does not have to be someone who dominates you in an obvious way. It might be someone who does no more than moan, or criticise, or embarrass you, or who is always negative and pessimistic; someone who you would rather not be around more than is necessary. This might be difficult if he or she also happens to be someone of whom you are fond.

A case of loving someone in spite of himself! Here the trick is one of mental detachment. Once understood, the unwanted influence can be set aside and their negativity, put down to something that is just a part of that person – and ignoring IT without ignoring him.

Identifying people who are having a negative influence is where it all begins. Become aware of when you mood comes down. Even when it is low there are people who can make you feel even lower. Ask yourself WHO was with you, or of whom were you thinking when your mood lowered? Who were you talking to, who were you about to meet, who had just left you? Who left you with the sense that you had just lost something, that your world is somehow emptier or that you feel unsettled and dissatisfied? Who has taken the colour out of your life and painted a picture of your world in grey?

Examination of the effects of your relationships may throw up some interesting and perhaps confusing results. A change of mood may not be directly attributable to the person with whom you have associated a change of mood. Your mood change could be due to a subconscious reaction triggered by a mannerism, word, tone of voice or turn of phrase associated with an earlier negative experience involving someone else. In other words you begin to run on automatic, experiencing the feelings and mood associated with a past encounter of a D.P., you may or may not be aware of who that person was.

Identifying a change of mood is as important as identifying the source of the influence. You can choose the level of mood in which you want to stay by mentally removing external influences. Of course if you want to punish the person concerned by all means demonstrate how unhappy he or she is making you – be angry, miserable, unhelpful or do whatever is necessary to make your feelings clear. In doing so you have submitted to that person's dominating effect because you have stopped being yourself, you have become what someone else has made you.

It is then important to decide whether the cause is past or present. Have you experienced a triggered reaction, rather than having fallen under the influence of someone who is having an immediate dominating effect?

The question is not quite as difficult as it might at first seem. It will soon become apparent whether the other person's behaviour reinforces the effect or moves past it. Triggered reactions tend to come out of the blue and have no real connection to the matter in hand. The way to handle an isolated negative reaction occurring within an otherwise positive conversation or relationship is to deal with it simply and directly.

Remember that it is quite normal for subconscious reactions to be triggered by innocent and insignificant things that have no true relationship to present time. Knowing that there is no real basis for your negative reaction and change of mood you can begin to control your reactions by setting aside any disquieting effects and bringing your attention back to the matter in hand.

Not ignoring your reaction but instead mentally putting it aside while you evaluate its validity. This can only be done by placing your attention on the reality of the present moment. If, having done so, you find your mood lifts, and you maintain or return to a comfortable exchange of views and ideas, you will have realised both self control through self understanding without jeopardising a relationship and the outcome of your present engagement.

The real bonus in exerting self-control in this way is the effect you have on the behaviour of other people, especially D.P.'s to whom you are attached. Because you avoid re-runs of old behaviour patterns and dismiss impulses to react submissively, the nature of your relationship changes.

It is not that you have suddenly become assertive or challenging, only that in choosing not to react to the words and behaviour of someone else, you are simply 'being yourself'. The process is calculated and your behaviour controlled carefully, but passively. From such small changes come great ones – guaranteed!

When a D.P. to whom you are attached finds that he cannot provoke you to react subordinately or defensively it is the D.P. who is left questioning. The roles you each play within your relationship are no longer clear and uncertainty results in a sense of insecurity. At this point the D.P. begins to lose confidence. *His* reaction may to be question you, demanding to know what has got into you and why you are behaving so strangely. Or he may try to exert even more pressure. You need do nothing more than remain on an even keel, gently rebuffing unreasonable arguments and requests, each time you do so, reinforcing your independence.

What else can you do when faced with a Dominant Personality, perhaps one who is in your life right now? Someone who is making you do things you would rather not do, or preventing you from doing things important to you personally? Someone who is spoiling life for you in a variety of little ways, that in themselves seem too small to comment on, but which have the effect of suppressing your natural energies, desires and achievement of happiness? Someone who always seem to be able to make it seem that it is *you* who is being unreasonable and that whatever goes wrong is always your fault?

Firstly it is important to try to understand what motivates the D.P. to act the way he does. (As throughout I use the term 'he' for simplicity only, as all applies equally to men and women).

Does he know what he is doing, the effect he is having on you? (Have you told him?)

Does he behave coldly and act without feeling? (Emotionally defensive behaviour).

Has he always behaved in a dominant way? (if not, his change of behaviour may be linked to an incident or matter not yet properly resolved).

Does he sincerely believe that his domination is no more than guidance and he has your best interests at heart? (Maybe genuinely misguided; maybe justifiable in certain instances, perhaps delusional and covering his own lack of confidence – explore).

Does he act dominantly/intolerantly towards most or many people? (A basically insecure person.)

Does he act dominantly towards you only in private, almost secretly? (A bully and very insecure person who appears very different to other people.)

Whatever the circumstances, it should be understood that the Dominant Personality behaves in the way he does FOR HIS OWN REASONS. It should also be understood that whatever these reasons are, they likely go unrecognised by the D.P. himself. Typically a case of "It's obvious that I am right and if you can't see that, then that's your problem!"

While your natural reaction to being subjected to the influence of a D.P. is to feel pressured, guilty, lack confidence and self-question negatively, this reality is a totally reactive and subjective. They may sustain and encourage the D.P.'s behaviour, but neither they nor you, cause it. The D.P.'s behaviour is not a reflection of your personally. Whatever you do will be open to the criticism of a D.P., implied or direct. You just happen to be the person unfortunate enough to be attached to or in the firing line of such a person. If it were not you then it would be someone else. If you happen to be a spouse or partner than you were probably chosen in part for your apparent submissiveness. You would not be aware of this and may only act submissively when in the presence of your D.P. spouse. This makes him or her feel good and, in his or her eyes, also appear good by comparison.

The whole 'act' is to show you, and other people, how much you need him/her. If you are ill your D.P. partner will give every outward sign of aiding your recovery but, and it is a significant but, he will use the opportunity to enhance his position and keep you from recovering. This D.P., will give you every encouragement to take your time in getting better and because this kid-glove control is disguised as sympathetic care it is difficult to detect, resist or criticise. Subtly you are discouraged from making the effort necessary to establish independence fully. Should you 'overdo it' you will be criticised and made to feel you cannot judge for yourself what you can or cannot do. Eventually the effort to overcome the restraining effect of the D.P. may be too great and there is acquiescence into submission.

At this point your stifled resistance prompts a further reaction; that you redress a unacceptable situation and switch the balance of power in your favour. The D.P. controls your life but now you use your condition, situation and circumstances to control his – resorting to a means of effective communication left open to you by the D.P. The negative aspect of this is that in order to maintain control, you have to remain 'ill'.

D.P.'s are dominant in their behaviour and effect because the resulting sense of power makes them feel superior. D.P.'s are people whose sense of inferiority demands they not only redress the perceived inequality but raise themselves sufficiently above other people as to avoid their criticism. These views of relativity are entirely subjective but for one person to feel superior another must be regarded as inferior and bringing that person to actually behave in an inferior manner reinforces the perception.

In the patterns of behaviour occurring around a D.P. there is an overlap of words used to describe the dominating experience.

Ask yourself, do you feel inferior, subordinate or junior to the D.P. in question?

Do you regard him or her as behaving in a superior, dominating or senior way?

Does the D.P. in question share your view of his or her behaviour?

The dominating effect of a D.P. may be exercised over just one person, or many: it may be limited to a particular place or circumstance, such as the home or workplace, or all the time, everywhere.

Whatever the case, it is a pattern of behaviour designed to protect the D.P. from blame or criticism, to avoid having to explain or make decisions. It has nothing to do with the needs, wishes or behaviour of the subordinated recipient.

A D.P. does not usually recognise that there is any problem or that his or her behaviour is having such a negative and disruptive effect, or creating the unhappiness it inevitably does. It is the unfortunate victim or victims who are driven to seek help as mental and physical health suffer.

Of paramount importance is to recognise that the cause of the problem, the essence of this manifestation of human behaviour, is rooted in the Dominating Personality, not in his victims. If you are unfortunate enough to be connected to a D.P., remedial action can be taken.

1. Control/Manage

Recognise Dominant Personalities through their effect and behaviour, and in response, adopt the pattern of behaviour you feel most appropriate to prevailing circumstances and most able to follow, either:

a)   Make or break.

Through gentle assertion and non-compliance, demonstrate resistance to D.P. pressure. In so doing, reaffirming your own self-reliance, depriving the D.P. of feed-back and demonstrating that his behaviour is ineffective. The D.P. will then face accepting you as you are and adapt, or avoid contact.

b)   Live your own life

Understand the D.P.'s need to behave in the way he does. Because you are unable to avoid or do not wish to separate from this person, accept the situation and act compliantly. Give the impression of submission but continue to be true to yourself and do your own thing. Your behaviour can be misinterpreted by other people who see you as 'downtrodden' and you may become secretive to avoid discovery of your 'real life' but so long as this is a chosen path it can remain positive and fulfilling.

2. Disconnect

You can remove yourself from the presence of the Dominating Personality. Divorce or separation, leave home, change your job; do whatever is necessary to regain freedom in the Self in which you can make personal choices.

Temporary disconnection may be beneficial, separation for a period of several weeks, during which time the victim undertakes remedial counselling, can be effective in establishing the basis for a more balanced relationship. The act of separation, albeit temporary, may encourage the D.P. to look at his behaviour; it is equally likely he may see it as an opportunity to say how the victim 'cannot cope' and needs him even more!

If control or disconnection is not effected, life for someone attached to a Dominant Personality will deteriorate.

The Negative Personality.

The effect of a Negative Personality in your life can be even more devastating than that of a simply dominant one. A more detailed definition of the Negative Personality follows but it is worth mentioning than many D.P.'s have a very negative outlook and appear to behave subordinately, but this is misleading.

As an example take to case of a quiet, home loving man, inoffensive and to all appearances a nice chap. However, his wife and children see him differently: to them he is an unapproachable ogre, impatient, bigoted, intolerant and uncommunicative. A man who imposes his will through denial, who will not explain or discuss, who wants nothing more than 'peace and quiet'. He has scant regards for the wishes of the rest of the family and lets them get on with their lives while he reads the paper, and criticises whatever they do. He may be loved but it is in spite of his behaviour, and he will be resented and avoided: 'Don't tell your father' is an oft used phrase.

A Negative Personality does not quite go so far as to actually impose his will on others directly. His effect is to diminish their sense of self-worth, turning people into failures in their own right. Having done so he is happy to let them alone, bar being critical of any decisions they make. Failures are judged by the his standards and are not really failures at all: here the effective force is accusation, doubt and circumstance, not reality.

The Negative Personality appears to make decisions but really only denies those of other people. The N.P. appears compliant and easy going but is neither.

Take the following example:

You ask the N.P. where he would like to spend the family holiday. He says he doesn't mind and will fit in with what you and the rest of the family want. From the moment you voice your 'wish list' you will know you have created problems. The NP will undermine your decision with doubt as to the wisdom of your choice – traffic, location and any number of factors that could be problematic. When the time comes, you go on holiday and none of the feared 'failures' have arisen, more lay in store. If the traffic is bad, it is your fault, if the weather is bad, it is your fault and so it goes on, no matter what goes wrong it is your fault because YOU decided where to go on holiday. Nothing is the fault of the N.P. because he made no decisions. Had it been left to him, he would have done the same as last year. This lack of confidence leads the N.P. to find comfort in the familiar, no matter how bad that familiar might be.

Because of a lack of confidence, the N.P. always finds a reason for not making a change. Change only occurs when it is enforced or used to increase to effect subordination through criticism.

Negative Personalities are stuck in what they see as their own failures, that they have failed in some way and have not been as successful as they should have been. The ways in which they have 'failed' is less important that the feeling of failure itself. The perception of failure may have arisen through unfavourable comparisons made with other people, wasted opportunities, fear of taking a risk, moving house and so on. Behaviour is typified by playing safe and taking safe advice from other people.

Negative Personalities may appear to take risks and make changes but the real reason behind these 'successes' is usually a partner or spouse who is there to take or share the blame.

The Negative Personality will build a wall behind which he can hide; a wall of apparent sureness and knowledgeable certainty. He will often seem openly dominant and authoritarian in manner and speech; the thrust of his words will tend to be critical and destructive rather than evaluative and constructive.

He will talk in generalities, loudly and in a way that makes even the simplest statement seem like a challenge. A challenge the average person finds difficult or embarrassing to meet, or which those better versed and of greater understanding let pass them by. He is rarely a good listener, the exception being when he is out of depth, when keeping quiet and appearing sympathetic is to his own advantage.

Typical phrases used by negative/dominant people include the following.

"Everybody knows that" (I speak for all people)

"We all think this." (I speak for those concerned)

"All reasonable people believe it is the best thing." (I am reasonable)

"It is a known fact." (Known by whom, judged factual by whom?)

"It is obvious to anyone with half a brain." (Will you admit to not seeing the obvious?)

"The fact of the matter is this." (Facts are truths and truths are perceptions, not absolute.)

"There can be no doubt of this." (A direct challenge, put up contrary proof or shut up)

As a general rule, doubt or question the validity of statements phrased in any of these ways. In fact, should you doubt the validity of this general rule? If you see what I mean? You don't - I thought it was obvious...and on and on...

A Negative Personality is someone who specialises in the invalidation of another person, his wishes, desires and his purposes. The N.P. will tell you directly or by implication that you have failed, or will fail; that you are stupid; you are inexperienced therefore have no worthwhile view; and are unreasonable because you cannot accept his view. Having invalidated just about everything in your life and destroyed your confidence he will give you a purpose in life – to be like him, and in doing so, show him that he was right all along. The two of you can then go about destroying the rest of the world.

The Negative Personality allows you to win a little and makes you feel guilty for doing so.

The effect of the Negative Personality is to stimulate your subconscious to remind you of memories and feelings associated with your own past failures, which should otherwise be no more than your own tool of self-improvement, making you feel unsure and embarrassed. You become weak in his presence and so turn to him for guidance or approval – the ultimate submission. Domination is complete.

Yet in this there is a paradox. The D.P. wants you to depend on him but at the same time wants/needs you to take responsibility for decision making and risk taking. You are his way

212

out. Disguised as sympathetic concern and seemingly generous cooperation his domination continues. Distinguishing between sincere loving care and manipulative control can be difficult and subjective. Even the negative D.P. may not be aware of the underlying motivation behind his behaviour, calling for understanding rather than critical judgement.

The most effective way to break free is to understand and manage rather than judge and confront. When you begin to experience a negative reaction, recognise the trigger and the element of your relationship this reveals. Then take a mental step back, deny the effect of the reaction and in doing so you also deny the effect the D.P. would have had.

Remember how the behaviour of a Negative Personality will often appear reasonable at first sight, especially in front of other people. He will fit in with your plans and appear blameless in every respect – which he usually is because of having avoided making any decisions.

Typically he will question your decisions; and give you plenty of reasons for NOT doing things, most of which do not bear up to close examination, all of which take up valuable time in discussion, leading inevitably to argument, frustration and no decision! When challenged and invited to make the decision the likely response will be that it is not his problem, it is up to you.

Examples of negative behaviour.

You are getting ready to go out.

"Oh you're not going out are you?"

"It looks like rain, when will you be back, have you got your coat....?"

"What shall I do if so-and-so calls?"

"Do you want me to do anything before you get back?"

"Mind the traffic, it will be busy today?"

All implying you are incapable of thinking of these things for yourself, making you think about questions you have already considered, delaying you, spoiling 'the moment' and unsettling you before leave.

You are looking at holiday brochures and mention a particular location.

"Is that holiday firm OK, can you trust them, you know how many go bust?"

"What about the food there, you know my sensitive stomach?"

"Will it be safe to leave the car parked outside, you don't know the area?"

"What about the drive there, do you know the roads, we don't want to get stuck in traffic."

Most of the questions are unanswerable, most holiday booking is done on trust and by recommendation, friends, travel guides and so on. No matter what you suggest, the questions remain. You either give up of take the responsibility and blame, and you know before you set out that you will be blamed for anything and everything that goes wrong. Food, weather, beds, beach, the list of 'faults' for which you alone are responsible is endless.

"We should have come last week.."

"Did you bring my......?"

"We should have come earlier and avoided this queue."

"I've got sunburned?"

You recognise the picture. The Negative D.P. will arrange it so that you make all the decisions, even to the point of what he should wear, and then blame you when it rains, or is too hot/cold cloudy/sunny, or his clothes are uncomfortable, or that you forget his favourite shirt..just about anything at all.

The Negative D.P. will question you about your decisions; give you unending and unanswerable reasons for not doing something and generally invalidate you ability to make decisions. Ask him to make a decision and he will likely procrastinate and be evasive.

"It's not my problem."

"It's up to you, you do what you like."

"Wait and see what happens, don't chance it just yet."

"I don't think we should risk it just now."

"Do you really want me to decide?"

"I don't mind what you want to do, I just thought....."

"Well go ahead but don't blame me."

Domination and Jealousy.

Jealous people are often insecure people, lacking confidence and self-worth; attributes also found in Dominant Personalities. The overtly jealous person demonstrates the Master-Slave syndrome and is fearfully mistrustful of his 'slave'.

The jealous D.P. may be more subtle in the way and manner in which he achieves domination but exercises just as much control.

Jealous people also often have difficulty in accepting responsibility and fear being found to have done something wrong. Similarly a common characteristic of the D.P. is a fear of criticism and the inability to handle criticism constructively.

The D.P. will have a tendency to feel threatened by the most innocent remark and when he does, will reverse roles quickly, making counter accusations to divert attention away from himself. He will bring the most routine situation into doubt, bring the motives of other people into question, be generally suspicious and ask pointless questions unendingly. Where have you been, why, with whom, what have you been doing and so on. You will be unable to 'prove' the veracity of your replies and so remain permanently 'under suspicion'.

The jealous D.P. feels justified in questioning you and if you object may use a past occasion (repeatedly), when you unable to 'prove' yourself to him (and in which you were made to feel guilty), as justification. The occasion in question may have been twenty years ago but in his mind and for his purposes it was only yesterday.

The circle is complete. At some time in the past you became subordinated by your own sense of guilt, leaving him with reasons to doubt you. Now he will use that occasion to disadvantage you whenever you show sign of independence, or from 'slipping out from under'. No matter what you now do you can NEVER win and in trying to justify yourself and prove your point you are playing his game; and as he makes the rules it is a game you cannot win.

It is easy to ask a question but not always as easy to answer one. The fool can ask the unanswerable of the wise. Do not fall into the trap of placing credence on questions or mistaking them for sincere interest or a quest for knowledge. A question can make a powerful weapon, disabling the unwary with confusion and doubt.

"Have you stopped beating your wife?"

Remedial.

Control or disconnection.

Do you continue to suffer the pressure, humiliation and undermining effects of a Dominant and or Negative Personality, manage them in a particular way or disconnect from the person completely? This is a singularly personal choice.

The choice is yours, the problem is his. He may not see it that way, or want to. You may see his behaviour as a barrier to love and happiness , he may not: the problem is yours, and everyone else's, not his. He is fine: his pleasure simple; self-indulgent and immediate. You, and other people, are simple there to serve........

21.   Space Invaders

The erosion of personal territory.

The need for personal space and perhaps more importantly, for a "sense" of entitlement to individual space and other kinds of personal territory is now well established.

The denial, to an individual, of personal space and the accompanying sense of privacy it provides creates is associated with behavioural changes, including social withdrawal and destructive behaviour.

This is associated with the perception or factual denial of that most basic of human rights, the right of an individual to exist.

If one believes and feels that one has the right to exist, simply because one does, then presumably one is entitled also to space in which to exist. The amount of space one is allowed is less important than the recognition of and adherence to the principle of one's entitlement by other people.

Physical space may be limited and we find means of supplementing ways in which this basic desire for territory may be satisfied.

We resented and resist the actions of people who attempt to deny us use of our territory or in some way interfere with our use of what we see as our "personal space". Space Invaders are the cause of much bad feeling and arguments within groups of all sizes, from families to nations.

The term Space as an expression of measure can be applied to almost anything. Below are some examples and ways in which people endeavour to establish their own personal space.

SPACE TERRITORY.

The need to establish personal territory, e.g. my room, my desk, my house, my garden, my land.

The need to define personal space by use of markers, e.g. doors, fences, walls, desk dividers, etc..

To satisfy the need to demonstrate the right to be admitted to public spaces, e.g. the countryside, rivers, sea, parks, roads etc..

To be able to satisfy the need to move freely within one's personal territory.

The need to feel, as a citizen of a land, to be able to travel lawfully, unhindered and unquestioned through open public spaces, the countryside, roads, rivers and the seas without restriction.

INVADERS of space territory

Parents, siblings and other household members who violate the right to privacy in whatever areas of home life are possible; employers, fellow employees who fail to recognize the need for and right to personal workspace. The denial of a sense of personal territory in early life may be one reason why children so affected become *control freaks* in adulthood.

TIME TERRITORY.

The need for personal solitary time, e.g. privacy.

The need for time in which to complete tasks without interference.

TIME invaders.

A time invader is *anyone* whose intrusion into the life of another is unwanted, perhaps too frequently, uninvited, e.g. family members, neighbours, gossips, salespeople, colleagues and so on.

Time invaders need not necessarily be people. Mobile 'phones, e-mails, television, radio, mail and a host of other ways in which modern communication impinge on the individual's time take their toll to the extent that for some people it is almost impossible to feel free from the threat through the use of these means.

SOUND TERRITORY.

The need for quietness as a right.
The need for quietness in personal time.

SOUND invaders.

Persistent localized noise created by domestic equipment and appliances, e.g. washing machines, fans, cleaners, kitchen equipment, mechanical and electronic toys, pets, radios, televisions, etc..

The regular and/or persistent intrusion of environmental noise such as that from neighbours, traffic, aircraft, garden equipment, animals, children etc..

The irregular intrusion by road repairs, builders, ice-cream vans, professional gardeners, etc..

Intrusion of social environmental noise including that originating from the use of licensed premises, clubs, shops, schools, churches, demonstrations and so on.

A further category might also be included, that of

FOOD TERRITORY

The need for wholesome, nutritional sustenance, e.g. good food and clean water (and the time, space and privacy in which to enjoy it).

FOOD INVADERS

Non-food, i.e. food having little or no nutritional value and containing high quantities of fats, sugars and profit making fillers.

Food additives designed to preserve, colour and enhance appearance and flavour for no reason beyond that of manufacturing and retailing convenience and profit.

Toxic substances introduced to food by way of poor and contaminated soil, artificial growing techniques such as hydroponics, manufacturing processes, unhygienic storage and cooking practices, etc.

THE COST OF TERRITORIAL INVASION

The combined effects of a loss or lack of adequate personal

space, a lack of privacy and an inability to escape sound or noise intrusion has immeasurably serious consequences. The additional effects of a poor diet combined with the toxic effects of additives and poisons make for a potentially alarming scenario.

The rise of anti-social, destructive behaviour may be associated with these factors. Much neuroses, anxiety and depression is rooted in the social consequences of a society which shows little respect for the territorial needs of the individual. Everything from spy-cameras, 'phone signal tracking, road-charging, credit, debit and loyalty card tracking and analysis, policing and secret policing deny and control the rights of the individual ever more greatly. Too many people know where we are, what we are doing, and what we are buying; what we have and don't have, even what we say and write.

When space is at a premium any claim to space is vigorously defended and jealously guarded. Privacy may be equally difficult to secure and achieved only with great difficulty. Timber-framed houses with poor sound insulation, open plan offices and other work-space areas and communal public transport all make it difficult to avoid social intrusion in our lives. Not, I hasten to add, communication or meaningful contact, just intrusion.

From 'phone and e-mail interceptions to more over-managed public spaces, privacy may at best ever only partial and conditional.

Sound is invasive and pervasion in almost every direction and location of modern society. Traffic noise from roads can travel for miles across an otherwise deserted landscape. Air-traffic noise is even more far reaching – stand a mountain almost anywhere and find out!

Time is its own master but with increasing pressure to 'buy' space and privacy the cost is high. Long working hours and a seemingly infinite number of artificial and costly ways in which to enjoy one's leisure time are the result of an almost permanent round of getting and spending. Finding enjoyment in the process is the reward we give ourselves. Well actually no. It is the reward we buy from others who make it possible for us to first get and then spend. The fortunate few who find the 'off-switch' become beacons of light.

22.   Dominating Personalities – Superior Inferiority

To many people the term Inferiority Complex brings to mind a picture of someone withdrawn and lacking confidence and while the latter is certainly true, the former could not be further from reality. That the dominating effect many people have on others is also due to this condition and similarly is not widely understood.

Before addressing the question of *dominance* it is important to distinguish between dominance and prominence. Throughout life we encounter people who play a dominant part in our upbringing and development but this is not to say that all such people are also are dominant people. Many life-lessons and nuggets of wisdom come from people whose prominence we recognise only because of that which they have imparted to us. Often with hindsight.

Behaviour typical of the obviously dominant person includes greediness, bullying, critical, constant and repetitive moaning, lacking consideration for others, bossiness, the accumulation of wealth or goods, impatience, the display of encyclopaedic knowledge (often on a single subject), resistant to change, single track focus, vague or incurable non life-threatening but useful illnesses.

Most people display these facets of human behaviour at times but the Dominant Personality displays many, and in extreme cases all and manifests them to an alarming degree.

The behaviour of the Dominant Personality with an underlying inferiority complex, is designed to bring recognition of success and enhanced status. Behaviour is hinged around a display of power, the ability to accumulate wealth, to demonstrate insight.

In an endeavour to elicit the reassurance that one has 'the best' the D.P.'s behaviour can become ostentatious or exaggerated.

Here 'the best' is always related to immediate circumstances and will vary according to ability and opportunity to demonstrate superiority. The D.P. will be knowledgeable in the company of the ignorant, demonstrate his or her comparative wealth when in company of the less so, and strong in the presence of the weak.

When the D.P. finds himself in 'unknown territory', amongst people he does not know and whose protocol for behaviour he is unsure, he will appear quiet and interested until he has their measure. Natural behaviour for most people but the D.P. is always looking for an opportunity to demonstrate 'superiority' in some way. When faced with little or no opportunity to demonstrate his superiority, he will tend to call upon a disadvantaging condition, poverty, poor school, etc.. to explain his lack of achievement.

Status is only status among equals, clothes being an example. Exclusive designer labels affordable only to the few being mimicked in the High Street in a proliferation of 'exclusive' London, Paris, New York labels in an ever changing array of 'fashionable' clothes – meaningful only to those who value such things or who use possessions as signs of wealth.

An inferiority complex may be disguised by the D.P. by his insistent and urgent need to dress in the 'best' clothes, drive the 'best' car, live in the 'best' neighbourhood, be seen in the 'best' places. The 'best' is always relative, the best car may be the least oldest or noticeably different in some way, the best house may simply be unusual in some way.

When the 'best' cannot be achieved, another person's best can always be criticised. Faced with comparisons finding himself lacking in all respects the D.P. will become 'invisible' or absent himself on some pretext.

When the 'best' is truly unattainable, where the D.P. is impoverished, without talent or other obvious attribute, justifications for these circumstances abound. The absence of having or owning 'the best' can always be explained away by: lack of opportunity; poor health; favouritism; deprived of good schooling; family ties; discrimination; let down by other people – the list is complete only when inventiveness is exhausted.

However, the need to dominate persists and opportunities to gain power over another are to be found when sought. But why should one person want to dominate another when subordination is so obviously resented and resisted?

For some people, any sense of feeling inferior is intolerable. This may lead them to react self-protectively when faced with a situation in which they would feel inferior. It is a reaction to their own self-perception of a reality which exists only in their own minds but which is sufficient to provoke them behaving in an overbearing or superior manner.

The feeling, or fear of feeling inferior produces an anxiety reaction based on *fight or flight.*

Habitually the most usual reaction is that of 'fight' and the best form of defence is attack. When there is a likelihood that superiority cannot be demonstrated, the sufferer will fall back on 'flight' and refuse to place himself in the feared situation. If neither is an option, the sufferer of an Inferiority Complex will become compliant to his situation, disguising his fear and sense of inferiority with whatever social graces he can muster.

The D.P. will firstly 'fight'. And only when unable to demonstrate his superiority, will he 'take flight', either by absenting himself or making a point of ignoring someone who is a source of superiority. When placed in the position of having to listen to someone else, he will make it his idea that the other person speaks. He will become the centre of attraction just long enough to demonstrate his largesse. Then it is he who invites or gives the other person permission to hold the floor,

The sources of these feelings of inferiority are usually imaginary. The D.P. sees comparison and weakness where none exists or is intended. Reactions to an often innocent remark may be sudden and explosive. When the D.P. feels his response to the perceived threat will be inadequate he will withdraw, usually in bad humour. The merest hint of criticism will be regarded as patronising arrogance.

The D.P.'s reactive defence mechanism is designed to reverse perceived roles and elevate the threatened D.P. to a position of relative authority. The grounds for the 'fight' will be selected carefully. Victory must be total and absolute and leave no room for doubt. Emphasis on the role of 'mine-host' enables avoidance of weaknesses in other areas. Relief and ease of mind can come only when superiority is acknowledged by others and he feels in charge of the particular domain *he or she has chosen.*

Here then is someone doomed to failure; someone who fears a threat lies around every corner. Repeated confrontations bring increasing isolation and friends become increasingly scarce. The sense of isolation is one of perception rather than reality, a perception justified by feeling misunderstood, with talents unrecognised or envied unkindly. Misguided self-perception extends his sense of isolation to the point where a sense of uniqueness becomes the ultimate superiority.

The fear or sense of feeling or actually being inferior, especially in an unkind social sense, is a basic fear common to most people. The root of this feeling lies possibly in the innate knowledge that inferiority equates to vulnerability and potential annihilation. Because strength and security prospects are increased by joining forces with others, social acceptance is also important.

While it may appear unnecessary to carry these fears and principles into everyday life it would be unreasonable to expect them to be absent from human behaviour. Hence when confronted by new or feared situations there is a tendency to revert to basic traits and characteristics. Behaviour that is little more than a hang-over from not so distant primitive times. At the root of this behaviour are basic survival reactions which may manifest disproportionately, harshly and cruelly.

The fearful Dominant Personality lacks tact, acts unkindly and inconsiderately. He is a destroyer of relationships subjecting those around him to subordinated misery. Husbands, wives, friends and family all devalued and robbed of confidence as they submit to positions of servility, watching their every word, resentful and unhappy.

Should the effort of achieving or maintaining superiority become too great, the D.P. may adopt a paradoxical position of absolute inferiority. In doing so, the D.P. becomes 'the best' by achieving the lowest possible level of miserably happy existence, painful as it may be.

In presenting mental and physical symptoms (the origins of

which can usually be diagnostically attributed to anxiety) the D.P. can maintain a state of total defeat in which he need prove nothing, using his condition as means to achieve control of those around him as they adjust their lives to accommodate his needs.

This person is no hypochondriac, remaining unaware of the reactive subconscious processes that have created the situation he now enjoys and endures. Relieved of the need to struggle to any pinnacle of superiority he may now rest in his condition. His behaviour fails to disguise his true nature. The behaviour of this D.P. is typified by false humility, constant apologies that soon ring hollow in their repetition, and criticism. Suffering is a state from which no change is sought.

For the D.P. who has fallen back on illness any effort to change becomes increasingly difficult. Despite all efforts he may seem to make there is little progress and his illness continues to dominate the lives of those around him.

One reason for this is that a D.P. needs totality, there can be no half measures, why he is also critical of 'everything'. Perfection is 100%, 99% is unacceptable. Perfection is essential. Progress is therefore relative to an unachievable perfection, perpetuating illness in the guise of imperfection.

The D.P. finds both comfort and status in maintaining his illness, explaining that no one can really help me, "I'm too complicated." "I've seen lots of doctors but they don't seem to be able to do much to help." "I'll just have to live with it." "I don't blame you for not being able to help or understand, don't worry about me." The effect can create a sense of guilt and sympathy but also possibly anger and frustration. It may seem a heartless act when a 'carer' leaves his or her sick partner but there may be deeper elements of their situation that make such action necessary.

Another variation is in complementing the doctor on his skill and patience. The D.P. has complete faith in his medical care (avoiding personal responsibility and failure) and hopes that 'one day' a cure will be found. He then embarks on what has already become firmly established in his own mind – semi-permanent treatment, surgery and hospital visits, trials of this and that, and of course, praise for being so helpful, cooperative and uncomplaining.

At which point it must be pointed out that there are many instances where long term, palliative and remedial care is essential and genuinely necessary and that such patients are not to be confused with Dominant Personalities, the subject of this chapter.

The unhappy partner of a D.P. may be driven to seek some kind of separation in order to regain control of his or her own life. The threat of such action will provoke retaliatory measures aimed at preventing change and maintaining the status-quo. It is unlikely that any such action will be focussed on peaceful reconciliation.

Symptomatic illness is a commonly used threat. "You'll killing me you know." "If you go, the consequences will be on your head, not mine." Threats of suicide and ruin and of social disgrace may be enough to prevent the husband or wife from leaving.

It is to be remembered that while the threats sound real, they are threats made by someone who needs to be seen as someone who is self-confident and self-reliant *and* someone who needs to blame another for his situation. If separation does occur, then the D.P. has a new reason for his failure – his ex-partner. There is then new opportunity for sympathetic ears, and their subordination.

Even the prospect of isolation becomes acceptable in the light of insurmountable incompatibility - "I tried to help but it made no difference." "I gave her everything but it became impossible." "He was impossible to work with, so unreliable and untidy."

The successful inferiority complex enjoys the victories of always being right, of criticising others in the variety of their faults, and by dismissing those unwilling to submit to his inflexible behaviour and to follow his lead as unreasonable.

Causes of the syndrome of an Inferiority Complex are often found in childhood, originating in experiences that have produced excessively emotional feelings. An emotional excess, of being overwhelmed by feelings of hurt and insecurity, leading to the development of complex patterns of behaviour designed to avoid their repetition.

These heightened emotional reactions may include feelings of fear, guilt, inferiority, embarrassment, frustration or exclusion; experiences common to most children. However, when these feelings are dramatised as a momentarily overwhelming experience, that moment becomes a turning point. Leading to the development of avoidance behaviour in which the complex is now rooted.

This kind of situation occurs after an individual has been subjected to cruel, degrading or thoughtless acts of 'superiority'. Parents, siblings, family and friends, teachers and others may all be responsible, albeit unwittingly, for causing inferiority complexes in those in their care.

The broader effect of sometimes questionable attitudes and actions of police, civil service bureaucrats and governments can be a factor creating and perpetuating these fears. Fears and reactions underlying private and public emotional outbursts and demonstrations which range from passive non-compliance to mindless violence and a disrespect of authority in general.

Ways out by overcoming symptoms.

Spiritually.

The D.P. will probably have a superficial acceptance of the idea of there being a 'God'. Because his views are likely to be narrow and his experiences shallow and lacking in emotion, any appeal to change on grounds of belief or faith may seem pointless.

Unfortunately it is often those of a sensitive, spiritual or psychic nature who are easily shocked and brutalised in childhood. People who may consequently develop a complex nature which distances them from their spiritual path.

The prospect of a selfless love towards other people – the true basis of spirituality – is, to the D.P., the prospect of being defenceless, vulnerable, weak and at the mercy of all who would take advantage of such a 'push-over'.

There are approaches that can make an abandonment to faith, attractive to the D.P.. The sense of spirituality that gives rise to the birth of Faith, is uniquely personal. Unlike the doctrinal beliefs of religion, Faith, being internalised, cannot be subjected to scrutiny or critical examination,. The danger is that the D.P.'s abandonment is little more than a cop-out, providing a mental retreat and excusing aspects of behaviour that might otherwise be criticised.

One way of approaching the D.P. at a spiritual level is in showing love openly and, without reservation, enabling the D.P. to respond positively and return that love. The love felt for someone who is a D.P., can be revealed and offered through understanding his needs *without* needing to comply or become subordinated to his demands. Love based on honesty and mutual respect. Ultimately the D.P. finds confidence in such uncompromising, loving mutuality from which may grow a relationship based on trust.

The 'Self-reliant'.

Where a childhood experience involves a loss of love, the adult response may be one of withdrawal. A reluctance to enter into any close relationship in which love may subsequently be denied, resulting in 'another' loss of love. This can become an inhibiting factor affecting future relationships as the D.P. denies his own feelings and distances himself emotionally from other people.

To admit and succumb to experience emotional desire or hunger equates to an admission of a want that cannot be provided solely by oneself. If this admission is seen as a reliance on another person it may also be regarded as an intolerable weakness, resulting in a denial of desire. This is the hallmark of the 'loner'.

The solution or way out of this situation is difficult because whatever anyone gives, and no matter how genuinely 'gifted' help may be, it may not be repeated, repeatable or constant. The act or the person is then seen by the D.P. as being inconsistent or unreliable. One-off's seem pointless to a D.P. who assumes insincerity and ulterior motives everywhere.

The answer may lay in another direction, one that offers potential without risk of loss. By encouraging spontaneous enjoyment of 'anything' – using the "Why not, there is nothing to lose?" argument, ways in which the D.P. may greater and more frequent opportunities of enjoyment, is opened. Instead of automatically saying No to anything new or which involves other people, the D.P. may be able to allow himself to explore opportunities for potential for enjoyment even though (and perhaps because) he himself has no immediate need, hence no weakness, hence no risk of loss.

The 'Stupid'.

Inferiority is not just a negative and critical state of mind, it is also the refusal to admit to the possibility of ignorance and the D.P.'s implied assumption of knowledge, even where there is none.

The D.P. will find it difficult to pay proper attention to instructions of almost any kind. His approach will be one of prior knowledge, assumption and misconception applied in the guise of 'common sense' and, when things go wrong, of criticising the instructions and they failed to make clear the knowledge they were intended to impart.

Apparently contradicting this kind of stupidity is the D.P. who says that he wants to 'understand', and in order to do so, wants to know 'everything'. This ploy is often implemented as a bullying tactic used to disguise the D.P.'s ignorance while at the same time, wearing down his opponent with his endless questioning. Typically, on finding himself embroiled in an argument or discussion in which he feels out of his depth, the D.P. will want to 'drag everything out into the open' or appear deeply interested in the other person 'opinion'.

All this is intended to switch attention away from the D.P. whose ability is to bring everything down to the level of the mundane, and destroy any element of individuality or value the subject or person may have once had. The 'stupid' D.P. is not so stupid when it comes to destroying other people's confidence and devaluing their ideals.

The stupid person needs to know all the answers and so must have all the facts! In order to do so he will drag out every last detail and triviality in order to get to the bottom of it, by which time everyone will have lost interest, lost the point and is happy to bring matters to a close. The D.P. has won! He is a bully and a bore, and as he sees it, he always wins.

For the socially inept D.P. who lacks confidence, Self therapy begins with saying, "I don't know." Closely followed by "What do you think?" And to accept that most things in life are matters of opinion, grey areas where no absolute truth exists and where opinions are valued more when they are shared than when they become dogmatic statements.

The folly of comparisons.

It is an overwhelming sense of inadequacy that brings the D.P. to doubt himself to such a degree that he turns the world on its head. The D.P. whose very sense of weakness becomes the bullying strength by which he rises to the top. A perspective so distorted that any true sense the value of differences, of equality between people, gender,, skill or ability is lost.

This, so to speak, opens the therapeutic door, and the D.P. can be approached fruitfully with philosophical and intellectual discourse. Of course this must be carried out patiently, allowing for individual ignorance of any particular subjects discussed, and without any hint of patronising.

An opening gambit might be the suggestion that, the individuality of human beings results in a uniqueness that defies comparison – discuss!

It is the uniqueness of every human being that makes comparison pointless and which offers humankind as a whole its ability to survive. A uniqueness in which all people are equal: and equally gifted in an infinite variety of personal skills and talents that mutually complement and compensate in effects that ultimately benefit the whole.

The Dominant Person suffering from an Inferiority Complex is dangerous because he or she weakens the world we share.

Compassionate understanding together with an indomitable resistance and refusal to submit to a D.P. is essential to both self preservation and bringing about a change in the D.P.'s behaviour.

To stress the pointlessness of comparison.

In a world-class field of athletes, each contestant prepares to race against the others, against his past performance and against the clock. He may be a representative racing for the honour of his country or club. Each contestant races against an opposition, or several opponents, of his own making. That he is in this race at all has been determined by people, events and circumstances far beyond his individual ability.

Each competitor has been selected on the basis of his previous performances and his potential. Each man is unique, born on a date and at a time and in a place unique to him; and probably of different parents. Raised in social and economic backgrounds not shared by other competitors, and with a naturally different bias of interests, philosophy, culture and sense of purpose. Each competitor with his own unique pattern of cycles determining mental, physical and intellectual peaks and troughs entrenched since birth and inescapably effective. Each with his bodily needs of nutrition, rest, activity and sleep. Each with his unique DNA matrix. One man will show best on the day, he will be declared the winner; every man will show his best on the day and every man will have won his own race. Where here is any true basis for comparison?

At best the race should be an opportunity for people sharing an interest to test themselves not against other people but against the performances of other people. Performances that act as a yardstick and a spur to personal greatness in a particular field. A race in which there are only winners.

To deny one's value, by not recognising it and by not honouring one's individuality, is to deny life itself and to turn one's back on life's ultimate questions.

"Who am I, what am I, why am I here and what is my purpose?"

Answers to be found within a sense of personal realisation.

23.   Identifying Dominant Behaviour

People who have a dominant effect on our lives do so in a variety of ways. Sometimes obvious; bullying, or threatening, overbearing or just plain boring; other times less so; being gently intrusive or persuasive, quietly persistent or implacably demanding.

For the purposes of this paper, being dominated means to relinquish the most basic of human rights, that to simply 'be'. All people are entitled to be left alone, to pursue their own paths without intrusion on others or being intruded upon. This is an over-simplistic ideal because for every action each of us takes, there is a consequential reaction that ultimately affects all other people, never the less, the principle stands.

We are all influenced by the presence, words and actions of other people; it is an inescapable consequence of human relationships, however distant and obscure those relationships may be. It is the nature of this influence that matters.

A single event may have a profoundly dominant effect that dramatically and irrevocably changes someone's life, or indeed many people's lives. Less obvious but equally powerful in its effect is the repeated exposure to a superficially insignificant influence, such the compliance to some daily routine or chore, or words.

In whatever way and by whatever means, domination equates having one's behaviour determined by another person's presence or influence: to unwanted subordination; The dominant effect may be consequential on nothing more than the imposition of an essential occupational routine but it may also be consequential of another person imposing his or her will for no other reason than personal gratification. In the direct sense of the domination, motivation is less important than the effect itself, but it should be remembered that even the motivation is that of the dominant person, not the subordinated one.

Individual reactions to dominating influences depend largely on when and how the presence of the dominating influence is detected. Behaviour that is obviously dominant may be seen for what it is and resisted. That which is less obvious may not be recognised for some time, at which point resentment is likely to be a factor of resistance.

Other factors affecting both the power to resist dominating behaviour and the wish to do so include the relationship between the parties concerned, such as that of husband and wife; employer and employee. Here additional emotional factors come into play, fear, love, hate, anger, respect, admiration and so on. Beyond this are personal feelings resulting from the recognition of allowing one's self to become subordinated, to doing or saying things that bring the person concerned to behave uncharacteristically. There is now a risk of self-loathing and an emotional pathway of extremes

The effects of a dominating influence remains long after dissociation from the source of the influence. Individual reactions become lost within the pattern of what is now termed 'ordinary' or characteristic behaviour. Identification of the origins of 'characteristic' traits and their attribution to another person similarly obscured as behaviour patterns of the individual become homogenised. Overall, the significance individuals have on the lives of other people is easily lost.

The reality is that the thoughts, words and actions of everyone reflects the influences to which they have individually been subjected. There are no exceptions. Some influences may have proved helpful, others less so and this brings us to the point where identifying the sources of less helpful influences may be more important than the attribution of praise and gratitude to those that have proved beneficial.

Self-improvement is a commonly held desire that involves the divestment of negative, destructive or harmful thoughts, words or deeds from our lives. This involves firstly identifying the negative aspect and then taking appropriate steps to eliminate it. However, appropriate steps may be more than simply having the willpower or technique to change one's self in some way. Identification of the source, or reason why this negative effect came into being is also important, perhaps critically so.

Here we come back to the function of the sub-conscious

mind and its ability to stimulate the individual to re-act in a given circumstance. Subconscious alarm bells begin to ring at the very thought of changing what has become an habitual pattern of behaviour. Control is beyond reason but may be implemented by counteracting the original command instructions, that is, the dominating effect of another person. The initial effect, or bias, may have originated in something read in a book, a misunderstanding of something overheard – the list is almost endless.

The fact remains that a particular facet of an individual's behaviour exists only because of the influence of another person. This fact is important because identifying the source of this influence, acknowledging and accepting of the root cause of its, opens the door to an argument to change that the subconscious can find acceptable.

Self realisation in the form of an affirmation to accompany wilful self-changing action.

"I know that on certain occasions I react in a negative way and I no longer wish to do this. I know that this originally came about because of (something that happened a long time ago that I remember OR that I do not remember). That time has now gone, I have moved on and no longer need to react in a way that is now pointless and which has a negative effect on my life."

For persistent reactions that stubbornly resist change, further analysis can be helpful, and this can still be a self-help project towards which the counsellor can guide the client. The instruction is this.

A self-help project to help identify sources of negative reactions.

Begin by making a list of people you have known, including anyone you feel has been a special influence. This is no small task but in its power to absorb the attention it has merit beyond the immediate exercise. It involves a process of taking stock and of sorting out one's thoughts. There will be a lot of names and a good place to start is with the earliest birthday; remember who was present. Think about who you knew at that time; relative, neighbours, friends, shopkeepers – let your mind wander and think about those early years. Let one name lead you to another, picture the people concerned, all the time adding to your list.

Make four columns on a large sheet of paper. Write the names of all the people you can remember down the left hand column. Then, in the second, beside each name, write down how you saw or regarded that person. In the third column write down how you felt about that person and what feelings he or she engender/ed in you. In the right hand column write down whether you see that persons influence as helpful or otherwise. Use your own words, good, bad, hurtful, kind, unkind, loving and so on. Be brief, succinct and spontaneous.

WHO contributed WHAT in making YOU who you are?

Making your list may take days, weeks or even months, and many sheets of paper. Go at your own speed, after all you are shaping the future of a life that has taken many years to reach this point. Persistence is the key: once begun, disinclination to pursue this course of action is a subconscious reaction to prevent change

As you complete your lists, taking a chunk of your life at a time, take a look at the range of feelings you have aroused by doing this. How do the good influences compare with the bad? What do you feel is the net overall result?

While you are looking through your lists remember that you are actually looking at yourself. Perhaps you will reconsider how you saw people then compared with how you see them now. You may begin to see how some of your present day reactions and habits came about. Take your time.

We all have characteristics we feel we might be better without. By identifying the origins of those reactions we may more easily overcome them. In knowing others we come to know ourselves, in understanding ourselves we may understand others more easily.

Remember that in looking at how you were affected by other

people, the focus is on your reactions to them and how they influenced you. Those people who influenced you may not know that they have done so. Similarly, you have influenced every person you have ever met!

24.   Responsibility as a Source of Discontent.

Part 1

Responsibility-Choice-Decision-Blame-Risk-Credit-Liability-Duty-Obligation

Most relationships entail a sharing of responsibilities both personal and those which arise as a consequence of the relationship.

The mutual agreement of responsibilities is essential to the achievement and maintenance of the happiness of those concerned, and the successful development of their relationship.

A mutually agreed sharing of responsibilities is more important than the proportion in which those responsibilities are shared. Seldom are the skills, desires, abilities and opportunities of two people within a partnership identical. A flexible approach to deciding 'who-does-what' is called for and it is a melding of strengths combined with a sharing of ideals or objectives that produces an outcome conducive to cementing a relationship.

The ideal is not always easily achieved as circumstances conspire to place responsibilities on a partner either less suited to undertake them or who does so reluctantly. A partner may too eagerly assume certain responsibilities and make decisions, resulting in the other partner's anger and resentment.

Imbalances in the sharing of day to day responsibilities that leads to friction, frustration or resentment cannot be ignored without cost to the happiness of one or both partners. Such imbalances should be approached in a simple and straightforward way that avoids emotive issues and blame. The objective is to rectify what one or both partners see as an imbalance that has developed within their relationship as a whole. Seeking a practical solution the restores equilibrium.

There will be occasions where it is practical or necessary for a partner to accept responsibility for something he or she would prefer not to undertake. The response of both partners to this situation reveals their ability to compromise their ideals and desires within the relationship.

To help avoid imbalances of this kind becoming a source of discontent, I have put together a questionnaire enabling partners to become more aware of both their own responsibilities and those of their partner.

The following questions reflect some commonly encountered within domestic partnerships. As you read through them, take time to reflect on your true situation, it is easy to assume responsibility for something without actually taking responsibility. Tick as appropriate and leave the extreme right-hand column blank.

There may be some questions to which you feel the answer is unclear, for instance, holidays, when the timing is determined by an employer or school closure. Answer is you can.

The objective is to highlight to both self and each other, not only who does what but what each *thinks* and perhaps more importantly *recognises* and *acknowledges*, who does what.

On completion, partners exchange questionnaires.

Statistics can be made to prove anything so be careful in looking at compared responses. Decisions of magnitude may take only minutes to make and demand no further involvement whereas responsibilities of a more mundane nature may take up vast amounts of time each day. One 'tick' does not equal another.

More revealing is the way in which partners see each other, and importantly, what they don't see. Duties can ever be shared equally, or responsibilities compared – how can a decision concerning a child's future be compared with that of what to plant in the garden?

More important is a balancing of the *weight* of the duties and responsibilities – does each partner have sufficient time in which to carry out that for which he or she is responsible *and* have time for him/herself, or is each day a tail-chasing exercise? Is free-time equally shared? Is the spread between mental and physical activity shared fairly and/or to each partner's satisfaction?

First and foremost this process must be regarded as an

opportunity to develop both individuals within the context of a happy and fruitful relationship. Where imbalances and their attendant resentments and frustrations have arisen, as they undoubtedly do, blame is set aside in favour of an open and frank exchange by which everyone wins.

Important aspects include.

Do not become blind to another's efforts.

Where one partner hands over responsibility for a particular matter, then he or she should be both appreciative and supportive of what is done on his or her behalf. Constant criticism or unhelpfulness damage the relationship and create unnecessary and harmful stress. Where persistent criticism is a problem, the criticised partner should perhaps hand over responsibility to he or she who 'knows better'.

Do not make decisions on another's person's behalf.

Generally it is demeaning to have decisions made on one's behalf. Not to be consulted on anything relating to the partnership, including personal decisions that affect one's partner and family, could be seen as uncaring disregard for both, whether or not this is intended. Consult, consult, consult.

Do not have decisions made for you.

Sometimes it is easier to go along with what someone else suggests than go through the hassle of disagreement. If you are to be involved and have a view it is your responsibility to share in the decisions making. If you don't you forego the right to criticise the outcome or blame anyone else for a situation in which you placed yourself by abdicating responsibility.

He or she who has the responsibility also has the authority.

Do not argue with decisions made by someone to whom you have delegated authority. By virtue of letting that person take responsibility for a certain decisions and to undertake certain work you must allow that persons achievements to be your own. If you don't like what is happening and change cannot be achieved by discussion, shut up or take over!

Harshly put perhaps but there comes a time for plain speaking. Not every situation can be recovered, no one is perfect and compromise is essential. Desire may not always be accompanied by ability but sincerity of desire and earnest effort are to be valued more highly than perfection in terms of a successful relationship.

Balances are to be made, outcomes to be enjoyed, compensations to be found. Above all, loving helpfulness ensures any outcome is more likely to one mutually enjoyed.

There will be questions of responsibility about which you disagree.

Return questionnaires to each other and now with your own sheet, go through the list again. Question by question, what is just a simple misunderstanding or case of drifting into an accidental imbalance. Having sorted these issues, of what remains, ask yourself, "Do I resent this situation?"

Do you resent doing or not be allowed to do something; expected to be responsible for or excluded from something? If you do, put an 'R' in the right-hand column.

As you consider this, ask yourself whether there is an alternative solution to that which you resent? Is your partner capable of undertaking the 'something' in question; could you reasonably be involved in or make the 'decision' in question?

When you have each done this, again compare, and more importantly, discuss.

More than anything else it is gentle confrontation of a relationship that is based on more than just agreeing or not agreeing about this or that.

It is to do with flexibility and consideration between partners in their loving desire to realise happiness.

Give and take, finding friendly shoulders and listening ears in each other.

Isn't that what love is all about?

Part 2

Responsibility a source of discontent

Could Your partner do this?	Who decides/decided; choose or chose, did or does is responsible for these things?	Self	Partner	Both or shared	R'
	Who proposed marriage/living together				
	-what kind of wedding you should have				
	-made the wedding arrangements				
	-where to go on honeymoon				
	-where to live				
	-what house to buy				
	-whether to rent or to buy the family home				
	-colour and design of décor				
	does the interior decorating				
	-the furnishings, curtains, carpets				
	furniture				
	-garden design, what should be grown, etc.				
	gardening, lawn mowing, weeding etc.				
	What kind of car to buy				
	what make of car				
	how much should be spent on buying a car				
	In whose name is the car financed/registered				
	whether to have more than one car				
	who does the driving when travelling together				
	-manages the household				

	budget				
	-how your income is shared and used				
	-how your partner's income is shared and used				
	whether you have a joint bank account				
	whether you have a personal bank account				
	whether your partner has a personal bank account				
	for insuring the home				
	for arranging life insurance				
	for arranging pensions				
	whether you should work				
	whether your partner should work				
	usually initiates intimacy				
	usually takes the active role in sex				
	decides whether to have child/ren				
	takes responsibility for contraception				
	when you spend time alone				
	when your partner spends time alone			.	
	when and where you shop				
	does the main household shopping				
	what clothes you buy				
	what clothes your partner buys				
	makes complaints to tradespeople when necessary				
	makes retirement plans				
	decides when you go out socially				
	decides when/where you go out for pleasure				

243

decides when to go on holiday				
decides where to go on holiday				
arranges the holiday				
chooses what food is bought/cooked/eaten				
is responsible for preparing meals				
is responsible for clearing away/washing up after meals				
does household cleaning				
does household washing and ironing				
decides on television/radio programme selection				
takes charge in emergencies				
takes responsibility for family health matters				
chooses the child/rens name(s)				
looks after the baby				
decides on religious education of child/ren				
disciplines the child/ren				
in whom does the child/ren confide?				
decides on 'big buy' items such a t.v.'s, computers, etc.				
buys Christmas/birthday presents for friends				
Wraps and arranges/delivers presents				
writes Christmas/Birthday cards				
remembers anniversaries				
invites people to the house – social, business, etc.				
acts as host to visitors				

	decides whether to have a pet				
	who looks after pet(s)				
	decides when to go to bed				

25.   In The Mood

Definition: MOOD – an affective outlook or attitude enduring for some time,

characterized by particular emotions in a condition of sub-excitation, to be readily evoked: irritable, cheerful etc.

Moods are changes in our state of mind, our state of being, that makes us act, feel and respond in ways that are characteristic of a particular mood.

A Mood appears to be a particular state of mind that occurs reactively, the precise trigger for the reaction not always being obvious. (See chapter on Conscious-Subconscious Minds).

Moods are an important part of life. Moods bring about changes in perception and responsiveness that govern much of how well people inter-relate, sympathise and cooperate. Given their importance it is surprising we do not give more weight to their effects and the question of how we might be able to control or manage our moods more effectively.

Why are we unable to experience life without becoming involved in ways which change our mood and perception? We cannot we remain the impartial observer?

To answer these questions it is necessary to have an understanding of the ways in which the human mind works. Not the way in which the brain works but rather the ways in which the product of brain activity, mind function or mental perception, appears to operate.

The human mind receives information from sources external to the body through the five senses – sight, sound, touch, taste and smell; and internally through the nervous systems monitoring and managing the body's state of being. The information received from all sources collectively becomes, the human memory.

When a memory is recalled we 'see' or experience a comprehensive snapshot of the event in question. What happened, what we did and how we felt. The recollection includes not only the facts as they appeared but the personal feelings that accompanied the experience. Within the Mind there is therefore a 'store' of old feelings, each of which is attached to a particular memory.

In recalling a particular memory we may also bring to mind the associated mood. Similarly, on experiencing a mood, we more easily recall an experience that in the past created the same feeling. As a learning tool, we are more likely to remember something if the mood in which it was first experienced is recreated.

Because thoughts and the focus of one's attention can be controlled to some degree, so too can some level of control be exerted in the creation of a chosen state of mind.

Most people are unable to maintain a comfortable 'middle-ground' of mood indefinitely because of the many factors influencing Mind function. These factors or influences include subtle physical and mental changes, the causal factors of which go unnoticed consciously. This category might include chemicals occurring in food or drink, allergic reactions, even chronic low level pain.

The following list will give some idea of causal pathways to mood changes, but it is by no means comprehensive.

The physical state alters the mental state.

A change of activity results in a change of physical state which in turn alters the mental state. The change results from the chemical and hormonal fluctuations induced by participation in a particular activity.

A physical change results in a mental change.

A change of activity brings about a change of sensory and mental focus. In the light of perceived risk in the new situation, information relative to survival is brought into mind, re-stimulating old 'risk' memories and their associated fears.

A change of mental activity results in mental change.

Without change in physical activity, the mind can be brought to focus on something new by an outside stimulus or imaginative or creative thought. The new focal point will bring associated memories into mind.

The mental state alters the physical state.

As mental changes occur, appropriate changes take place in the body. The processes by which these changes are brought about is automatic, for the most part there is little or no distinction between mental imagery and external reality.

Environmental factors change physical and mental states.

The physical state (body) is dependent upon adequate nutrition in order to perform properly. Chemicals, infections, toxins, mal-nutrition, excesses of foodstuffs, including caffeine and sugar, all produce mind/mood changing characteristics.

There are many combinations of these mood/mind changing causal effects and it is important the counsellor is aware of the possibility of their presence when undertaking therapeutic work with a client. Background information should therefore include dietary habits, lifestyle, exercise regimes and so on.

Circumstances can arise where the Mind enters a downward spiral of changes with a accompanying lowering of mood. Physical change, perhaps traumatic, results in a mental change which, when combined with some physical limitation, lowers motivation. In turn this brings less mobility, less physical activity, less mental activity, leading to less stimulation and further mental changes.

The human mind has a tendency to hold on to patterns of

behaviour, including patterns of thought, which encourages 'more of the same'. The longer a state of being exists, or the more frequently it is experienced, the more difficult it is to break free from its persistence and recurrence.

One way of deliberately bringing about a change of mood is to concentrate on the memory of something known to be accompanied by a 'good' feeling. This need not involve any physical activity but does require mental concentration. Listening to a favourite piece of music is often a good aid to this process.

The process is effective in any direction and so the preoccupation with something that is worrying will result in a drop in mood regardless of otherwise good circumstances prevailing. The way out of such a situation is to engage in an activity completely unconnected with one's self thus shifting mental focus outside one's mind.

Because negative or low moods are those which concern us most, it is those on which these notes concentrate.

Changes in mood come about through physical, mental and environmental causes and it is not difficult to see how one thing can very easily lead to another. Simple thought association mixing past and present. One moment feeling on top of the world, only to find those happy, light-hearted feelings fade and be replaced by the dullness of depressing or worrying thoughts.

The change or the causes of change may cause resentment or frustration at the inability to hold onto the good mood and the optimism that preceded the change. These additional negative feelings then feed into the cycle promoting even greater changes. Without early resolution the thoughts go round and round, internal tension mounts and mood deepens.

From this point a number of things may happen – here are five.
1. Feelings are vented off in a forceful outburst involving someone else.
2. Feelings escape to be expressed in uncontrolled rage, verbal or physical violence.
3. Conscious control prevents an outburst and a state of quiet surly resentment persists.

4. In isolation, walking or working silently, the mood is allowed to dispel.
5. Realising what is happening, rationale overcomes reactions and activity is allowed to displace negativity with feelings of optimism and control.

Any physical activity that releases tension will help relieve a negative mood state. Angry people tend to put more physical effort into their work simply because the tension created by their frustration, anger or whatever, gives them greater energy. This factor may be exploited by sports coaches who needle their teams in action, building on hate, pride, fear of humiliation and anything else opportunistically presenting itself to building tension and physical and mental energies to breaking point. A unfortunate by-product is the violent outbursts to be seen in sporting arenas.

Fortunately there is are better alternatives that can be used to far greater effect in building confidence, energy and determination. These are usually centred around self-belief, whether for an individual or a team, and are based on reality. The challenge of what can and cannot be done, and of course the wise trainer or coach knows that the absence of certainty can be use to advantage. If you don't know that you will win, you don't know that you will lose. Here the focus determines a positive and optimistic mood – it is a matter of choice.

Both approaches help teams win. The former in a destructive way where losing results in misery and a loss of confidence; the latter in a constructive way where losing is a learning experience spurring to greater endeavour. As it is with teams, so also the individual. At extremes people tend to be either aggressive, needing to win and beat the opposition in order to maintain self-esteem; or is a dedicated enthusiast aiming for the ultimate performance, winning bringing acknowledgement of that success.

The perception of whether one wins or loses is a purely personal one. If a participant relies on beating the opposition, then winning success depends on the opposition agreeing that they have been beaten. When a participant tests himself against others the outcome is one of judgement relative to the performance of the others. The relevant differences between coming last, third, second or first are all important to the competitor accepting of himself and others.

The would-be participant who lacks confidence in himself, or who judges himself poorly against the performance of his competitors will inevitably find his mood depressed and likewise his motivation; no recipe for assertive training. This negative self-assessment will undoubtedly have its roots in the past. While it may have been triggered by a more recent event, an earlier experience will have been affecting performance for some time.

Someone who suffers depression and who is fighting back will pass through a minefield of 'reminders'. Subconscious memories of every failure, loss or poor performance of any kind lurk in the background awaiting revival. Memories; any one of which can trigger a depressive phase in mood, depressing motivation as it kicks in.

The result can be erratic mood changes, one minute optimistic and energetic, the next, plunging into the depths of despair. The sufferer is likely unaware of the true cause of the change, attributing it to something topical or pre-occupational. This can be as frustrating for anyone trying to help a depressed person as much as it is for the sufferer. To restore confidence, patience and understanding is needed by both.

It is to be remembered that if there is any single symptom of depression that stands out above all others it is a sense of loss; the inevitable sense of loss accompanying the lowering mood. Loss of appetite, loss of interest, loss of sex drive, loss of just about anything you care to name.

Sometimes good things carry bad or sad associations and mixed feelings. Being a beneficiary of the will of a close friend or relative, or a happy and enjoyable day ending in some misfortune.

At this point I must stress that we are not talking about mood depression categorised as 'clinical depression' for which see separate chapter.

Moods have been analysed and placed in comparative tables

inviting practitioners of many disciplines to use this information diagnostically and a behavioural risk-indicator. Much of this work is speculative but it can be helpful to a counsellor or therapist to understand the relativity of moods, even if not quite as precise as list might appear.

Part of the control we can exert over moods is in knowing just what mood we are in, what we might experience in changing mood for the better, and what dangers there may be for be if it should lower.

A mood can be a general state and characteristic; or a short lasting and reactionary. Moods can be habitual or isolated, predictable or unexpected. Most moods come and go, at worst lasting a few days and often just an hour or so. The process of mood changes occurs in most people and is a natural part of life. Mood problems begin when one gets stuck in a mood inappropriate to one's circumstances, or mood enhancement is sought by use of drugs, prescribed or otherwise.

Because moods are natural, their acceptance and their subsequent control should also be natural. Something of which we may too easily lose sight.

It is also important to remember that the ability to communicate is almost always a problem for someone who is in a depressed state of mind. The lower the mood, to greater the difficulty in communication, even in so-called positive state. It is easy to communicate enthusiastically when feeling good and up-beat. Not so easy though when the mood is lowered: anger, pain, hurt, frustration and apathy inhibit the desire and ability to communicate, or be communicated to.

The following table of moods helps put the positive and negative mood state into a broader perspective. Almost everyone experiences changes of mood every day, their depth and nature determined by a host of circumstances, their precise causes not always obvious. The subject is not one in which to become preoccupied, just to be understood a little more deeply in order to make mood management more easy.

Individually described negative moods describe feelings that can be partially and transiently experienced with other states.

Depth of feeling or mood is related to impact and persistence of the causal experience, which may be physical, mental or environmental.

Physical health is an important factor and must be taken into consideration. For example, toxins produced by infection, such as those resulting from Candida Albicans, when encountered persistently will produce almost permanent moods symptoms (mainly depression) which will not be broken by psychotherapy, counselling or medication.

Similarly, mood reactions to pressures and the influences of other people may persist without counselling intervention as to their management, for as long as those outside sources persist.

It will be noted that in transition from a negative to positive state a *zero point* is encountered. It is at this point, whether going down in mood or going up, an unstable state exists in which to sufferer is faced with self-acceptance and responsibility. This is a point around which suicidal or wholly negative guilt and hopelessness can fleetingly exist.

Spiritual and/or therapeutic help may be necessary for the symptomatic denial of ability to accept the responsibilities of self-determination.

A scale of identifiable Moods or states of mind

Presented in descending order

Serenity – total presence, spirituality.

Exhilaration – resulting from mental or physical engagement.

Action – participation.

Enthusiasm – optimistic.

Interest – mental/physical activity.

Conservative – conformity.

Boredom – disengaged, without purpose.

Antagonistic – argumentative, lacks sense of humour.

Pain – suffering, irritability, distraction.

Anger – threatening, aggrieved.

Unsympathetic – suppressed anger, cruel, calm, 'cold'.

Covert hostility – a gossip, defensive, fixed smile.

Fear – anxious, cowardly, defensive, indecisive.

Sympathetic – afraid of hurting others, collects 'downers'.

Appeasing – do-gooder, can't say NO, intending to change.

Grief – dwelling in the past, may feel betrayed, painful.

Amend making – sympathy seeking, a 'yes-man'.

Apathy – fatalistic, given up, addictive, may pretend to have found peace.

Stages above this point may be considered positive.

Zero – doubt, confused, guilt, negative self-judgement, suicidal.

Stages below this point may be considered negative.

Regret – self-questioning, dwelling on own actions.

Shame – acceptance of own actions.

Blame – non-acceptance of own actions, outward looking.

Hope – unsustainable and non-specific optimism.

Demanding - help seeking, wants improvement, dissatisfaction.

Need change – self-aware, mildly motivated.

Fear of worsening - self aware, anxious, help seeking.

Suffering – awareness of physical and mental depletion.

Ruin – distorted perspective.

Despair – no sense of perspective.

Hiding – physical and/or mental withdrawal.

Numbness - shutting off.

Introversion – energy and focus inwards.

Disaster – unable to cope.

Delusion – experiencing alternative realities, highly imaginative.

Shock – begins to cut off, loss of physical and mental mobility.

Detachment – feeling unreal, dissociated from reality.

Catatonia – stares into space.

26.   Aspects of Depression

Identification and treatment

In general terms, depression is a disorder of mood: protracted disproportionate melancholy.

Exaggerated misery accompanied by an impairment of all mental and physical processes and functions, including appetite, sleep, motivation and work.

Broadly speaking Depression is a condition of 'losses'.

There are many circumstances and situations to which melancholy and a depressed mood are normal responses, such as following a bereavement. While someone in such circumstance may become depressed, sadness itself, together with a natural preoccupation, should not be mistaken for depression.

Furthermore, some people are pessimistic and gloomy by nature and while this outlook can be modified or changed, it should not be regarded as abnormal.

Depression is recognised clinically when a person's lowered mood meets certain criteria. Depression may be described as an emotional attitude involving feelings of inadequacy and hopelessness. These feelings may be overwhelming and accompanied by a general lowering of mental and physical activity.

A diagnostic criteria for Primary Major Depression could be as follows.

A. A distinct period of depressed, hopeless, irritable or low mood accompanied by a loss of interest or pleasure in usual activities.

B. That such period is of a duration of at least two weeks.

C. At least four of the following symptoms are present.

    i. Poor appetite or weight loss.

    ii. Sleeplessness of excessive sleeping.

    iii. Agitation or a slowing down (retardation) of physical activity.

    iv. Loss of interest or pleasure in usual activities,

decreased sexual drive.
v. Loss of energy or fatigue.
vi. Feelings of worthlessness, guilt, or self-condemnation (which may or may not be delusional.
vii. Inability to think or concentrate, slowed thinking, marked indecisiveness.
viii. Recurrent thoughts of death or suicide, suicide attempt.
D. NOT superimposed upon/accompanied by any of the following.
1. Schizophrenia or Schizoid disorder, paranoid disorder or other psychiatric disorder of illness which precedes depression.
2. Organic mental disorder due to drug use, influenza, hypothyroidism, any life-threatening disease, Alzheimer's disease, senility or other brain disease leading to dementia.
3. Bereavement, particularly the death of a relative or close friend.

From this it can be seen that while most people suffer bouts of depression, they do not suffer them to the extent or duration sufficient to be classified or categorized as clinically depressed, that is to say, in need of drug or other clinical treatment.

In the vast majority of such cases, a brief spell away from the source or location of the depression, a short holiday perhaps, and the opportunity for mental and physical relaxation, followed by gentle re-stimulation is sufficient.

Almost everyone suffers depressed feelings at some time in their lives but within the normal range of fluctuating moods and the feelings last just a short while. In everyday circumstances the Mind is distracted from its depression by something of greater interest or urgency, so breaking the mood. Or the sufferer recognizes he or she is feeling 'down', and makes an effort to bring about a change of mood.

When the cause of the depressed state is so great that depressing thoughts dominate all else, there is likely a withdrawal into the Mind and an isolation in which depression may take hold more firmly. The sufferer is then held by his or her own thoughts in a preoccupation of gloom. Concentration or focus on anything else, including the ability to change, seems impossible. Self and self-misery remain uppermost.

Depression is a state of reaction rather than one of choice or consent. There is little point to tell a clinically depressed person to 'buck-up' and snap out of it. No one stays depressed from choice.

When Depression is experienced in infancy, possibly associated with the deprivation of love, the same feelings may be subconsciously reactivated later in life'. The trigger being a time when the sufferer feels love is either withheld, denied or lost.

This, as with all subconscious reactions, is determined by the sufferer's perception rather than any factual reality. The situation giving rise to the reaction may be innocent and the person 'responsible', unknowing, creating a barrier to any truly meaningful communication. Which in turn increase the sufferer's sense of hurt and isolation.

Feeling unloved or ignored, perhaps as a means of punishment or manipulation, is sufficient to revive old feelings of depression. The unhappiness caused by such a reaction may be wholly disproportionate to present circumstances but it is the genuine unhappiness of the child. The child who lives on within the mind.

Happily situations of this kind are of simple, reactive depression. Often the solution is little more than the sufferer finding reassurance that he or she is loved, offering the opportunity to express love. The cycle is then broken.

Depression can also arise from the frustration of forbidden desires. Forbidden only in the sense of their denial or disapproval by a person essential to their fulfilment. Frustration leads to despair and every time the desire is aroused, even without the sufferer being consciously aware of it, depression follows.

Common causes are sexual in origin and have their roots in childhood. Desires of this kind may be simple and straightforward or unusual, even illegal. The true nature of the problem will only be revealed through careful counselling whereby the sufferer feels able to disclose his or her 'secret'.

The sufferer must understand that the presence of desire does not initiate any right of its fulfilment. There may be common ground to be found between partners or exploration of a means of outlet, but equally there may not.

More important is the removal of guilt and even the sense of shame that can accompany the forbidden desire.

For the counsellor, a client with this kind of problem poses difficult choices and very careful handling. The forbidden desires may be illegal or morally unacceptable. Once there is clarity, it is up to the counsellor to draw the line. Only then can truly appropriate help be given.

The menopause may be responsible for depression in some women. This can be due to physical factors, including uneven/irregular hormonal activity and the recurrence of distressing and uncomfortable feelings and symptoms.

There may also be an element of psychological distress arising from confronting the realisation of the inability to have children. Depression of this nature may be spasmodic and spoken of a moodiness. A similar kind of depression may follow an hysterectomy.

In either case an additional factor can be the stress encountered in coming to terms with a new level of sexual activity. This may also carry connotations of how much, or indeed whether one is 'loved'.

There may be a decline in sexual drive that is not matched by a partner. Alternately, a new sense of sexual freedom may result in an increase in sexual drive, also not matched. Where a sexual mismatch between partners previously existed this may be may be equalized, or exacerbated.

Postnatal depression usually results from hormonal changes combining with fatigue and feelings inadequacy in the face of the demands of childcare. The mildest form of postnatal depression is the 'baby-blues'. Developing within the first week after childbirth, depression of this kind is often short lived.

Postnatal exhaustion can begin any time following childbirth and when it lingers, can predispose those mothers to the risk of a state of clinical post natal depression. Postnatal depression may begin at any time during the twelve months following birth, perhaps longer. The higher risk period is within the first three months.

Postnatal depression, when suspected is best left to clinical doctors and associated experts in the field as hormonal and other physical changes in the body nay be a, or the cause.

Postnatal depression is not something to be dabbled in by well-meaning amateurs

Pointers to help identify Postnatal depression and indicating referral.

Extremes of postnatal depression are symptomised by total rejection and disinterest in the baby or very strong fears of losing control and injuring the baby. Disinterest or destruction – feelings potentially putting the baby at risk – are symptoms of depression, NOT expressions of wish or desire.

Depression can result from months/years of living in an almost constant state of anxiety. Or it can arrive unexpectedly, even mysteriously; both point either a subconscious reactive source or attachment to an incompatible or negatively affective Dominant Personality (See separate chapter)for its origins.

When it comes, whatever its causes, the sufferer feels unable to cope with his or her feelings and, importantly, the effect those feelings have on other people. For the sufferer it is a time when maximum demands are being made of someone with minimal resources.

There is evidence for biochemical various causes of mental disturbances, including depression. Beyond the use of drugs, cannabis, heroine and other illegal substances, vitamin and mineral deficiencies can cause depression and/or make it worse.

Many symptoms of 'mental illness' can be switched on and off by altering vitamin levels in the body. Folic Acid is but one example. I have used Folic Acid to treat cases of mild depression with particular efficacy. This is supported by research which has also shown that the majority of the mentally and emotionally 'ill' are deficient in one or more B-Complex vitamins or Vitamin C.

Before continuing with this theme I stress the importance of study and research into the properties of vitamins, minerals, herbs and any supplements you, as practitioner or patient, may be consider using, recommending or prescribing. While I have used or recommended the use of certain supplements I have done so cautiously and with the full cooperation of my patient, having discussed research and reported findings. Sometimes it has been my patient who brought something to my attention and we have then studied the effects.

When in doubt make no recommendation.

A broad spectrum supplementation containing a balanced supply of most essential vitamins and minerals can be the basis for a restorative regime. In addition, the following have been found helpful but NO mega-doses. Always follow manufacturer's advice and adhere to warnings and contra-indicators. Always discuss openly and fully with patient and advise that **it is for the patient to decide on whether or not to use any supplementation** discussed.

Vitamin B1. Thiamine. Significant amounts appear to energise depressed people and tranquillise those who are anxious.

Vitamin B6. Pyridoxine. Is important for the function of the adrenal cortex, part of the body's system of adaptation to stress and ultimately related to general health.

Pantothenic Acid. This has a tension relieving effect.

Vitamin C. Essential to combating stress, the formation of red blood cells and the absorption and utilization of vitamins and minerals and essential nutrients, and the maintenance of the immune system.

Vitamin E, alpha-tocopherol – aids oxygen transmission to brain cells.

Zinc aids brain function.

Magnesium. Necessary for nerve function and has anti-stress properties.

Calcium appears to help people relax and feel less jumpy.

These are observations and while based upon, are not meant to represent scientific study.

Single supplements should be used cautiously as they may interfere with the absorption and function of other nutrients or with any medication currently in use.

It could be said that the difference between depression and anxiety is that anxiety can persist without serious loss of ability to respond and make an effort, and is without loss of hope. Depression seriously impairs ability and exists when hope has been abandoned.

While the symptoms of depression can be readily identified, the causes may not be obvious. Because of the inseparability of Mind and Body, complex cycles of actions and reactions between the two make the isolation of a specific cause difficult. There is a danger that symptoms are taken in isolation are misdiagnosed. The result is that apparently successful treatment and control is short-lived, and the underlying condition, i.e. depression remains untreated.

Medical and clinical practitioners classify depression as being one of two types, according to the presented symptoms and apparent nature of the origin of the condition.

Reactive Depression

This term is used when the depression appears to have been caused be some external event. The trigger may be one associated with a personal loss; reaction to an acute disappointment; or the result of prolonged and unresolved anxiety.

As stated, this kind of depression occurs as a result of a reaction to a sense of loss of some kind. The cause for this sense of loss may not always be obvious, when there is the suggestion that the sufferer is in denial of such loss. Examples of denial could include the slow or reluctant realisation of a deteriorating life situation; work, marriage, relationship, unfulfilled dream, and so on. The acceptance of which would bring unbearable sorrow or trauma. More obvious are losses of bereavement, (usually more appropriately diagnosed as grief, which is understandable and 'normal') divorce and redundancy.

Endogenous Depression.

There <u>seems</u> to be no obvious cause for this type of depression and it arrives unexpectedly.

It may occur following: years of unresolved, and perhaps unrecognised stress; physical debility; hormone disturbance or imbalance; drug use or ceasing to take drugs; severe injury or disease.

Symptoms are usually more physical and noticeable than in cases of reactive depression, a main characteristic being that the patient tends to think, move and respond very slowly. There is also appetite loss and early morning waking.

While a clinical separation between reactive and endogenous depression may help a doctor or psychiatrist determine the kind of help he can offer, and the urgency with which that help is given, it can be said that ALL depression is REACTIVE. All depressed states arise from the experiences of the patient and the patient's reactions to those experiences.

Further, given the opportunity, most psychologically formed or caused depression, that is to say, depression NOT CAUSED by drugs, illness or injury, can be overcome or cured by counselling and analysis. In addition, without the identification of the underlying cause, the rewards of effective counselling and analysis, depression may become cyclic with the additional risk of drug/medication dependency.

The descent into Depression.

As said, depression can arrive out of the blue or follow a bout of anxiety, worry or trauma; it can be associated with injury, illness and medication. Whatever the underlying cause may be, there is often a path of noticeable mood changes that can be identified. While these changes are often easier to see retrospectively, they are an aid to diagnosis and in certain circumstances can provide an insight on future behaviour.

When looking at cases of depression, there are certain types of behaviour which, while they seem negative are in fact quite definitely positive.

Some recognisable moods are listed below in descending order;

In pain – the patient is suffering, perhaps secretly; is irritable and avoids being touched.

Angry – the patient holds a grudge, again perhaps secretly; acts in a threatening manner.

Unsympathetic – appears disinterested, calm, cold; very 'matter of fact'. Closing down.

Fearful – anxious, defensive, indecisive. (weighed down by unspoken fears).

Sympathetic – obsessive agreement, afraid of hurting others, collects 'losers'. Switches attention away from self, unable to deal with problems or confront people.

Appeasing – can't say No, intends to change but doesn't. (Help seeking, switching off).

Grief – dwelling in the past, collects grievances, feels betrayed. (inward looking, unable to face present, suspicious, UN-trusting, increasingly withdrawn).

Amending – sympathy seeking, blind loyalty. (a last ditch effort).

Apathy – fatalistic, addictive, repetitive, pretends/self-deludes to have found peace (patient has is giving up, incapable of further effort, sinks into self.)

Switch Off – coldly looks at self regretfully and guiltily; recognises own actions; suicidal.

The following are wholly negative states of mind.

Regret – dwelling on own actions.
Shame – acceptance of own actions. Inward looking.
Blame – non-acceptance of own actions. Outward looking.
Hope – that is vague and unsustainable.
Demanding – seeks help, impatiently.
Ruin – distorted perspective.
Despair – lacking perspective.
Numbness – no feelings, shut-off.
Delusional – highly imaginative, 'sees' alternate realities.
Hysteria – fearful, distorted perception.
Catatonic – stares into space.
Oblivion – unaware of self or location.

It is important to remember that the ability to communicate is affected by mood. The lower the mood the more difficult it is to communicate. When feeling happy and well it is easy to be enthusiastic, make conversation and talk. Not the case **when the mood is low, when anger, pain, frustration and grief inhibit the desire to communicate or even listen.**

Treating and Beating Depression

The treatment of depression tends to follow a path chosen by, or imposed upon, the patient. Broadly speaking there are three levels of diagnosis and treatment.

<u>Minor to moderate depression</u>, of either type, and which is contained by the sufferer and his or her family, often without referral to a medical practitioner. Bouts may be repetitive and accepted as part of the sufferer's make-up. These periods of depression are of sufficiently short duration to be endured rather than treated.

Home treatment may be in the form of herbal or vitamin/mineral supplements, withdrawal or other form of isolation, or help from complementary health practitioners.

<u>Moderate to serious depression</u> that is treated by the sufferer's doctor.

There sufferer may resist or decline psychiatric care or therapy, opting instead for the range of treatment and medication available through the general practitioner. Drug therapy is often the first choice, using one of a range of anti-depressant drugs, perhaps even a tranquilliser where precise diagnosis is unclear.

The range of suitable drugs changes with the passage of time and the practitioner should acquaint him or herself with those currently in use. History has show that all drug treatments carry risk of physical and mental side effects; these should be studied thoroughly.

<u>Moderate to serious depression</u> where the patient receives specialist psychiatric treatment. The sufferer may be admitted as an in-patient to a psychiatric unit, or consultant on an out-patient basis, perhaps with additional care in the community. Treatment

is usually assumed to be a mid to long term prospect. Medication is almost always part of treatment at this level of intervention.

There may be need for constant or close supervision, which can be at home.

There are many things the sufferer and his or her family can do to help dispel depression and overcome the problem. The process begins by understanding the nature of the depression and how it effects the sufferer. Also in accepting that the condition is a natural part of life and not a mental 'illness'. (Exceptions to this are those depressive states that are chemically and physically induced.)

In the vast majority of cases, depression should be regarded as a built-in safety switch, that comes into effect when there is danger of a mental 'overload'. Frantic mental activity created by impossible choices and hopeless situations, places a high demand on mind/brain circuits. If this activity reaches a critical point the safety switch will be thrown and circuits shut down to protect the sufferer from further anguish.

The brain/mind itself does not need protecting and will not be damaged by intense use, but as a result of intense preoccupation, excessive nervous tension and the changes brought about by acute anxiety the well being of the sufferer may be placed in jeopardy.

Anxious depression gives way to an inability to think, be imaginative or enthusiastic, or make even simple decisions. **This is rest time**.

Family and friends must take away from the sufferer as much responsibility as possible, leaving him/her to rest and be lovingly cared for. Ideally the patient should be in comfortable, stress-free surroundings, away from work and other sources of worry, including the family home if appropriate.

Physical contact, even though it may be shunned or ignored, is of vital importance. Physical contact is the route back to physical and emotional reality. Loving care is touching care; gentle and patient support helping the sufferer back into the world.

The sufferer needs reassurance that can only come from

other people. To be reassured that this condition is a temporary one, that no matter how bad things seems now, this time will pass. That there was a time when things were not so bad and that time is still there, waiting to be touched. In little ways, and very gently, a glimmer of hope must be introduced into the patient's thinking. For him or her to allow others to see things differently, to accept their support, and their love which expects nothing in return.

Notes for the patient - 20 important things to remember

1 Try to hold onto the thought that you KNOW that you do not really want to feel the way you do.
2 It is OK to do nothing for a while, there is no pressure on you to 'get better'.
3 That time will come just as soon as it can.
4 It is pointless comparing yourself with someone else, someone you think has coped with life better than you.
5 No two people have the same lives, needs or abilities.
6 We all have our hills to climb and sometimes we need a helping hand to get to the summit.
7 A rest may be called for before you can journey on.
8 Remember the power of thought. It is the power of your mind that places you in the position you now enjoy, yes enjoy!
9 Your mind is not working against you.
10 Rest a while and let your mind work out the problems that overwhelmed you.
11 If you are coming to terms with something that has affected you deeply, a trauma or the loss of a loved one, move into your memories gently, you now have the time to do so.
12 Don't feel threatened by memories. They remain in the past and you can now look at from your safe place, here in the present.
13 Bring to life all the treasured memories you have been gifted now by your mind.
14 It may seem impossible to concentrate on anything beyond yourself or work things out in your mind – that is how it is,

that is what depression is. Go with the flow.

15 Remember how there was a time when you were not depressed – and that a time will come again when you are not depressed.

16 You will be happy again.

17 If you feel that your depression is like fighting a part of yourself, then in a sense you a right. Willpower, your conscious effort, is trying to overcome the feelings of depression that are coming from a subconscious reaction.

18 Remember that the reaction is protective even though your may feel it is misplaced. So, rather than fight in an aggressive way, be patient.

19 In quietness begin to ignore depressive thoughts and feelings, look around you, look beyond yourself.

20 Don't try to think, just look, and listen, that's all.

If you feel tired, weak and lethargic, you may feel that you are relaxed, but this tiredness is a result of the depressive nature of your condition, not of natural relaxation. It is important to learn to relax deeply, to passively 'let go' and 'go with the flow'. Keeping to a daily routine can be of great help, perhaps following a recording of a guided relaxation. Your routine should not involve any visualisation or place any real demands on mental function beyond systematic relaxation and abandonment to your body's natural ability to balance and restore itself. A recorded session containing gently positive suggestions or affirmations can also benefit.

Loss of appetite is not uncommon and to ensure you are adequately nourished, you could consider taking a basic, broad-spectrum vitamin and mineral complex as a daily supplement to your diet. Discuss vitamin and mineral supplementation with your doctor or therapist, especially if you are taking prescribed medication.

Ask your doctor for referral to a counsellor skilled in treating depression.

Here are some 20 further changes you might wish to consider.

1   If someone close to you cannot, or will not, talk about your depression, or seems not to understand, try not to resent this. He or she may feel unable to offer any help, or is overwhelmed by the thought of what might be involved. Instead of seeming to ask for help, simply make a statement to the effect that you understand how difficult it is for anyone else to understand; also that you do not want to feel the way you do, and that it will pass, but for the time being it is the way it is. Also that you do not want them to do anything special, just give you a bit of breathing room, some space. Tell them that you know how hard it is for them and how your depression must affect them.

You might feel unable to do this, or to even want to bother. Stop that thinking and TRY. This is part of the deal – try, it is only mental effort and you need to hear the words as much as someone else.

2   Remember that someone close to you may have been suffering as well. Feeling the pressure of your need for help, and the feeling of isolation your withdrawal from their life has brought. He or she may also have personal or emotional problems to deal with, perhaps brought up as a result of your own condition. This is not bad but it is an added pressure of which you may not be aware. If you can, talk openly, not only about your own feelings but to encourage other people to share their own feelings as well. Talk!

3   Give vent to your feelings. If you feel angry then shout, slam doors, get rid of your anger – feel your feelings – when you do this you are not feeling depressed! If you feel sad, cry, it is all part of getting back in touch with yourself.

4   Move about. Don't sit and dwell on your own thoughts. Make an effort of some kind, no matter how small. Go out into the garden, walk to the end of the road. Move!

5   Wash, shave, put on some make-up, comb your hair, cut and clean your nails. Get up, get dressed. Don't live in your dressing gown.

6   Look as good as you can, even if you really couldn't care less about how you look. It takes no more effort to put on clean, smart clothes than old, tired or dirty ones. Why bother, you say? And I reply, if it really doesn't matter, then why not? It is much easier to feel good if you look good, whatever looking good means to you.

How you feel depends to some degree on how other people see and react to you, and how you feel other people see you. Looking a mess is one way of saying how uncared for you are and that is unfair on those who care for and about you, as well as on yourself – you are worth more.

7   If you have something to say then do so. Speak it or write it down though even the effort of beginning to do so may seem beyond you, try. If there is something special that you want to say but cannot find a way to do so, or are afraid of doing so, talk to a counsellor, but talk.

8   Make some small changes in your daily routine. If you go out, take a different route to the shops or wherever it is that you are going. If you stay indoors try not to sit in the same room or chair each time. Sit at a table to eat meals, not in an easy chair in front of the television. Stimulate your mind by making simple changes.

9   Do something for yourself, something that needs just a little effort on your part. Walk to the park, to town or somewhere new. Buy a magazine from a shop, take a bus ride. Do something different, simply because you can, you have the time, you do not need any more reason that that.

10   When you can, in odd moments of thoughtful mind-wandering, make some plans, no matter how small. Put a little faith in the future. Make a list of some jobs you would like to see done or something you would like to get for the house. Everyone is entitled to escape into their dreams.

11   When the time comes, to show even greater faith, look ahead to what you will be able to do when you feel up to it. Give yourself something towards which you can work – the

only commitment is the goal, not how or when it may be realised – and no one need know but you.

12 Plan to visit someone or somewhere, think about making a journey, perhaps even to stay away for a day or so. Do no more than think about it. There are no barriers in the mind, but it is the starting point in which the future you choose to live can begin to take form. These are your ideas, your thoughts, not those of your husband or wife or friend. These precious thoughts are your own. Treasure them. Keep them to yourself until you feel the time is right to share them.

13 Don't expect miracles. Set small goals, attempt something, finish something, if unfinished, go back and try again. Gently and quietly, in your own time. No one is judging you but you. Lose some weight, gain some weight, whatever you feel is needed, get fitter.

14 Try to get involved in your own special project. Something simple. It could be a notebook, your comments on what happens around you, or just special things, how you feel – good and bad! Make a scrapbook using anything to hand.

15 Start a diary – be honest about how you feel, even how you feel about keeping a diary.

16 Write a letter, to a friend, to the editor of a newspaper, anybody at all – make an effort and you make an impact on the world.

17 Don't try to justify what you do, or how you feel, or find reasons for why you feel depressed. You are who you are and there is no need to explain or excuse yourself. All will become clear in time. There will be plenty of time for explanations and decisions, when the time comes, perhaps with the help of a counsellor or friend.

18 Listen to what other people have to say. It may be polite chat, it might be concerned interest or helpful suggestions. Equally it might be complete rubbish, but it is their rubbish so learn a little patience. Be patient, be spontaneous, be relaxed, enjoy human contact when you can.

19 Often small-talk seems impossible simply because that is what it is – boring, insignificant gossip but it is part of life for

many people. No one says you should be interested but remember that it works both ways. Much of what you say will be uninteresting to other people.

20 If you do not want the company of other people for a while, say so. Just get on with getting yourself together in your own way. If you feel you need some privacy and peace and quiet say so – but not all the time.

Don't be afraid of asking for professional help. You do not have all the answers, nobody does, but a little help and guidance can be invaluable in breaking through the depression barrier.

Don't just sit there doing nothing. If you can't get going by yourself, allow someone else to help you, be led, be loved.

Don't just sit there thinking about what has happened – you can't change the past but you can stop blaming yourself or other people.

Don't just sit there feeling a failure. Your achievements cannot be erased and the help you have given others grows in value all of their lives.

Don't just sit there seeing no tomorrow. Your tomorrow is there, as it is for everyone; a blank page on which to write.

Don't just sit there trying to justify what you have done, or what you think you have done. The circumstances that have brought you to this point in your life may be impossible to explain at the moment but an understanding of what has happened will fall into place in your mind when the time is right. When you can comfortably do so.

It is in overcoming that we learn to overcome; every day we learn to overcome something, even if that something is ourselves. Smile, even if you don't feel like it, because a smile changes the way we look at something. The muscles we use to smile is associated with a happiness response and will trigger an automatic reaction that colours your outlook positively. Don't take my word for it, try it and see. Life is like a mirror and your smile will come back to you in the happiness you generate in other people.

You may feel that nothing and no one can help you, that nobody can understand, after all, why should they? Your suffering is your own. No one can get into your head and know how miserable and unhappy you feel so how could that help?

Your feelings are you own but that does not mean people do not care, or that people do not want to help. You may not know how they can help, or why they want to. Perhaps because they have been there themselves and do know what you are suffering, but does it matter? Let the fact that help is offered be sufficient.

Depression is a temporary state of mind that will pass but when you are in its grasp, in the depths of blackness, all you can do is survive – and in whatever ways possible, remind yourself of who you really are and the world of which you remain a part.

27. Loneliness Observed

Lonely people may feel sad but sadness need not be loneliness. Nor is loneliness the same as unhappiness, although people who feel lonely are usually unhappy.

Being alone and on one's own is not loneliness: many people live solitary lives but do not feel lonely.

Feeling frightened of being alone is not fear of loneliness, though it a fear common to many.

Loneliness is not the same as feeling unloved.

Deprivation need not bring loneliness, money cannot buy friendship nor poverty deny it.

Loneliness may come about as a result of self-exclusion, brought about by the fear of what another might demand.

 Loneliness may be a consequence of insensitivity, when the needs and feelings of other people have been ignored or suffering brought about through selfishness.

Loneliness follows resentment like a dark shadow.

Loneliness is withholding love, or having love withheld.

Loneliness is being shut away in one's own mind.

Loneliness is in not meeting one's responsibilities, not knowing one's true value and therefore not realising one's obligations. It is a denial of one's position in life.

Loneliness is to do with a lack of communication. The absence of meaningful communication with another human being. Of not feeling a part of creation and the absence of any sense of communion with the environment of one's birth.

Loneliness is about emotions and an inability to express or reveal one's emotional feelings in a spontaneous and fulfilling way. Not an explosive, uncontrolled reactionary outburst of feeling that repels but a sincere revealing of the self.

Loneliness is about judgement and about response. It is an inability to respond to other people in a mutuality of trust and openness.

Loneliness is to be private to a degree of secrecy that is un-sharing and which reserves all things creates a barrier which another has to breach should he or she wish to become a friend.

Reserved and private people are happy to remain so if their reserve is not a sacrificial withdrawal from society and cause of loneliness. Many people are very happy in their solitude.

Loneliness is not solely about giving or sharing. Active willing people may also be shy and modest, their relationships regarded as being one of acquaintance rather than friend. Many such acquaintances may indeed feel that they are friends of someone who obviously cares about them and is interesting in them, but is an illusion of circumstances rather than fact.

One who is a friend to all may have no friends at all.

Loneliness is not about going out, meeting people and mixing. It is about knowing that no matter how full is the day, how busy the hour, the time draws closer, inevitably bringing that which for some is their haven of peace and tranquillity but which for others is the hollow ring of an empty house and loneliness.

Loneliness is in closing the doors tightly against an uncaring and hurtful world. Awaiting another's helping hand, the keys of trust and hope and love lie motionless in rusty locks too stiff to turn alone.

28.   Embarrassment

To feel embarrassed could be described as feeling uncomfortable in a very personal way; feeling awkward, out of place and self-conscious. Embarrassment is a feeling or emotion that most people have experienced at some time in their lives. The feeling may be purely personal, or one that is shared by several people sharing an experience in common.

The cause of embarrassment may be someone else's behaviour or one's own; personal awkwardness caused by another person, or limited to one's purely personal self-consciousness

Reactions accompanying embarrassment include wanting to run away, hide, disappear, become invisible, be somewhere else. The emotional discomfort may be so acute that the sufferer actually flees, failing this we tough it out, avoid eye contact, generally feel at a loss for words and just try to be as inconspicuous as possible.

Translated into stress we can see the basic 'fight or flight' response in action but biased almost entirely to the 'flight' factor. This is because the source of the embarrassment is being overwhelmed by one's own sense of inadequacy, making the 'fight' factor appear pointless. Feelings of embarrassment can severely diminish self-confidence, not only in the immediacy of a particular situation for some time.

It is important to separate this type of embarrassment from more run of the mill situations. Sufferers of severe and limiting anxiety reactions and symptoms caused by other commonly encountered embarrassing situations are often able to disguise their reactions and other people are often unaware of an individual's problem.

Not so someone acutely embarrassed and whose reactions are almost impossible to conceal.

Acute embarrassment produces disabling reactions that reduce to sufferer to bow-headed silence or immediate and speedy withdrawal. This state may last for only a short time but for that time its power can be overwhelming following which, its effects long-lasting.

Embarrassment is essentially a social condition that arises when we become aware of a breach of social etiquette: unacceptable, inappropriate or inept behaviour. A breach of this kind may occur accidentally, through ignorance or oversight, or through amateurish over-confidence.

Embarrassment is not simply an anxiety state as it usually contains an element of offence or offensive behaviour. Behaviour that offends the conscience. To this can be added a sense of moral and/or social judgement as we compare our behaviour with that of another person or group of people, who we assume judge us.

When we (are made to) feel that we compare unfavourably or that our performance has been found wanting, either by our own sense of comparison or by the words and actions of another, the result is embarrassment.

Here it may be appropriate for the counsellor to introduce to the sufferer, a broader spectrum within which he might see himself differently. Suggest that Embarrassment arises from a judgemental attitude, and is therefore unjustifiable because any personal judgement is entirely subjective. While a person may be entitled to his or her point of view or opinion, the right to hold such opinion is not also the right to impose it on others.

When one's embarrassment takes place in the public arena and witnessed by many, the prospect of then being ridiculed or rejected brings additional fear.

Arising from the feeling of having done the wrong thing, of having let someone down, i.e. causing someone else to feel embarrassed, or uncomfortable Guilt may lie at the core of the embarrassment, imagining, how another person might now feel; whose misplaced or misjudged sense of ability or occasion now makes one squirm even more.

Embarrassment can also be derived from a subconscious reaction following an earlier, and perhaps undisclosed embarrassing incident. A situation, devoid of problems, may reactivate the circumstances of a similar situation but which happened under different circumstances. (See notes on

Conscious and Subconscious Mind)

Here, it may be that a key word triggers feelings surrounding this earlier sensitive time, bringing a sense of guilt and the fear that this secret may somehow be betrayed. Guilt from sexual thoughts and activities can be a source of this kind of reaction.

In overcoming embarrassment, actual and potential, it is important to identify the true nature of the experience, i.e. was/is it appropriate to feel embarrassed or has the situation simply been misread.

It is also important to establish a philosophy reflecting a practical sense of Self and of rights of self existence. For example, being seen as inappropriately dressed, should be no cause for embarrassment – amusement and comment perhaps, but not embarrassment.

The reaction of embarrassment may contain any or all of the following.

1   Embarrassment related to inner personal guilt-feelings reactivated by present circumstances.
2   Embarrassment as a result of feelings of guilt caused by being accused of something.
3   Embarrassment caused by someone else's behaviour.
4   Embarrassment arising from being judged a found wanting, i.e. 'failure'.
5   Embarrassment arising as a consequence of being misunderstood and hence misjudged.
6   Embarrassment arising from a sense of shame, rejection, isolation and loss of face.
7   Embarrassment arising from unfavourable self-comparison and harsh self-judgement.

Summarising, within the complex reactions of embarrassment is: a preoccupation with past guilt; fear of unfavourable revelation; perceived judgement; fear of failure, rejection and isolation; sense of shame; loss of self-esteem and status.

Small wonder that at such times we feel that we cannot cope!

It is important to remember that many embarrassing moments occur in childhood years, when 'grown-ups' unkindly make fun of childish antics and ignorance. Children are eager to learn, with open minds that are vulnerable to impression, favourable and unfavourable. It is to be regretted that many adults, including teachers, use this vulnerability and adolescent ineptitude to create embarrassment as a means of discipline and cheap humour.

Overcoming embarrassment and self-consciousness.

In overcoming the fear of embarrassment and overly sensitive self-consciousness it is necessary to rationalise which of these seven factors apply; also to talk out past embarrassing experiences.

Taking the last point first. Yesterday has gone and whatever happened cannot be changed. If it is necessary and possible to put right some misunderstanding which still causes anguish, then do so as quickly and simply as possible. The less fuss is made about it, the less likely other people will make anything of it. We never get to know what other people say about us in our absence. Being straight forward and honest without being over-sensitive or approval seeking secures a good prospect in which untrue gossip will be given less credence.

Looking now at each of the seven points listed.

1. Embarrassment relating to personal guilt.

In dealing with inner-guilt that is brought to the surface from time to time, it is helpful to do one of two things.

A. Find the origin of the reaction; see it for what it <u>was</u> and in reality <u>is</u> and come to terms with it. It is possible to do this if the 'trigger' to the reaction is obvious, that is to say a word, subject or situation known to give rise to its resurrection. Then, go back in your thoughts and try to identify when this first happened, identify the original experience which left you feeling guilty or foolish. Professional help involving some form of analysis may be necessary.

B. Accept that everyone has irrational reactions and that

279

they can be controlled to a far greater degree than most people imagine. An essential part of human reactions and behaviour exists as a result of past experiences. Human beings are capable of handling new experiences and as they do so, also naturally modify their behaviour and reactions. This is happening naturally day by day throughout a human beings entire life span offering great potential for behavioural change.

Human beings are also capable of wilful action. A combination of these two naturally inherent abilities offers the possibility of almost limitless changes of ability and perspective.

Simple familiarity, through deliberate exposure to 'newness', by making small changes in routine and increasing exposure to known sources of mental discomfort, brings great benefit. Suggestive hypnotherapy can be very helpful in speeding up the process of change and minimising reactions.

2.   Embarrassment caused deliberately by another person.

It is not difficult to put someone at a disadvantage by drawing attention to him or her-self, or to something he has done that can be criticised; or by asking for an explanation or comment. Few people like to make any form of public address and if there is a negative aspect to be confronted it can be especially difficult. Here are two effective ways of dealing with this kind of situation, or person.

A.   Respond to being drawn into the spotlight by simply refusing to accept the invitation or otherwise join in without giving any explanation. While this sounds dramatic and difficult it is neither as the emphasis stays with the person creating the situation, who, as you stay in control, is being disempowered, publicly. All that is required is a firm, polite response. "No thank you". "No, I have nothing to add." "No, I will leave that to you."
Expect some pressure but gently stand your ground. Look directly at the person who is challenging you and, if necessary, simply repeat your answer. The tables are quickly reversed as you show yourself both unresponsive to his demands and obviously in control of yourself and

the situation. Nothing and no-one can make you comply. He/she can rant, verbally bully, rave, ridicule, shout and end up looking rather silly while all you do is – nothing!

B. Alternatively is to pretend not to have heard the accusation or invitation; to deliberately ignore the initial challenge. As the response is looked for, and you remain unresponsive, in the silence that follows you say, "Sorry, what was that again." or "Would you mind repeating that?"(Which amounts to a counter challenge). Without the initial spontaneity, any challenge has lost its impact and is now easier to handle. You have also shown that you were not paying attention to the person concerned, disempowering him even before the matter in question has been broached. If the challenge is repeated you answer as in 2a above OR offer a counter challenge. ""Why do you say that?" "What would be the point?" "How is that relevant?"

By playing naïve and not joining in the best timing in the world falls flat.

3. When another person's behaviour causes embarrassment.

A typical example of collective embarrassment can arise in the public witnessing of an inept or inappropriate performance of some kind. These feeling arise from the assumption that although we may personally be able to understand, excuse or ignore such behaviour, others may not be so able and we feel embarrassed on both their behalf and on behalf of the person in question.

Such reaction is both unnecessary and presumptive. We are each responsible for our actions, including the situations in which we put ourselves. If someone really feels unhappy or uncomfortable with a situation, it is most likely he leave it if he wishes. If unable to leave, observe.

4. Embarrassment from a sense of failure.

It is rare to find someone who has not experienced the fear of failure. Early years of life are dominated by the imposition of competitive behaviour, performance tables, examinations and positioning and grading of various kinds. Little wonder then we grow to adulthood with memories of failure and of its consequences, real and imagined. In a quest of self-establishment, we relate to other children in a variety of ways. Winning or being 'best' at anything is regarded as a personal success. Tallest; fastest; most skilful at this or that; gaining most, or least marks; best or worst behaved; – the opportunities seem endless and of course, as children we seize any opportunity to demonstrate our success. Some of that success will be no more than recognition of our individuality or uniqueness but it is all part of the person self-assessment we carry forward into adulthood.

Through relationships, interviews and encounters, personal endeavours and creations from the way in which we dress to the way in which we speak we expose ourselves to the judgement of other people. In the process we experience many (self perceived) 'failures' as we see our efforts fall short of the competition or overlooking, devalued or ridiculed. In short we are made to feel that we are a failure.

This can only happen in a competitive atmosphere where those who do their best and who achieve much in their lives and in their work, are compared unfavourably with those whose achievements are lauded. No one is good at everything. Only one person can ever be 'best'. Everybody 'loses' at something.

The moment we stop being competitive in our thinking and accept that there can never be any comparison between individuals beyond their suitability for a particular circumstance, we free ourselves to explore our own potential. The moment we do something because we want to do it, or because it needs doing, or because we are best placed to be able to do it, we open ourselves to opportunities of gaining personal satisfaction and enjoyment that is not reliant on the views of other people.

5.   Embarrassment as a result of being misunderstood.

Listening carefully to what other people the care we take in communicating and responding goes a long way to avoid misunderstandings. Try not to make assumptions, waiting to see the whole picture; holding back rather than jumping in at the first opportunity helps avoid many pitfalls.

It is not always easy to stop other people from making assumptions and drawing conclusions in comparative ignorance; nor from misreading innocent and unintentional remarks, but clarity goes a long way to minimise the risk of their doing so.

When there is opportunity to speak there is opportunity for clarity. If at any point you sense you have given a misleading impression, put matters right as quickly as possible. Do so without implying you think you may have given the wrong impression, instead, reiterate what you have said in another way. As a fail-safe, invite questions.

6. Shame and embarrassment.

As we go through childhood and adolescence, we encounter situations when our behaviour is deemed to be 'wrong', and if we persist in doing this 'wrong thing' it will lead to us not being liked – or worse. Examples of this may include words including: "Don't do that, it's dirty, nice people don't do that." "No one likes a boy who cheats." "Mummy doesn't love little girls who are cruel."

As an adult, our sense of values matures and crystallises and gives us latitude to interpret our actions, and those of other people, with relevance to circumstances and a broader understanding of human nature.

We may be accused of being cruel or of cheating and although we have not done so, still feel an element of guilt or shame. We may feel justified in taking a certain course of action but knowing there is a risk that other people might not see it in the same light, behave secretly as if we had done something wrong.

To avoid this kind of embarrassment demands you are honest with yourself, and this requires confrontation. Write down what it is that you keep secret, what it is that you feel justified in doing but which you feel may be interpreted differently by other people. It may be just one thing or you might end up with a list. Here are some examples.

I keep back some housekeeping money for my own use. (*This could feel like stealing from your husband or family but, unlike your husband and children, you have no separate allowance from the family purse or budget)*

I masturbate. *(This could feel like a betrayal within a marriage, or something reprehensible or dirty but it is your body,; a body designed to give pleasure and for you to enjoy and in no way reflects on anyone else.)*

I have not told anyone about a lover I had in the past. *(Here, enjoying old memories could make you feel that you were being unfaithful but your thoughts are private and again need not affect anyone else. Privacy of thought is a right of everyone.)*

Consider your list. Differentiate between secrecy and privacy. Simply remembering something is not the same as being disloyal. There is no obligation to recount every thought, dream, fear or fantasy to anyone – in fact it would be impossible to do so. You interpret and relive your experiences in a way no one else can for a very good reason – they are uniquely yours, to suffer or to enjoy, and, usually, to keep to yourself. There is a time for self and a time for sharing, something it is important to be clear about.

The person who wants to know *everything* about you, to share every moment of your life, is being intrusive, inconsiderate and demonstrating a lack of respect.

Face yourself and your secrets and your objectives, your sense of fairness and your desire to maintain and comfortable equilibrium between yourself and other people, including your family. Part of this is in not making any unnecessary ripples in the pond you all share. That is being thoughtful and kind to other people as well as to yourself.

7. Embarrassment resulting in a loss of status.

"How can I ever face him/her/them again?" is a common enough thought or exclamation. It is based on the assumption that him, her or them see you as a lesser person because of something you have said or done. As a result you feel embarrassed and uncomfortable at this loss of respect.

To deal with this effectively, the embarrassing incident must be viewed with the utmost clarity and with an expansiveness of thought that encompasses other relevant factors. This process should take into account the 6 major points above. Then , put the entire incident into perspective, not just considering the moment in which the incident happened but what had taken place in the preceding hour, or hours.

Then identify who was present, why they were present and what each may have expected of you, as individuals not as a group. Ask yourself, who created the situation in which you feel you let yourself down and was it accidental or deliberate? If the answer is one person, look at what might have motivated this person to bring about the circumstances in question.

Get the broadest picture you can into your mind. See the innocence or the connivance. Ask yourself whether your views of what happened are likely to be shared by others, if not, why not. The picture will clear.

If you did lose face or status in the eyes of another, showing that you do not share or accept their judgement, and making it known to that person that his or her views are not universally shared will speed reinstatement or resolution, in any event, closure.

We all make mistakes and are misunderstood and manipulated by other people at times. These things can become damaging to us personally. If they go unrecognised for what they are, little blips in time that count for little in the world beyond your own, and if we fail to maintain our independence of thought and fail to accept responsibility for our actions.

As the old saying goes, the person who has made no mistakes is unlikely to have made anything else.

29.   Aspects of Guilt

Guilt: A sense of one's wrong doing; an emotional attitude generally involving emotional conflict, arising out of a real or imagined contravention of moral or social standards, in act or thought. Also, anxiety aroused by threats created in one's own mind (punishment).

Generally, feelings of guilt spring from subconscious reactions, the source usually beyond conscious reasoning, and are experienced in the wake of a thought, deed or with-holding that is regarded (subconsciously)as morally questionable in some way.

Moral values, though commonly shared in many instances, are uniquely personal. The moral values each person holds are a combination of the effects of that individual's upbringing and the moral, social and legal values and limitations imposed by society as a whole.

The strength of feelings of guilt may be disproportionate to the nature or magnitude of the offending act, when viewed objectively. However, guilt is a very subjective emotion. What is a matter of little importance to one person may be significant to another. Acts of omission can be as powerful as acts of deed; both can be contrived or spontaneous. Whichever the way, and in almost any circumstance, feelings of guilt make their presence known, perhaps suddenly, even unexpectedly.

Once in place, a sense of guilt can be very hard to displace.

Guilt is the consequence of the realisation that one's action, inaction or thought is, or may be found unacceptable, either by one's self or by another. This reaction of unacceptability may be termed as an expression of one's conscience; which for these purposes is regarded as part of the reactive subconscious mind.

If one also believes in the existence of one's soul additional guilt associated with the transgression of a code of conduct and behaviour even greater than sensed in a breach of social or cultural ethic or law, may also exist.

Does everyone have a conscience?

In broad terms the answer is yes but a rider must be added.

Conscience seems to be inextricably linked with brain function and in particular with the subconscious. Therefore the existence and expression of conscience is reliant (to a greater or lesser degree) on physical brain function. Brain function is affected by cell condition/damage. Damage can occur as a result of physical trauma, including those arising during foetal development and birthing, those resulting from dietary extremes; chemical, including hormonal influences, electrical and electromagnetic disturbance fields and other sources. In short, through accident, design or intervention, brain function can be deficient in scope or expression.

Having said this, for the most part the assumption is made that all people have some sense of conscience but that is not to say that all consciences agree.

A major part of one's conscience develops in the early, formative years of life, particularly during the first eight. The most impressionable early years have most formative value. Aspects of conscience developed here may have the strongest and longest lasting effects. Individual experiences of indoctrination is both personal, in the sense of private, personal experiences, and communal in the sense of more broadly shared experiences.

Private, personal experiences may give rise to inhibited or unbridled behavlour which when demonstrated may prove puzzling to other people, or be criticised by them. Differences of cultural or religious conscience also gives rise to problems and behavioural conflict. One person's code may seek 'an eye for an eye'; while another's seeks to 'turn the other cheek'. Aggression verses forgiveness, both seemingly justified by religious doctrinal law. Contradictory, doctrinal opinion, the former doomed to failure, the latter destined always to win. Just why this should be so will become clear.

One thing that is clear is the way in which arguments of conscience tend to justify their position by deferring to a teaching or doctrine appropriately supportive and ignoring those contrary to their point of view. People can demonstrate remarkable flexibility in their choice of terms of reference.

Justification is a revealing hallmark of a *sense* of guilt, though not that it is necessarily deserved.

An example of simple justification is the employee who steals from his or her employer. Pilfering stationery, inflating expenses claims, over-booking time spent on a job typify this kind of theft. Common arguments for these and similar acts include, 'it's a perk of the job', 'everyone does it', 'a little means nothing to t*hem* but a lot to me', 'it compensates for the times when *they* take advantage of me'.

An employee may feel that it is part of the deal, compensation for not being paid enough or taking something that might otherwise be wasted. Whatever the justification, the act is carried out furtively, covertly, secretly and in the knowledge that there is a risk of being caught or found out, all feelings of conscience telling the perpetrator that what he or she is doing is wrong.

Need for justification reveals a troubled conscience. The practical and honest alternative would be to ask for whatever is wanted.

However, the terms practical and honest are also subjective in their interpretation. What is practical and honest to one person may not be so to another. It now becomes important to separate genuine differences of conscience. Consider the difference between these following examples.

An act considered by the perpetrator to be wrong, but which is considered not wrong by the person who would otherwise be 'wronged'. The perpetrator who sees wrong in what he is doing and who feels justified in his actions which are then considered to be not wrong by the person affected by them. The justified act of someone who feels he is doing wrong but still goes ahead and does it and then feels guilty. The guilt unrecognised and so unsupported by the one supposedly 'wronged who therefore sees no need to forgive.

Conscience is not simply a question of what is right or wrong, good or bad. Arguably opposing views each needing the other for their comparative and highly subjective existence.

To take the life of another person is considered to be wrong by most people. But this tenet is conditional upon circumstance; acts of war and acts of self defence being sited exceptional circumstances and exceptions.

For the pacifist, the life preserver, there are no exceptions, all life is sacred and each must run its destined course. For the mystic nihilist, the cold hearted killer, there are no exceptions; life is a transitory experience, death of the body no more than the release of its soul; part of its destined experience. Apparent opposites sharing an acceptance of destiny, each implicit in the part they will play in its unfolding – who is to say which is right and which is wrong, or why?

Conscience is to do with living with one's self regardless of how other people view one's acts. It is also living with the consequences, of suffering the effects of comparative injustices and punishment metered out against one's personal 'innocence'.

When a person does something he knows deep down is wrong he must find ways he can live with himself and his conscience. He may try to justify his actions only to find that despite all the 'reasons' he puts forward to explain and justify his circumstances the sense of guilt remains. In time this sense of guilt may wane. To return on those occasions when he, or his subconscious are reminded of what *he* has done. If the deed has caused suffering to another and consequences are unavoidable, the sense of guilt may deepen, resulting in depression, regret and self-punishment to the extreme of suicide.

An answer that stands out above all others is the perpetrator's acceptance of Divine forgiveness. In an abandonment to Faith, acceptance of wrongdoing, absolution through contrition and resolution by good living the perpetrator may return to living in good conscience. The subject of forgiveness is dealt with more fully in another chapter.

The mental struggle to come to terms with knowledge of the consequences of our actions is made more difficult by there being no clear standard by which all people live. Even within single-religion communities, interpretation of religious law will be brought into question, need updating and so on, resulting in a community splitting into different factions. In the end we are all left with personal choice, that by which we shall find a sense of inner peace that is an expression of the free-will accorded to all people by birth.

Thus it is that within this apparent dilemma, the answer forms as we each first suffer the imposition of the common codes of our upbringing, and later as we choose those we find attractive and with which we individually find compatibility. A process culminating in our final personal choices, a sense of conscience comprising the code of ethics and morals by which we try to live.

The process.

Following entry into this world we learn the social, moral and legal codes of the society in which we have been born. Initially this is relatively simple, restricted to the rules imposed by our parents and relatives – our family code of behaviour. Even here though there is choice when one parent's view differs from that of the other. The child soon learns who will most likely permit a certain action and who will most likely refuse it.

We also learn that not all family codes are the same. What can be done at home may not be allowed elsewhere, and vice-versa.

As we grow up we find that some rules change, there are new rules, and there are rules which apply to certain activities. Some rules apply to everyone, some to just a few, some to just other people. At school, certain rules that apply to children do not apply to teachers. Rules applied by one teacher may not be applied by another. Rules may be applied to girls differently from their administration to boys. Rules may be administered differently by women teachers and men teachers. Children of achievement may earn privileges freeing them of restrictions which remain for others. Laws can be applied or ignored, hardened or softened according to whim, desire or agenda.

Perhaps the most important lesson learned in early years is that the interpretation of law, or rules, is not absolute. It is in childhood we are likely to experience injustice at first hand. Early lessons in how rules can be applied or ignored according to need, desire, bias and ignorance. Lessons which shape the way in which we come to view our society's moral and legal framework.

We learn that we can question rules presenting obstacles to things we want to do; or we can join a branch of society open that the type of behaviour we want to enjoy. Sex is a powerful motivator and where families and society set standards found unrealistic by young people, those standards are ignored. What is acceptable to one family may be abhorrent to another. The stuff of classic conflict, age old and enduring. Who is right and who is wrong? There is no answer.

In early years we have the codes of family, school, clubs, teams, scouts, guides, church, society as a whole, and later those of employer, supervisor, union, police, the law, courts, community, husband or wife.......

Choices are to be made, often as opportunities of choice present themselves in an ever changing world and society. One can be one's Self, constant in the sureness of living closely to one's own conscience regardless of others. One can accommodate the needs of changing circumstance, 'when in Rome, do as the Romans'. One can find a middle way balancing sense and sensibility, conscience and conflict.

The process continues throughout one's life, ending only when a point of pure personal existence is reached, where the codes of others cease to present cause for doubt or inner conflict. Such state may come through an increased acceptance and tolerance of other people and their ways of living. Equally it may come when a point of such absolute certainty makes deviation from one's chosen path wholly unacceptable.

For the truly fortunate, and perhaps inevitably for us all, there comes a point of realisation or awakening when 'all becomes clear'; in a moment of unequalled perspective our understanding of life is complete.

We are looking at three typical examples of adult perception, namely:

Willing humanistic coexistence.

Individual anarchic separatism.

Spirituality and acceptance through personal serenity

291

It is likely that most people experience the first two states to some degree for much of the time. However, social acceptability demands behaviour be modified to avoid reflecting their true feelings.

Many people experience moments of realisation in which they find themselves able to accept all people lovingly. A state difficult to sustain but one which having been experienced provides an enduring source of aspiration.

There will also be some people who are so attracted to abstract, spiritual or pseudo-spiritual states, they seek to absent themselves from worldly reality. Their routes to abstraction may be extreme religious or physical practices, the use of drugs or isolation.

None of the states describe is dependent on any other state, or approval or acceptance by other people.

Most personal rules of conscience have their origins in external sources; rules that have been observed and subsequently become empowered internally, personally. Some from childhood and unquestioned, others relating to very specific circumstances and social or other social layers or groups. This is an important factor to take into account when trying to understand the power underlying a sense of guilt as presented by a client.

Does it arise from a deep seated sense of right and wrong or more simply from the transgressing of a code of ethics or social rules adopted perhaps loosely and comparatively more recently? Is there an inner conflict?

The question then becomes: which rule is to take precedence?

The foundation of personal belief and the foundations of the beliefs of society lie at the core of conscience and at the core of the sub-conscious. Within this core, the most basic are those things which give us our singular and collective understanding of what is 'good' and what is 'bad', 'right or wrong'. Remember too that somewhere in every society is an element of spirituality, or other-worldliness. Space must be allowed for the existence of the illogical, which be implication is therefore also unchallengeable.

From these core beliefs spring the most powerful forces of coexistence.

Core beliefs that are reflected throughout the society to which we belong. In everything we read, from comic books and fairy tales to the literary classics, the Bible, Koran or book of prayer; in almost everything we see, from a game of football to a stage performance or a television programme, we are presented with aspects of good and bad behaviour.

In the execution of rules, whether they be rules of a game or rules of society, when and where discovered, the 'bad' suffers a penalty. Evil is punished in favour of righteousness. This does not mean that good is rewarded or that the righteous will win. It does however imply that the bad will be denied true enjoyment knowing their success was born of deceit rather than skill.

This fundamental aspect of the human learning experience has deep-seated, long-lasting effects and in the context of conscience and guilt, one specific effect. That of expectation.

We (choose to) do the right or good thing (and feel good)

or we (choose to) do the wrong or bad thing.

and go in fear or expectation of our 'just deserts'.

This reactionary process is reinforced throughout childhood. As children we are rewarded and praised for doing the 'right' thing and for not doing the 'wrong' thing. This often incorporates an aspect of achievement, through school work where hard work is rewarded with success, or playing games where practice and diligence is rewarded with winning. Doing the right or 'good' thing incorporates effort, hard work, diligence and perseverance. Therefore, we equate not doing those things with the wrong or 'bad' thing.

It also follows that failing, as opposed to succeeding is also somehow wrong. Losing as opposed to winning is but a short step away in the mind.

As children, if we do something wrong and are found out, we expect to be scolded or punished. The absence of reward or a withholding of privileges also comes to be regarded as punishment.

Children are also scolded or punished for 'not trying' and for being lazy, the equivalent to not achieving, and for being made to feel they are doing the wrong thing.

"The Devil finds work for idle (lazy) hands." Laziness is now EVIL.

From this it would seem that winning is important because it is associated with achievement and the assumption that achievement follows effort, discipline and application; themselves all praiseworthy. Winning is therefore virtuous, and brings praise and reward. To the victor go the spoils. But there can only ever be one winner, everyone else 'loses'......

Coming second, third or where ever, does not mean losing in any way apart from the competitive element of the challenge in question. Beyond this, winning or losing need have little to do with the amount of energy and diligence applied by an individual. Appreciation and success are subjective.

Failing does not mean losing, nor does it mean having done something bad. Nor does achieving necessarily mean winning or having done something good.

Good people who do good things for good reasons may not be successful in their endeavours or if they are, may not find their achievements recognised or rewarded. Appreciation and reward are subjective.

Bad people who do bad things for all the wrong reasons may succeed and go unpunished. Recognition and guilt are subjective.

Perhaps because of the collective nature of guilt, there prevails the notion that a perpetrator of bad things will be ultimately punished. There is strong argument to suggest that it is the perpetrator's subjective sense of guilt that eventually leads to 'circumstantial punishment'; when he or she deliberately, albeit subconsciously creates the circumstances that will release their guilt.

An effect of childhood indoctrination is then, growing up with an expectation of punishment or reward. A reward of some kind is sought or expected following a good deed or achievement. That this is part of 'fair play'. The other side of the coin is where punishment is accepted for wrong doing. While this may be true in the long run and almost certainly true of the world as a whole, it is by no means true for the individual in the short term.

"Inasmuch as I have benefited from the
efforts and sacrifices of others, so too will my
deeds benefit other people, even though I may
not seem to benefit from them myself. It is not
fitting to expect to reap the harvest of that which
I sow when much of what I do reap, has been
sown by others."

Motivation - Why does a person do something he or she knows is "wrong" and will result in them feeling guilty?

Motivation to action is complex and while personal choice is at the root of an individual's actions, other pressures include sense of duty, desire for money or status, pursuit of success or winning, and emotional factors – anger, resentment, love and compassion and so on.

To reduce the motivating process to its simplest component, pose the following questions.

"Why should I do this thing?"

"Do I want to do this thing?"

"Will I feel good or bad, better or worse for doing this thing?"

Answers to these questions will likely expose external and reactive influences revealing underlying considerations more easily. Intuitive feelings should not be ignored as while they may lack the clarity of reasoned argument may reveal the presence of deeper understanding.

Acting without motivation?

One can act altruistically, without motivation and still find one's self accused of having done something "wrong"

Basic principles of giving without motivation, beyond the simplicity of the act itself, may be seen in the following example. If we give lovingly, or give love itself and that gift of love goes unacknowledged we may feel hurt or rejected. Love though, like any other gift offered freely, is offered that it may be accepted freely and without obligation or declined freely without explanation.

"Whether you accept or decline the love I offer, in this gift, I will hold within me those loving feelings which are truly mine."

What though if the loving act is considered inappropriate?

The expectation syndrome applies when we do something wrong; when we then fear punishment should our misdeed be discovered. If not discovered, feelings of guilt, combined with a lack of punishment can bring heartfelt and wretched feelings of remorse.

The pressure created by these feeling results in an almost unbearable urge to confess, to suffer punishment and rid oneself of the guilt. Adultery is an example where the perpetrator, finding him or herself unable to justify adultery or face confession, adopts a pattern of behaviour subconsciously designed to arouse suspicion and invite discovery.

Responsibility is then felt to be shared as revelation is consequential on the actions of the enquiring partner, who may then also be made to feel guilty or at least responsible in some way.

However, confession may not be the straightforward answer it at first appears. To whom does one confess? What hurt will be inflicted on other people in the aftermath of confession?

The circumstances under which adultery is committed are many. Two extremes are:

    A. an isolated, spontaneous incident that is regretted immediately and

    B. a contrived, long-running affair that is deceitfully justified.

Whatever the circumstances, at some point following the act of adultery, feelings of guilt emerge. Regret, remorse and fear of discovery cannot be ignored: actions cannot be justified and rationalization becomes necessary.

Many separate transgressions of one's moral code may lie at the core of this guilt, for example: broken promises, betrayal, breach of religious law, dishonesty. deception, and untruths.

The question of resolving the situation now arises. Assuming the adultery is regretted and concluded, the prime objective is a return to a happy married life. For the adulterer this is easy and straightforward: terminate the adulterous relationship and 'get back to normal', letting the affair slip into the background quietly and quickly.

For the wronged partner, should the adultery be revealed, and assuming the marriage continues, there follows a lengthy period of adjustment and re-establishment of trust. For the adulterer the strongest single need is to confess, get things out in the open and be 'honest'. The trouble is that being 'honest' may not be the best thing for other people, for the situation as a whole, or indeed for the adulterer.

Guilt demands punishment! But what should that punishment be and by whom will it be administered? Who is to judge and pass sentence? Should the responsibility of judgement and punishment be placed on someone else, especially the aggrieved? Should the injured party be expected to play judge, jury and hangman? Can one judge one's self? Who is to punish?

Guilt, is but one side of this particular coin, on the other is forgiveness. Again we most pose these same questions. Can one forgive one's self? Ultimately, who is to forgive?

Taking a case of adultery as an example, deciding which is more appropriate or most beneficial, punishment or forgiveness, is firstly the responsibility of the adulterer and secondly, and only following revelation, the responsibility of the aggrieved.

Given that the primary responsibility is that of the adulterer, his or her first consideration should be the effect that a confession will likely have on his or her partner.

What benefit is there in a wife telling her husband (or vice-versa) that she has committed adultery, regrets having done so and is now sorry? Arguably the only real benefit is to the wife who rids herself of guilt. However, in doing so she hurts her partner, unnecessarily, and whose subsequent suffering will likely cause the adulterer more guilt. Importantly, their relationship is changed, never to be the same again.

It could be said that here is a case where confession is the selfish act of someone unable to carry the weight of guilt, which is the REAL punishment. Here we are faced with a true test of conscience. Can the adulterer rise above her miserable plight, contain their sense of guilt and carry on silently without causing harm to other people?

Here we should not confuse honesty with confession. Not confessing is not being dishonest.

The act of adultery was dishonest and its honest admission results in the guilt now felt. Regret in the wake of that guilt is therefore also honest. True regret, arising from the depths of conscience. From which will come honest and careful behaviour in the future. A beneficial outcome without confession.

How then shall the burden of guilt be born, or set down?

Firstly by not trying to justify or excuse our actions.

Secondly, in accepting that guilt is normal and there for a reason, guilt becomes a tool of improvement; a reminder, that we have done something contrary to our ideology and beliefs.

Thirdly, by accepting that our own guilt punishes us surely and severely. What we think of ourselves and our behaviour governs our behaviour in the future and makes us what we are. Lessons are to be learned, some first hand, some by mistakes; this is simple process of self-improvement.

Fourthly, by accepting that punishment is only part of the process of improvement, the second part being forgiveness. Confession can be to any person thought appropriate, God, priest, counsellor, friend or someone wronged.

Fifthly by accepting one can be forgiven in favour of (further [self]) punishment, further accepting that in order to honour that forgiveness, one must also forgive one's self.

In accepting responsibility for our acts, and that the mental suffering created by guilt is punishment, regret and remorse will shape our lives to the greater good of all.

30.   Aspects of Forgiveness

As an integral part of the processes of guilt, the acts of forgiveness or non-forgiveness, indicate of the presence of an emotional wound. This does not mean that the wound in question was intentional or inconsiderate, only that the recipient felt it to be so.

A need to forgive, or an inability to do so (implying a need to punish), demands subjective, accusative judgement leading to a sense of 'hurt'. Such sense of hurt can arise in a variety of ways: breach of trust, breach of confidence, act of disloyalty, being illegally wronged, a physical injury, loss of property or possession, the withdrawal of love or affection, a broken promise, being slighted by untruth, slandered or libelled, being unjustly accused, an unrealised expectation.

Whatever the cause and however the suffering comes about, someone has been judged to have been uncaring, selfish, thoughtless, cruel, unkind, greedy, irresponsible, and so on. Blame has been attached to someone, perhaps even to the sufferer him or herself; in all cases, judgement has been made and blame placed.

Without judgement there can be no blame and judgement is easily combined with a verdict and sentence passed. Without forgiveness the sentence calls for punishment of the guilty. The punishment may be in the form of redress, revenge, withholding privileges, verbal cut-off, prosecution at law, persecution or other means of retribution, all carried out in the guise of 'justice' masquerading as justifiable action.

True justice demands proof and intent then, where appropriate the guilty person be allowed to demonstrate regret and remorse and to offer means of reparation.

The alternative to punishment is forgiveness, perhaps in the light of remorse and reparation.

While religious or philosophical principles may make it simpler for someone to forgive all things, specific situations may test to the limit an individual's ability to do so. Less obvious situations can lead to forgiveness being with-held mistakenly.

For purposes of illustration here are three categories or types of forgiveness.

1. To forgive a debt, to waive, cancel or excuse a claim.
2. To forgive an insult or 'sin'; to overlook, pardon or renounce need of penalty.
3. To forgive one's enemies; to cease to bear anger or resentment, to show clemency.
4. In general terms, to forego the desire for revenge or demand punishment.

To forgive a debt.

In order a debt may be forgiven, a debt must first be incurred.

In the formal sense a debt relates to an agreement of some kind between a lender and a borrower but there are other kinds of debt which blur the lines of responsibility. Such as debts of gratitude; a gift, where the giver feels no debt is due; and receipt of some benefit where the recipient feels no debt has been incurred.

A debt involves two parties, a lender and a borrower and however well intentioned their respective intentions may be, the two parties may not be agreement. One party may feel no debt is incurred while the other assumes a sense of obligation now exists between them.

For example, a work colleague explains that he has forgotten his wallet and asks you to loan him a small amount until tomorrow. As the amount is small, you agree; the risk is minimal and you can afford to 'lose' the money if it is not repaid. The money is given and the debt incurred.

Both parties are agreed upon the debt and the conditions under which it was incurred. What happens then if, tomorrow, for whatever circumstance, the loan is not repaid? Or if borrower and lender are destined not to meet again how should each regard the debt? The borrow may feel guilty for not keeping to his part of the agreement, the lender may forego the debt knowing it will not now be repaid. Despite the lender's forgiveness, the borrower's guilt remains forever. The experience has brought both parties to consider their actions, in the light of which they may act differently in the future. Many people have lost or gained a book or treasured possession in this way.

A common source of misunderstanding is in the giving of time. In one way or another we are all asked to give up some of this precious commodity. Called upon to give a hand to someone in need, help out with the odd job; kept waiting when appointments are broken.

The circumstances under which time-giving takes place are many, varying from the occasional emergency to the habitual call from someone you suspect is taking advantage of your generosity. The manner and means by which you respond will be determined by such factors but it is still considered time given freely, not a job of work for which remuneration is sought.

You might feel hurt if payment were forced upon you, equally hurt if you perceive no recognition or consideration of the time you have given. Your reaction is determined by your 'judgement' of the situation as a whole from which you create an 'expectation'.

You may do something without thought of reward; or alternatively feel that you are now owed a favour in return, should a hypothetical need arise. This concept is integral with much religious teaching – *do as you would be done by* – *we reap what we sow* – *a good deed is always repaid*, which is idealistic and perhaps relatives more to the larger picture rather than one of individual circumstance.

Within a society or group of living collectively, we cannot expect to reap all that we sow when much of what we reap has been sown by others. Individuals within a society invariably share creative and collective resources

Your reaction also depends on how you regard your action. Are you doing a good deed and if so, is your motivation one of duty, social pressure or something more personal? Of course we all need a sense of conscience, and the act itself is important, but so too are the roots of our desire to give. These roots point us to know who we really are, the depth of our willingness to coexist and to work in harmony; to respond according to the greater need and the benefit of all. Our ability and the ease with which we are able to forgive is also to be found in the same roots.

If you feel that you will be repaid in some way you have created a sense of expectation and a mental note of someone you now feel 'owes you'. This thinking may affect your judgement adversely when, in the future, you need a favour done for you. Instead of asking the person best suited and placed to do you a favour you may instead look first at who owes you a favour, regardless of whether he is best able to help.

If your request is declined by one who 'owes you' your sense of disappointment will sour your outlook further. How many times have we heard, "After all I have done for him or her, etc..." If, on the other hand, that same debtor accepts your request for help, simply in order to be free of you, you may not have the best or most willing person for the job.

Some people have a way of asking for something that makes refusal difficult. The sort of person who makes you feel guilty for not helping, even though you know that your wishes or circumstances are not being considered and that refusal is perfectly reasonable. The sort of person who takes other people for granted, who is inconsiderate and domineering, who fails to see the other person's point of view, and who seems able to get his or her way always.

Only by acting in conscience and to your own accord can you deal with such a person.

Before responding to pressured requests of this kind, a certain amount of self questioning is called for, for example.

"Is what is asked of me reasonable?"

"Do I have time to do what is asked of me?"

"Am I able to do properly what is asked of me?"

"Am I being asked to help someone out of a self-created problem, one that he would better get himself out of?"

"Do I want do this thing I am asked?"

"If I do what is asked of me, will I have to let someone else down?"

"Do I agree with what is being asked of me?"

"Will I be held responsible for the outcome of doing what is requested of me?"

When the answer to any one of these question is NO, then you should feel comfortably able to refuse or decline, and if pressed say why.

The determined and habitual 'people user' will have scant regard for the wishes of other people and whatever reasons you give as grounds for refusing their requests may be ignored, ridiculed, devalued and dismissed.

You should not take this as being a personal reflection and remind yourself that you are going about your business as passively as one can, without need for involvement in fulfilling the wishes of others.

If you accede to another's wishes, knowing you do not really want to, you risk resenting the person who has asked, resent doing what has been requested, and resent yourself for being 'weak'.

If you say no and have a twinge of conscience you can always reflect further on the matter.

The most valuable gift we can give anyone is our time. Time is the one commodity everyone has an equal share of. By nature, man is a hoarder and possessor and some people who want acquire extra time for themselves by using other people's.

Time can be bought, borrowed or stolen. For some people, time is something to be sought and captured, people for whom there is never enough: but because we can each live only one life, extra time can only be gained from using some of that allocated to someone else. Another person's time can be bought by employing workers, companions, housekeepers and so on. Often buying time in this way gives the purchaser a feeling of power and reinforces the social status of bother 'master and servant'.

People who demand and buy the time of others unnecessarily may be disguising a sense of inferiority, insecurity or fear of failure.

An alternative to buying someone's time is to steal their time through manipulation. By using some strategy, leading people to give up their own pursuits and entitlements. The bullying employer who seems to get more work time from an employee than he pays for, the 'lame duck' always in need of rescue, the gossip and party-bore' all fall into this category. Time-vampires from whom one cannot escape without 'killing' the relationship for while it is alive, the threat of control over one's life exists.

In time-vampire situations, the debt of time felt by the giver goes unnoticed or ignored by the receiver. Scarce consideration is given by time-vampires who feel it is your duty to give up your time to boost their ego's and who feel entitled to make demands of you. Or for you to listen to their moans, whinges and boastful diatribes which, they feel, cannot fail to impress or improve you.

If such situations persist, where the giver, unable to escape, surrenders to the habit of giving; the giver feels increasingly resentful and lives in a state of anxious hopelessness. In extremes, a situation that leads to illness and even death. Not dying through overwork but through being taken for granted, feeling imprisoned and unloved. Employer/employee, nurse/patient, carer/invalid; whichever way around when an opportunity for exploitation exists.

Forgiving and insult.

Insults arise in all manner of ways from name-calling, in the course of an heated argument, to the unjust failure to acknowledge achievement. jealousy is the cause of many insults and potential motives of the parties concerned be examined carefully.

A sense of personal failure may lead to a reluctance to acknowledge another person's achievement.

It is easy to feel hurt when something you have done, of which you are rightly proud, goes unrecognised or is dismissed lightly, but need you?

Ask yourself why have you achieved this particular thing? Did you do it for yourself, for reasons of personal need or conscience, or to gain praise and status? Of course praise is nice and can encourage one to even greater things but should praise be anticipated, expected or demanded by right? Why should you be hurt if you are not openly recognised for who you are and for what you may have done. Remember that much praise, as well as gratitude, goes unspoken. How much have we all benefited from the achievements of others whom we can never thank?

Perhaps the reaction to a sense of personal insult rises from deep within the subconscious mind, somehow attached to one of our strongest reactive feelings, that of the sense of (right and) wrong as seen in cases of injustice and unfairness.

The ability to forgive begins through understanding your own sense of purpose, with the knowledge that the actions of most people carry a sense of self-judgement and that everything you do, you judge to be right or wrong in your own eyes. That your actions may be judged by other people may be a major factor, one which brings people into disagreement as individual opinions of what is either right or wrong vary. However, ultimately you must live with yourself and here self-judgement reigns.

On this basis we should allow other people to act in good conscience even if in ways contrary to our own. Forgiveness means accepting the rights of individuality of another person. It does not mean another person goes without punishment within

305

a society amongst whom the rules of that society are accepted or imposed, and where transgression carries a penalty. It does mean that for victims of such transgressions can understand how the nature of their suffering is brought about by individuality and circumstance.

To forgive a sin.

To be able to forgive a sin is rather different because first you have to decide what a sin is, then, is that sin one which affects you personally, and finally, whether you have, or anyone, has been sinned against.

The use of the word sin indicates the presence of religious thought and an association with religious teaching and here may arise a contradiction. Followers of many religions are taught that is wrong to judge yet here is a situation in which we find judgement almost inevitable. Knowing what is acceptable or 'right' and what is unacceptable or 'wrong' and sinful, is essential to an individual living in good-conscience. He or she is therefore painfully aware of whether or not another person's thoughts, words or deeds are in accordance with the tenets of accepted belief or otherwise.

The question arises: is an individual is under any obligation to follow a particular doctrine. This is clear when the church or a religion is the basis for the social structure of a particular society and where the laws of that society are founded on accepted or imposed codes of conduct. Outside this example, one comes again to an individual's acceptance of personal responsibility.

Perhaps the point to be made is that one judges the act rather than the person. A good person may do a not-good thing and remain good. A person who is good in your eyes may do an not-good thing but remain good in his own eyes as he has done nothing outside his own good-conscience.

We can never know truly why a person thinks or acts in a particular way. There may seem reasons from which certain assumptions can be made, even the person concerned may not know the deeper reasons behind his thoughts and reactions. Collectively and singularly we become the creators of our reactive Selves and the environment in which we live, in turn impressing upon as, like a mirror, that for which we are responsible.

How then can one person judge another when all is nought but comparison and self-judgement? How can we refrain from judgement when the thoughts and actions of another run contrary to that which to us is our path of good-conscience? When so much of what is thought and done, is done in ignorance, who is to know that which is truly right? Who is to know the purpose of the Divine or Eternal Plan and the way in which it is to be played out?

Do we forgive the sin or the sinner?

The concept of sin is founded on the social and religious teachings of a society and as such inbred into the reactive, subconscious part of the mind. At a personal level, before an individual can forgive the sins of others he will take into account the way in which he reacts having committed one. His judgement will not be fair by any kind of comparison, simply that the sin of another person will remind him of his own sins and provoke a reaction based in part on his own emotional guilt.

He who can forgive himself will be more able to forgive another.

If an individual is unable to forgive himself he will likely have a very narrow and unforgiving outlook. In denying self-forgiveness, he will likely be unforgiving of others.

If an individual is forgiving of others but cannot forgive himself he is living a double standard: not affording himself the same common judgement and consequence he affords other people.

If one is capable of self-forgiveness, it is contrary to deny others similarly.

If one believes in a forgiving God it is contrary to deny forgiveness to oneself, or to another.

To forgive someone a sin is to offer forgiveness to the person who has sinned. Is this to forgive the act or to forgive the person who has committed the act? Can the sin be separated from the sinner?

Beyond any aspect of Faith or religion, forgiveness is a reflection of one's acceptance of the nature and reality of the variances of behaviour. In short, individually, we can only be who we are. Individual human beings moulded by genetic inheritance, the environment in which we live and the influences brought to bear by society as a whole and other people in singular measure. Who is to judge an act to be sinful, or any person a sinner when forgiveness is no more than acceptance of another as being as equally created as oneself?

To forgive is not to forget. To forgive is to accept and to love in the best sense, the nature and reality of another person; even one whose behaviour is found to be incompatible with one's own. Here judgement is commensurate with self-preservation and harmony without necessarily demanding retribution in any form beyond separation.

Trying to forget is attempting to push away the memory of something that makes us feel differently from how we want to feel. Only through acceptance and forgiveness can a memory be set aside comfortably, the matter in question having been completely and satisfactorily dealt with.

To forgive one's enemies. Definition: adversary, opponent, foe, adversary, rival...

Who are your enemies? Is your enemy the man down the road who keeps looking at your wife? Or is it the school bully who hits your children or the drunk who crashed into your car? Answering questions such as these, matters of conscience and practicality, seems at first relatively simple, but the reality is somewhat more complex.

Prejudice, propaganda and misinformation create divisions of society in which each right becomes another's wrong; a world of saints and sinners. Unknown and un-encountered people become established enemies, Blacks, Whites, Jews, Muslims, Catholics, Police and so on. Enemies with whom we have had little or no contact and who have been created historically, by the actions of a few individuals, or by political or religious propaganda. Nations have allies who are then considered to be 'friendly', while those who oppose us in some way are considered 'unfriendly'.

Who creates the situations in which such judgements are made? Who determines the policies by which allies and opponents are created? Who tells the people who are their country's enemies and friends? Invariably just one person, at best a handful.

It takes just one person who in name is representative of a nation, to declare war on another. There may be a social injustice motivating the person in question, social deprivation, oppression or inequality; but equally the powerfully placed representative may become consumed with power or misguided thinking that his judgement alone is sound. Fearful people are often gullible people eager to take any hand offered them.

Who has told you who your enemies are; more importantly why they are your enemies? Enemies can be handed down from generation to generation, passing on fears of persecution and in doing so preserving its essence. A distillation of centuries old injustices and intolerance kept alive by people who would otherwise make today's decisions based on today's situations.

In Faith and in good-conscience you hold all life to be sacred and basic rights common to all people. You feel it wrong to take the life of another person as you would feel it wrong for another person to deny you your own life. Here is the ultimate test of the ability to forgive. Can you forgive the person who takes the life of another, perhaps someone close to you, or who threatens to take your own life? Your answer reflects your spirituality, your understanding of human nature and your relationship with the source of your creation.

You are told that 'your enemy' wants to kill you and that you should feel threatened by his presence; and that if he comes too close, you should protect yourself. Why does he want to kill you? Who has told you of his intentions and he of yours? Does the rant and threat of an individual, who may invoke other people to take up arms where no hostility previously existed, deserve credence? The fortress built against such threats is little more than a costly prison in which the innocents live in fear.

It is a part of human nature that there are those who take pleasure in exerting their power over other people. Examples are commonplace at home, at work and at large. People in positions of power and responsibility who act wilfully and dictatorially without consideration for the needs of those their position demands they protect or represent. Yet it is we, the people who give power to such individuals. Giving someone power of authority can often prove easier than taking it away. History reveals how some leaders have proved most reluctant to relinquish their positions of power.

One person speaking for many, perhaps a Nation, whose words determine enemy or friend, war or peace, life or death: where dissent is seen as anarchy or treason.

A single man or woman thinking, speaking and making decisions; reacting and responding in just the same way as most people; processes governed by thoughts, fears and prejudices reflecting personal experiences, fears, desires and ambitions. Your president, first minister or other leader is no more able to make decisions than you or I. He or she may have greater detail and promulgate different agendas, but complexity and contradiction are no help in decision making.

Despite this somewhat gloomy prospect, the power of the individual NOT placed in any position of particular power, remains powerful. The individual stands all powerful in his or her right to, and expression of, self-determination. Even at the cost of his or her 'human' life, the individual stands alone and supreme in unassailable good-conscience.

Where is the line to be drawn between resistance and submission, revenge and forgiveness? How different from your own are the goals of other people and other nations? How similar are the objectives of religions and beliefs worldwide? In essence very little separates all peoples and their differences lie mainly in their relative inequalities.

The differences between those who have and those who have-not are some of the most powerful underlying forces fuelling strife and hostility. The means by which those seeking positions of power main gain their ambitions.

Yet the fact remains that no one can take away from you your personal belief, your Faith.

Not to forgive means that you remember constantly, or are reminded of the someone, or something that remains un-forgiven. You hold feelings of resentment that have to be repeatedly fed by thoughts of injustice and imaginary acts of punishment. You remain angry. All the while knowing that you feel happier, healthier and more at ease when you are in accord with other people. Happier than when your anger brings you into mental conflict with others.

The hurt, the physical or emotional pain that you feel may be very great, a betrayal, an unheeded call for help, an unwarranted attack and, try as you might, you cannot find any reason for its occurrence.

At such a time it is difficult to remain open and objective but it is essential to do so if the hurt is to be overcome. Very simply it is impossible to know the true circumstances or reasons leading to the suffering that presently dominates one's life. The essence of release lies in the ability to accept what has happened without recourse to endlessly trying to understand the reasons why it happened

It is natural to search for immediate and obvious reasons for the affront, to try and understand. The questioning mind and the need to remove any sense of guilt at possibly having been instrumental in its cause, must be satisfied. When this avenue of enquiry has been satisfied the subjective questioning must cease in favour of more general and objective considerations.

Another person's behaviour found to be strange may become understandable when viewed from a viewpoint, one offering a broader perspective. This does not make what has happened more agreeable or acceptable but any sense of understanding, no matter how vague, makes it easier to set aside.

Much of what happens in life results from ill considered words and deeds that bring unintentional consequences. Hurt and disadvantage may follow in the wake of circumstances, themselves the result of thoughtless acts or actions whose consequences are unpredictable.

No to forgive is to make judgement not just of the act but also of the motivation behind the act; to make assumptions and arrive at conclusions upon which punishment may be set. Punishment will reflect your anger and your efforts to bring the force of that anger to bear in some way. You are now at risk of hurting and creating unhappiness for another person, in turn creating unhappiness for those attached to that person, and in some way hurting yourself. Your energy and drive becomes a destructive force from which no good can ever come.

While directing this effort towards another and in fighting your own inner conflict, you neglect yourself. Your bitterness and unresolved source of anger creates illness. Your need to show others how you have been wronged perpetuates your pain.

You keep alive your suffering to justify your own feelings. You punish yourself.

Forgiveness is not simply being magnanimous or being big enough. Forgiveness is putting effort into living a life creative of a happier world; a world of equality and respect and where taking a stand against the oppressor, the feared and the fearful amounts to no more than living in good conscience. Refusing to support and ally with the perpetrators of fear and the abusers of power is opposition of the highest order.

Forgiveness is the reflection of a happy self able to accept those who have lost sight of the Sacred Path of humanity and spirituality.

Forgiveness is not to bear the false witness of assumption. The ability to forgive is the ability understand, to love and to be free within one's self; to remain un-assailed by the unwanted effects of other people; to look forward not back; to live peacefully.

Without forgiveness of the self there remains only punishment, which, in the absence of punishment inflicted by another person, becomes self punishment, the most insidious of all punishments. Self punishment sabotages the lives of many people unaware of the true cause of their failures and unhappiness.

Just as the acceptance of other people and their behaviour precedes the ability to forgive them their misdemeanours, self acceptance is the precursor to self forgiveness. Essential to happy living and to self-forgiveness is an acceptance of the person one finds one's self to be. Meaningful acceptance is no panacea or sop to indulgence but a 'warts and all' acceptance that spurs one to refine the life, the body, mind and spirit, which one has been gifted.

Acceptance is a prayer of gratitude for all that one is.

31.   Aspects of Love

There are many faces of love. There is the love that exists between parents and children, between siblings, between friends and even between strangers. The feeling of love can be felt for or centred upon anyone, even though the person concerned is unaware of the love so directed.

Love comes in many guises and has many forms of expression. The depth of its sensation may be beyond fathoming and its intensities unknown to anyone other than he or she experiencing the feelings. The forces generating this special kind of closeness, and for the maturing development of loving feelings, are aspects of humankind's urge to form attachments.

Attachment which may be to another person, or persons, a pet of some kind, or any living thing, and may even be directed towards inanimate objects, perhaps in some kind of misplaced substitution, in the way that pets become a surrogate child or lover.

The ability to express love varies from person to person, there is no norm beyond the idealistic abandonment of lovers in the Spring of their relationship. Some people are able to form deep and passionate relationships while others are content to enjoy a more light-hearted display of feelings, each equally sincere in their context of their love. Whatever way, whatever the needs, the ability to love is probably first learned in childhood, where experiences vary greatly.

As we grow to adulthood the weight of our experiences builds. Our encounters with kindness and unkindness and unkind words; with tender touching hands and harsh fists; of soft and understanding eyes, heated looks of anger and cold flashes of hatred; of embrace and rejection. Through all of these encounters, an individual's ability to love and need for love becomes systematically integrated.

For some, attachments come to easily, for others less so. Intense yearnings for love may result in indiscriminate attachments being formed that are doomed to failure; while the hesitant and cautious see opportunity after opportunity slip by without attachment.

After discovering for himself that he is another person, separate from those around him, the child, and later the adult, begins to make comparisons and accumulate positive and negative feelings about himself and about other people. From these early feelings grows a sense personal value and self-image; the way in which others are seen relative to the self, and vice-versa.

The undervalued person, who undervalues himself (as a result of being undervalued by other people) may become an escapist dreamer; or he may equally become boastful and over-assertive in seeking to disguise his insecurity. Such a person may behave jealously because in his unfavourable self-comparison with others he sees himself unworthy and unable to compete successfully with 'the opposition'. He is unable to believe anyone could really find him attractive or worthy of love.

The person who overvalues himself can be self-centred and inconsiderate; in extremes someone who feels persecuted or discriminated against because other people, who do not recognise his superiority, show resentment, which he mistakes for jealousy or envy. This person appears condescending and may be ignorant, or choose to ignore, social skills and because of his behaviour, is self-isolating.

Both undervaluing and overvaluing people have a dominating effect on their partners. Of course in reality we all over or under value ourselves in some way or ways, it is the stuff of insecurity and anxiety common to humankind. Recognising negatives traits and adjusting our behaviour is a part of our development. It is unfortunate that not all people are able to do this and must then carry the burden of their hurts and hardships throughout life.

Only a person who is balanced in outlook and self-appreciation, who respects others for who and what they are, can share himself freely.

Here is the person who sees others as his equal and this is perhaps the most important aspect of parental love, when guidance is given in an atmosphere of respect that permeates family life. Discipline and obedience is not enough and it can be reasonably argued that where the parental example is of loving respect, self-discipline and restraint, obedience comes more easily in the wake of the child's recognition of fairness and mutuality. Here, in the family circle, future patterns of loving relationships are established.

Love must be a supportive element within the family, not one that simply compensates or becomes remedial in patching up unequal, disrespectful partnerships.

Equality is the essential ingredient: equality of status and respect for individuality. Equality does not mean equal ability. Partners of differing abilities complement each other in their mutual respect; where sharing the load does not mean each doing half of the same job but each doing that at which he or she excels, enjoys doing or has opportunity to do.

When discipline borders on cruelty and the expression of love is withheld, the admonished child may take a lifetime to learn just how much he or she is capable of both receiving and giving freely. Such a person may leap at the first, or any opportunity to prove to himself that he is worthy of being loved, and is able to love freely in return, only to find himself incapable of fulfilling properly the role into which he has entered.

If the result is a failed marriage, then, without benefit of a truly understanding and caring partner, he may come to feel he is unworthy of ever being truly loved and is somehow incapable of loving sufficiently.

A child's love towards his parents, brothers and sisters and relatives undergoes many changes, and ups and downs until hopefully it settles into something respectful and productive. Sadly this is not always the case as the rifts that exist in many families bears out.

That children and families drift apart is not unnatural. Much historical example of close knit family life results from force of circumstance; economic need, lack of housing, limitations of work and so on. If an objective of family upbringing is to produce offspring able to make their ways in the world independently, then loving support is not dependent of location but of understanding.

Friendship is kind of open loving in a caring relationship. Keeping a friendship alive demands one's respecting the differences between friends and responding to each other's needs. A two-way understanding; open within chosen parameters and respecting privacy and choice. Where saying no, is as easy as saying yes and where love is exchanged gently and respectfully. Friendship between respondents is one example, pen-friends who may never meet beyond the pages of their correspondence.

Love has many faces, two of which are particularly distinctive. Love may have at its heart, or base, an intimate loving friendship or a close physical, sexual relationship. Many would see a combination of the two as the ideal.

The romantic image of love is that of a complex, emotional experience, the sexual element of which is either a natural but not essential, by-product of a loving relationship: or the pinnacle of its expression. Precisely which is a matter of personal characteristics and needs which demands strong compatibility between partners and/or a great depth emotional love, in order to survive.

A strong sexual attraction between two people may develop into a mutually loving relationship from which a long lasting partnership may evolve. Of course this need not be the case. The attraction and mutual gratification provided by their sexual union be sufficiently rewarding for its continuance.

Infatuation is a face of love that many people encounter at some time in their lives, particularly during adolescence. Infatuation is an adoration felt with an intensity and hysterical passion that can go beyond reason. There is often very little overt connection with sex but occasionally sex may be the stimulus that fulfils the need.

The intense feelings associated with a state of infatuation will usually start suddenly and stop in similar fashion. Their intensity can be very great and vary with social or cultural disparity and simple physical distance. The unattainable may prove attractive.

It is often a fantasy state, combined with intense, emotionally demanding and draining feelings, because of which, is impossible to sustain. Momentarily, consumed with desire, one may easily think oneself 'in love', and in a sense this is true. Unreality is not out of place where this emotion is concerned.

Infatuation is frequently the recognition, admiration and then adoration of a quality lacking in he or she so emotionally stricken. In 'possessing' the person one 'possesses' the quality the need or void for which is thus filled.

Here is a paradox. In this fantasy, the one infatuated seeks not to posses but to be possessed, in such possession being gifted the desired attributes, in turn becoming compatible and making the desired union agreeable or possible.

Infatuation dies because it is too demanding, too impatient, too impulsive and jealous – all things that love is not. Because of this, and the unreality of the situation, infatuation burns itself out.

Love is the fusion of two lives; an exchange, a process of building and of regard – infatuation is none of these things.

Infatuation with a dominant sexual emphasis is often sustained only until the sexual need is fulfilled. Love, whether sexually based or otherwise, grows with satisfaction and experience, is ever expanding, becomes more sure, less obsessional and more open to the partner's needs.

Love is not lust, nor lust love, but neither are they necessarily adversaries. A great love may also partner great lust in appreciation of that which and whom is also loved.

Feelings of mutual belonging and togetherness distinguish love from physical lust and transitory infatuation. While physical attraction may be a prelude to love and sexual intercourse an important expression of love, love can exist independently of sexual expression.

Love, based on mutual respect and understanding, can survive sexual decline, superficial disagreements and even infidelities which might destroy lesser based relationships.

True love may best be thought of as a spiritual experience and regarded as everlasting, a love that will continue to exist in unforeseen times and circumstances that go beyond this life. In which the trials and tribulations of this life hold relatively little significance. With this love there is no urgency, no sense of threat, no guilt, no regret, no remorse, no doubt – only existence in another's presence, whether that presence be spiritual, physical or whatever unknowing way may exist.

Unrequited love is another emotional experience that many people experience to some degree. The effects of unrequited love can be painful and distressing; an un-reciprocated love that can be a melancholic, sad and lonely feeling.

Any form of love, when rejected, ignored or unrecognised by he or she to whom it is directed, becomes unrequited.

Because of the nature of unrequited love, there is a danger that the intensity of feelings escalates to that of infatuation, with the subsequent risk of regret and self-recrimination. Should this occur, self-questioning, sense of regret and of shame, combined with an undervaluation of the self and perhaps awareness of social humiliation, increase the risk of suicide.

An outlet for these negative emotions can be self-wounding, which if unrecognised may persist to become habitual, a substitute for the sense of being loved.

In accepting the inevitability of a love being truly unrequited, the sufferer may actually enjoy his or her martyrdom. Free from any feelings of guilt, creating a fantasy around his/her position, he may become distanced from other people; or spin elaborate fanciful tales about his/her life and love. A fantasy world carried into everyday life, in case the objectivised person concerned should have a change of heart.

The persistent stalker might be such a person and it is not unknown for the 'victim' to give way in the face of intense and persistent 'loving' attention, if only in the hope that the unrequited infatuation might be brought to an end.

While many may use their imaginary world as an excuse to withdraw from real life and its problems, ultimately they find it difficult not to regret their wasted years, at which time life may seem to hold little meaning. Disillusioned and depressed the road back to a more positive state of mind and re-engagement with the world around them can be a long, slow process.

Within the vast range of human emotions and personalities lies one which seems shared universally – the response, urge, need or sensation we commonly call *love.*

Love is not just one emotion or state, it is a complex combination of reactions and responses taking place at all levels of personal existence and is far from being fully understood.

Body, mind and spirit overlapping, cascading and combining in a sensory wave that defies description. A Spiritual love tumbling in an ecstatic revelation of feelings that consume and subjugate body and mind. Emotionally loving feelings that embrace spirituality and which fire the passions of the body. Physical urges and reactions that become expressive of adoration and with which service is the highest ethic. All of this and more – such are the unimaginable dimensions of love.

Sexual attraction, an expressing of procreative urges, need involve no sense of loving, loving feelings or loving attraction. Lust is a healthy, human combination of response and reaction based on genetic factors that exist to ensure procreation. Historically, women might have several partners, not only to ensure pregnancy but also genetic variation; reasoning that then at least one child should prove to be a strong pro-creator.

Men and women can find themselves attracted to one another, despite other legal and social relationships. The unfaithful partner who explains that his or her infidelity 'meant nothing' can be telling a truth. Of course it is not a truth which sits comfortably beside present day beliefs and expectations, or necessarily reflects the state of a particular relationship. Like all other aspects of human behaviour, infidelity is as simple or as complex as we would like to make it.

A beautiful, sexually attractive woman may be found to be quite boring by her male companion: the most handsome of men may be totally lacking in wit, understanding or sexual competence. Sexual attraction may be the spur to an emotional commitment but it is the development of deeper understanding and of a mutually stimulating and satisfying relationship that will make that relationship an enduring one.

There develops within human consciousness, an image of what a husband or wife should be and the roles he and she should play within a marriage or committed relationship.

The choice of partner may be influenced by such psychological predisposition, including his or her physical attributes. Where these psychological images have been strongly impressed and reinforced (usually in childhood) the choice of partner can be strongly influenced on those programmed needs.

The result can be of a generation to generation cycle maintaining social and cultural characteristics reflecting particular aspects of behaviour peculiar to families or groups. Behaviour and practices not always understood or accepted by those outside the group. These can range from incest or other close relationship pairings to strict moral codes that prohibit activities commonly enjoyed by men and women.

Behaviour of all kinds can be passed along generations. The boy who sees his father disrespectful and uncaring toward his mother may grow up either abhorring this kind of behaviour or embracing it. Either way, no parental family example is without its consequences. In courtship, a girl who ignores the unpleasant or unacceptable behaviour of the man she none the less loves may enter marriage or close relationship only to find she regrets having done so.

The girl who grows up, having been carefully tutored by a mother (who does not want to see her daughter make the same mistakes she did), may, as a wife, be so critical and inflexible she is unable to find happiness within her marriage. No man can meet her expectations.

Attraction between two people may be simple and straightforward at first, each satisfying the others immediate needs. Over time, differences between them and their personal needs change, though the basis of their initial attraction remains. There follows a period of adjustment which, if mutually respectful, allows each to express preferences, likes and dislikes and each to accommodate the others needs.

Being a couple does not mean giving up individuality or foregoing the right to privacy, it means two people sharing the greater part of their lives with someone else. Trust and respect are built, love deepens, needs are met, happiness achieved.

Nobody fits entirely into a mould shaped by another person's needs and desires. Exploration and sharing of each other's body, mind and spirit should be an exploration of delight. Those aspects of desire which may go unfulfilled will likely prove insignificant and more than compensated by hidden delights waiting to be discovered.

Love cannot be sustained on flights of fancy or by trying to make a partner fit a role for which they are not either programmed or suited. Reality accepts the individual as it accepts change. People change as they age, as do physical abilities. Adaptation and adoption of new ways of doing things is essential to a happy and fulfilling relationship, including a sexual one.

A wife may be an attractive woman, expert lover and accomplished cook but is so critical and intolerant, other people, including her husband, find her difficult to live with. Her husband, while attracted to attributes signalling her suitability as a wife, may now find difficulty in living with her happily.

The marriage is put at risk by the presence or domination of characteristics previously ignored or tolerated but which were always really unacceptable. Not for no reason the saying that *love is blind*. No more so when desire and need are met by opportunity.

Without compromise, openness and honest self-evaluation such a marriage will only ever hold the potential for happiness. Ideally the time for compromise and evaluation is before marriage, reflected by another old saying, *marry in haste, repent at leisure*.

Within the many faces of love and the many aspects of love, there are stages of love: the way in which feelings develop, change and mature.

Infatuation – to burn bright and then die.

An unrequited love – to linger in some melancholic backwater of the mind.

A sexual union – so intensely fulfilling all else is obliterated.

Or just falling in love and in the happiest way, losing control.

Whichever way, and there are as many ways as there are people, the ability to grow is essential. To expand in thought and understanding, to compromise without loss of respect, the adjust without loss of identity, and to feel love change from an all-consuming passions to an all enveloping warmth, the inner glow of which is a reflection of the soul.

Love holds little respect for circumstance but it is, and must remain, beautiful. If it becomes a source of conflict, hurt and bitterness it is no longer love – it is only something perpetuated by a fear and anxious need, distorting reality and bringing unhappiness.

Patient, loving care can resolve almost any situation, if there is will to do so. The love that once burned bright may seem to have lost its flame but that it was once there is knowledge enough to entice its fanning once again.

Only you can know your heart's desire, only you can know your life's mission, only you can find yourself in a love that embraces more than you can ever know.

Love can be considered the ultimate human experience, transcending all other experiences, even the pain of death.

Love is of the spirit, the deepest part of the inner-most self. Alone on a mountain side, or by a silver stream, or in the quietness of a holy place, Love is the ecstasy of oneness.

Why am I loved?

What can anyone see in me?

Am I loved for what I am, or for what I lack?

Am I loved for what I give or for what I receive?

Am I loved for what I do and for what I allow to be done?

Am I loved for what I know or for what I seek?

Am I loved for touching or for accepting being touched

Am I loved for what I believe or for what I accept others believe?

Am I loved for what I offer or for what I demand?

Am I loved for being myself or for being what is sought?

I am loved for all and none of these things... only you who love me can know

I do not even know why I love you! I know only that I do.

32.   Jealousy

Jealousy: An emotional state, involving feelings of hatred toward another person because of the relations of both to a third; a common example being sexual or love-related.

Jealousy reveals itself as an emotional and illogical state, rather than a rational or intellectual one. From this it may be assumed that feelings of jealousy are reactive, therefore originating in the subconscious part of the mind.

A subconscious reaction is triggered by some thought, word or deed and in consequence throws doubts and fears into consciousness. The doubts are associated with the emotional 'trigger' and do not necessarily relate to a present situation, just a feared similarity and hence possible risk.

An example would be the conclusion drawn by a husband on seeing his wife in the company of another man, and without knowing the circumstances of their meeting. Taking this situation a stage further, the husband might find his sense of suspicion enhanced if some marital disharmony between him and his wife presently existed.

Speculation and suspicion in themselves do not amount to jealousy. If the husband does not ask his wife who the man was and how she had come to meet him, or if he is unconvinced with her explanation, his imagination may lead him further down the path leading to mistrust and jealousy. The possibility of an innocent explanation remains but in the absence of its realisation, the imagination rules. One possibility after another present themselves, hope followed by fear, clarity followed by confusion, trust followed by mistrust and possessiveness, questions without answers....

Once something is imagined, seen in the mind, it is there forever. The line between fact or fantasy increasingly blurred as all things become possible.

Eventually the situation is confronted and the wife's explanation proves to be simple and straightforward, at which point the episode should be closed. What though would be the effect of the husband catching sight of the couple together again, perhaps spending a lot of time together at a party or social function? What if there is a little gossip, a friend mentions seeing the couple in question in a cafe?

When trust is lost, suspicion ends and a sense of betrayal or jealousy or begins. Betrayal in itself is an intermediary step toward whatever action is to follow. When betrayal goes un-forgiven the relationship will be brought to a close but where love and desire persists, the sense of betrayal is superseded by feeling of jealousy.

Emotional hurt, resentment, anger and hatred, feelings attributed to the wife in betrayal, are now transferred to the 'other man/woman'. It is possible that even the husband's undying love cannot overcome the hurt and so the need to punish his wife remain.

Jealousy is a complex emotional state and one which, at its height, cannot be resolved logically – counsellors beware!

Hatred from such origins, coupled with a lack of confidence and fallen self-esteem can result in emotional outbursts. These may be violent, uncontrollable and have fatal results. Again, counsellors beware!

When jealousy continues to grow in the absence of any foundation for misgivings, the need to prove that suspicions are without foundation and the need for constant reassurance may become intolerable, to both parties. Continual questioning results in an emotionally explosive atmosphere. However, the questions arise from emotional reactions, self-doubt and imagination making any answer insufficient or unacceptable.

A jealous person usually feels threatened by the person he or she sees as a threat to a way of life and a valued relationship. A jealous person behaves possessively way and it is important to separate the emotions and feelings described thus far from other conditions of mind which may appear similar.

Jealousy. In general terms a jealous person distrusts him/herself, lacks confidence and feels inadequate and unable to 'compete'. He/she feels lacking of the personal qualities necessary to be found attractive to others, in this case, his/her partner.

Envy. Envy can be confused with jealousy but it is different in having the positive aspect of acting as a spur to achievement. To be envious of someone can result in personal efforts to emulate or surpass their achievement. This has elements of negativity in, for example, the 'Keeping up with the Jones'' aspect of envy. The difference is that while envy can have a detrimental effect on the person who is envious, it has little or no effect on the one who is envied.

Possessiveness. Possessiveness is associated with the symptoms of jealousy but requires no third party involvement. Possessive people seldom know what to do with themselves. Left alone they feel abandoned and tend to feel worthwhile only when someone cares for them by devoting sufficient attention to their needs.

Jealousy and possessiveness are both self-defeating. The more compulsive and insistent the sufferer, the less likeable or attractive he/she appears, with the effect of driving people away. The possessive person, like the jealous, inevitably ends up with an even greater sense of failure and lack of self worth. With deterioration, the sense of remorse and isolation leads to depression and a reclusive, bitter individual.

Suspicion. Suspicion is based on facts. Conclusions drawn from these facts may be faulty but beneath the misinterpretation and false supposition lies something concrete. To separate true suspicion from jealous imagination, the facts must be isolated and set out clearly. Facts can be examined, their validity questioned, their relevance placed in perspective; their worth will stand or fall on merit.

What happens when suspicion persists yet no fact can be found or proved?

The human brain is a powerful tool, working at remarkable speed; much of the information it receives, while filed away and stored, is not consciously evaluated. Our minds provide us with information from this store - our memory. Constantly updating us with things we need to know relevant to where we are and what we are doing. Usually we are so busy thinking about something that we are unaware of this constant flow of information and so our instantaneous answers come as a surprise. The brain serves us best when we trust it to provide the answers we seek, allowing answers to comes automatically to mind, instead of laboriously searching for them.

In much the same way the minds gives us feelings of unease without necessarily giving us its grounds for doing so. The grounds may well be some old subconscious reactive pattern with no foundation in present time beyond a similarity of circumstance. However, it may just be that sufficient tiny incidents, in themselves of little importance, have been collected in association with "suspicion", the sum then becoming greater than the parts. Without specific details there is now an awareness of the 'sum of the parts'. This awareness differs from the fear of irrational jealousy as it presents itself as an 'awakening' and something leading to further, and restrained, evaluation. Suspicions should be thought of as warnings of potential danger and treated logically and directly, this way preventing irrational imaginings and jealousy.

Overcoming jealousy.

Self-help steps/counselling base.

Firstly, in order to overcome feelings of jealousy it is essential to accept that these are YOUR feelings, based on YOUR perceptions and reactions. Any change must come through YOU and through YOUR thinking.

Any endeavours to create a more acceptable state of affairs by influencing the behaviour of other people will neither improve your relationships with those people or diminish your jealousy.

Secondly' there must be a reappraisal of the Self. Look in the mirror: what and who do you see? In the face looking back at you that of a worthwhile human being or someone struggling to exist? An accomplished person, good at what she/he does, no matter how humble it may be, or a wreck of humanity of little use to anyone? Perhaps you see a stranger you should get to know a little better, who you should evaluate through different eyes. Can you accept the person you see? Can you NOT accept the person you see, even if she/he is a stranger to you, after all, she/he does exist?

We are all, individually and collectively, the result of thought. Any change of appraisal, or action or of ability will originate with a thought. Before any change can take place you must know who and where you are, not who you thought yourself to be and where you think you are.

Look at the circumstances that brought you to this point in your life. What have you chosen and what have you just let happen, more importantly, what do you want? Before any change of self-determination can happen you have to accept yourself just as you are, known and unknown – to do otherwise is to deny the reality of your existence.

Thirdly, look at your objectives. What do you want, what are your objectives, now and for the future. What do you see as your purpose in life. Expand your thinking beyond yourself. Are your objectives so very different from those of other people? Most people want little but that little is so important that any denial of it seems so much.

Change comes through motivation and motivation exists in the presence of a goal, a pressing need or desire. What do you want? From whence comes your motivation?

Personal fulfilment is a goal common to most people and from its attainment comes contentment and satisfaction. Seldom are we in competition with one another for that which we seek is by nature a personal goal, something to be experienced inwardly, to be valued beyond all else.

Know yourself, respect yourself, respect other people and find your jealousy fading as you do so.

Sexual jealousy is probably the most common form of jealousy and here it is important to differentiate between sexual desire and love.

Sexual desire and attraction exists as a basic pro-creative reactive drive resulting in the stimulation of a variety of mental and physiological functions.

Love is an intangible bond felt to exist between two people; felt by one person toward another, or others.

Sexual response may exist as a consequence and an expression of feelings of love. In sexual desire the need for pair-bonding does not exist: sex and sexual pleasure exist as objectives in their own right. Internal stimulus is determined in part by individual psycho-neurological make up and basic physiology. The source of external stimulus is sensory driven, involving all of the senses resulting in feelings of extreme pleasure. Mild forms of this pleasure may be experienced in every-day situations such as having one's hair washed, a manicure or massage, and therapies involving touch. Sexual contact, stimulation and climax is usually regarded as the pinnacle of physical enjoyment, and of course no small degree of mental enjoyment as well.

With this in mind it might be considered unreasonable to expect someone holding sexual gratification as his or her main objective to be emotionally loyal to another person who is seen only as a sexual partner. Never the less that person is a valued partner, and both relationship and person should be honoured and respected is such. In terms of human relationships, unless the true nature of a sexual relationship is clearly understood, some misunderstandings are likely to arise!

Love exists in many different forms with similar underlying sentiments and emotions involving a variety of responses and obligations according to the nature of the relationship. Love can exist between husband and wife; brother and sister; father and daughter; nurse and patient; priest and congregation; friend and friend, and so on. Different relationships demonstrate the differences between 'loving' and being 'in love' and mistaking one for another is the cause of much unrequited love and jealousy.

Being 'in love' is associated with feelings that invade one's entire being and which demand almost constant attention; a loving distraction accompanied by actions of devotion and of giving.

Loving in a broader sense is to hold the value of all life above all else: it is the ability to forgive all things; a compassionate understanding that demands nothing in return: the gentle and uncritical acceptance of others; the creation of harmony. In its purest and most sincere form, 'loving' can touch a state of state of ecstatic joy.

True love is a gift, offered by one person to another, to be accepted or refused.

Loving always involves another person but it is not necessary for that other person to do anything in order to 'create' the love felt toward him/her.

So where does 'love' come from? Sexual attractiveness an arousal is triggered by instinctive reactions coupled with personal desires, but no so love. Love can exist without sexual attraction and vice-versa.

People able to strike a state of harmony or protectiveness with one another may experience feelings of love spontaneously. When reciprocated it is as if two or more people recognise a common spiritual element and mutual regard resulting in harmony and respect.

Difficulties can arise in the acceptance of a sexual responses to feelings of love, as much as their denial. Closeness and openness removing the last vestiges of privacy can be taken as a sign of commitment. When a sexual approach is matched with expectation and assumption of mutual agreement, that approach may disguise an absence of a true unity of feelings.

A psychological need demands attention and reassurance while the simple enjoyment of sex requires neither. A loving relationship seeks loyalty and freedom while the sexual partner seeks neither. The psychologically dependent partner demands the former and denies the latter.

Jealousy is not based on love. Love is gentle, kind, patient and understanding. Love is offered but never demanded. Love creates strength not vulnerability.

If you think that you love someone and also feel jealous, examine your feelings carefully before seeking proof of misplaced trust.

Points to address with a view to overcoming and avoiding jealous thoughts.

1   Be more tolerant of other people. Acceptance need not

be agreement.

2 Try to understand the needs of others. Understanding need not be fulfilling.

3 Be equable. Seek a reasonable and fair view on all things.

4 Be affectionate. Act spontaneously in showing your love for another.

5 Be respectful. Accept the responses another person gives: there is no right to demand them.

6 Enjoy life. Enjoy your own feelings. To deny your feelings is to deny yourself.

7 Shed feelings of resentment and frustration by voicing them uncritically.

8 Life part of your life just for yourself. Everyone is entitled to privacy.

9 Love without imposing conditions.

10 Accept love without imposing conditions.

33. Aspects of Sleep

Sleep is a unique period of consciousness during which the human body regularly and necessarily shuts down a considerable portion of its otherwise alert self. No longer alert and not simply resting, it is sleeping.

Sleep occurs in all warm-blooded creatures, including mankind and is observed to have two distinct states or phases. Orthodox-sleep is also known as normal, non-dreaming sleep, while Paradoxical sleep is known as dreaming or active sleep. Paradoxical-sleep incorporates, and is symptomised by, rapid-eye-movement, or R.E.M.. R.E.M. sleep is regarded as an essential and crucial ingredient of all sleep.

The time spent sleeping varies from species to species and for human beings it seems that about eight hours in twenty-four is average. In comparison, cows, donkeys, sheep and horses seen to require only two or three hours sleep for the same period.

R.E.M. sleep is commonly called Active-sleep because it is the active part of the normal sleep cycle. During active sleep, brain waves are more similar to those of wakefulness than those during 'ordinary' sleep. During this time heart beat and respiration are more irregular, blood flow to the brain is increased and there is extra arterial flow to the genital areas. Women experience increased in blood flow to their genitals during REM sleep, just as men and may find on waking up from deep sleep find themselves feeling highly aroused, or having just experienced an orgasm.

Humans have longer active-sleep as the night progresses but the interval between active and non-active sleep periods remains fairly constant at ninety minutes. Here though there appears to be a weight related factor. The heavier the person, the greater the interval between active-sleep periods. It is possible that periods of active-sleep evolved to meet the needs of warm-blooded animals; the bigger the body, the slower the rate of cooling and therefore less immediate need for the raise in temperature present during active periods.

A lack of sleep affects mental ability and the need for periods of sleep is unquestionable. However, there seems at present to be no general consensus as to the true purpose and processes of sleep.

Just after a period of sleep begins, the Pituitary gland releases considerable amounts of growth hormone. It has long been recognised that children deprived of, or allowed to have, little sleep, seem to remain smaller than their well-slept counterparts.

However, normal cell-division, being a process of growth, happens within the small hours whether we are sleeping or not. *If* the release of an adequate amount of growth hormone is to precede the process of cell division, there might be some truth in the old saying that *an hours sleep before midnight is worth two after midnight.*

The idea that sleep is a time for bodily restitution is questionable. Amino-acid oxidation and protein synthesis, both necessary for such restitution, are both reduced at night.

Human beings need sleep and cannot be deprived of sleep for even a few days. In various trials it has been shown that very few people can withstand more than eight days without sleep. Over time trials of sleep deprivation, have shown subjects became tired (obviously), irritable and suspicious, time-disoriented and unable to speak without slurring words. All effects to do with perception of both self and of environment.

Intellectually subjects found concentration difficult, particularly if the task was boring. Subjects could perform normally with I.Q. tests and brain wave readings (E.E.G).) remained standard. No signs of mental ill-health were observed in any sleep deprived subjects either during or after considerable deprivation.

Those of us who miss a night or two's sleep may feel, look, or even behave like zombies but in harsh reality we appear to be markedly unchanged. Sleep deprivation appears to bring only modest alterations to the body's internal workings. Cortico-steroids, which customarily rise with stress, are maintained at normal levels, blood pressure does not seem to change greatly, nor does heart beat. So far as bodily restitution can be measured, no ill effects have been found.

People deprived of sleep, sleep lengthily once the period of deprivation is over but even those deprived of sleep for seven consecutive nights did not sleep more than 16 hours and within a day or so were back to normal.

Many people erroneously claim they have had a sleepless night because it seemed, to them, that way. Also perhaps because, traditionally, in order to perform well, it is necessary to have a 'good night's sleep'. Infants are encouraged to sleep, perhaps against their will or natural need, by cradle rocking, the singing of lullabies, soporific car rides and so on, perhaps setting patterns of expectation and resistance. From bed makers to the manufacturers of milky drinks the virtues of a good night's sleep are extolled – aided by their product of course. Throughout life, reliance on high quality, regular sleep is reinforced, leading some people to worry should their nights be less than perfect.

Anticipation of a special occasion makes getting to sleep less easy, made worse by the thought that this is one time when a good night's sleep is important. There is even a danger that self confidence will be undermined by self-suggestions implying an inability to cope or do one's best because of a lack of sleep the previous night.

Basic human behaviour patterns are established in the formative years and give rise to unrealistic assumptions and expectations that may be not be conducive to circumstances in later years. For some, sleep becomes an worrying objective and not part of their natural daily cycle.

Some people feel that sleep is a time for energy conservation – a daily period of semi-hibernation but sleep is not really a time of torpor or semi-consciousness.

Sleep, from which the sleeper can be roused, is not the same as unconsciousness. Nor is it a time for bodily restitution as ordinary rest and deep relaxation are better for such repair.

However, sleep is a vital need and, perhaps puzzlingly, seems to have no significantly special relationship with the nervous system than any other.

Active-sleep periods are those during which dreams occur.

At this time eye-balls roll (R.E.M.), brain wave patterns change and sleep is deeper, though at the conclusion of a period of active-sleep, waking is more likely.

The purpose of dreaming has been the subject of much speculation over the years but as yet, brought few conclusions. One thing is certain is that dreaming is a necessary ingredient of a healthy sleep pattern for humans. As active-sleep and dreaming go together it is tempting to conclude that dreaming is an essential part of active-sleep and studies have seemed to prove this by subjects dreaming more often after a period when they were deprived of dream-time.

What is certain is that while is a sleeping state we experience a time of minimal mental distraction and one in which we are mainly immobile.

The possibility that another side of the 'self' is more active or accessible, the means for which measurement or scientific study is not yet to hand, should be considered. The inner, deeper or spiritual side of the 'self' may need time of expression that may also be tied in with dreaming.

Sleep is certainly a time when unusual experiences occur. Dreams can contain elements of precognition or inspirational insight. Dreams offer the dreamer the opportunity to experience hazardous situations without being put it risk. States of spiritual or other-body separation occur when what is called an out-of-body experiences takes place. Bodily healing can take place, with an awareness of the healing taking place. All of these things and more are experienced during sleep with most being beyond considered evaluation, the exception being pre-cognition, which is self-evident.

Perhaps sleep is a time for the spirit and a time in which the spirit can be free and in which it might make itself known. A portal through which we access other times and places which, because of their other-worldliness, seem dreamlike!

Sleep can be seen as a necessary part of the daily life-cycle and importantly, something that will happen sooner or later simply because it has to happen. Even those deprived of sleep do not remain wakeful indefinitely, following which natural processes quickly compensate for lost sleep. It is also true that during normal periods of sleep, everyone enters a dream state, probably several, though many remain unaware of having done so, or can remember their dreams on waking.

For people who find sleep difficult, for any reason, there is a commonly held belief that sleeplessness in unnatural. Such people also commonly have the expectation of suffering debilitating consequences the following day, which only adds to their anxiety and makes sleep more difficult to come by.

Some people who sleep for a short time, wake believing they should have remained asleep in the mistaken assumption that 'normal' people sleep until the alarm goes off, or they have had their proper 8 hours sleep.

Those who awake early may actually resent the fact that they are awake, perhaps resentful of being deprived the escape from life, from pain or whatever additional relief sleep offers. The real problem might not be of sleeping or not sleeping, but with coping with wakefulness and the coming day.

Being awake during the night, especially when others in the household are asleep, may pose give rise to problems of boredom, frustration or resentment. Such situation may well be a question of management rather than abnormality.

The reasons for not sleeping, or why sleep does not come easily, are many. Commonly the reasons for disturbed sleep are obvious, though not admitted, and include physical pain, irritated by a noise or less than perfect conditions, sexual frustration, hunger, over-eating, excitement, preoccupation, worry, self-criticism, regret and many more, all of which interfere with the brains ability to 'switch-off'.

Unable to sleep, some turn to prescribed drugs for help. Benzodiazepines are a group of drugs used to aid the onset of sleep, and may be helpful in the immediate term. Research has shown that beyond occasional or short-term use, these, and other sleep inducing drugs, have disturbing side effects.

Firstly, the human body accommodates or gets used to the presence of the drug quite quickly, building up a tolerance to its effects. The perceived effect is that the drug is less helpful, without increasing the dosage. If the dose is not increased and use is maintained, the user is at risk of developing a ritualistic bedtime routine essential to sleep, even though the drug's effect is minimal and in time, non-existent.

Secondly, while a sleep state may be induced initially, within a very short time, use of the drug interferes with normal sleep patterns. Psychologically, prescribing a sleep inducing drug for more than a week, supports the erroneous belief that natural or normal sleep is no longer possible.

Many people who think they are insomniacs and who are convinced they stay awake 'all night', in fact sleep almost as much as anyone else, it is a matter of perception: self-perception and the perception distortion of sleep times.

Sleeping pills reduce the time needed to fall asleep by as little as ten to twenty minutes and lengthen the period of sleep by less than an hour. Over time a residual concentration of the drug builds in the body and affects wakeful performance: alertness is impaired and there is risk of mental confusion, especially in the elderly. The ability to drive is impaired and the number of accidents attributable to tranquilliser and sleeping pill use can only be guessed at. It is never safe to drink alcohol when taking these drugs as the effect is multiplying and even a small amount of alcohol can result in severe mental and physical impairment.

On cessation, even after only a few weeks use, a period of what is called rebound-insomnia may be experienced, during which time the user may be tempted to return to drug use.

After long-term use, discontinuance is more difficult because of the double effects of psychological and physical dependency/addiction. Specialist help is required and withdrawal planned carefully.

There exist naturally occurring elements within our diets that help promote sleep. Many herbal remedies also exist but these should be regarded as medicinal and supplemental, not dietary.

Common to all living matter is an essential amino-acid named laevo-tryptophan. When taken at bedtime L-tryptophan may provoke paradoxical sleep without interfering with natural cycles of normal and active-sleep.

Certain foods and nutrients alter the brain's production of neuro-transmitter chemicals such as L-tryptophan and which a known to affect mood and behaviour. Carbohydrates such as pasta, sweets, bread and potatoes have a major influence on the production of serotonin, a brain chemical linked with feelings of sleepiness and tranquillity, and of reduction in pain and stress.

Serotonin is made in the brain by the L-tryptophan present in carbohydrate foods which, when digested prompt the release of insulin into the bloodstream. The presence of insulin in the bloodstream allows tryptophan to pass across the blood-brain barrier and to be made into serotonin. This is why foods and drinks high in tryptophan are helpful to sleep.

There are though other protein based amino-acids that compete with tryptophan to get through the blood-brain barrier and meats and other protein foods keep serotonin levels down and are best avoided at bedtime – and if suffering from anxiety or depression, kept to a minimum anyway.

Accepting that 'getting off to sleep' is a natural and essential occurrence that will happen as soon as it can; that you will get as much sleep as is both natural and possible on every occasion; and that your will wake having benefited from the sleep you have had, is a useful philosophy.

The onset of sleep can be aided by avoiding heavy meals late at night and avoiding protein foods in the hours before bedtime. The effect can be enhanced by having a warm carbohydrate drink with a biscuit or two, whilst avoiding coffee, tea and smoking up to three hours before retiring. A small measure of a favourite alcoholic drink can aid relaxation. Finally, after ensuring that you are warm and comfortable in bed, let nature and your mind and body do the rest.

Reading or listening to music helps many people rid their minds of thoughts of the day and makes it increasingly difficult to keep the eyes open. Purposefully relaxing and adopting a breathing routine can also help.

If there is a particular problem on your mind, address it and give your mind permission to continue working towards a solution while you are asleep. Then forget about it: very often the answer or solution is clear on waking.

Set the alarm for the chosen time of awakening and turn the face of the clock away from you. If you do wake there is no point in knowing what the time is. You need only know that the alarm will tell you when it is time to get up.

If sleep seems like a welcome escape from the day, or from wakefulness, perhaps it is time to look at those times and the problems or worries they contain. Not to do so risks those problems becoming intrusive at sleep-time, creating yet another worry.

We spend something like a third of our lives in bed. To see such a vast amount of time as being anything other than an opportunity to experience something that is not only beneficial but also pleasant is a missed opportunity.

34.   Aspects of Stress - Prevention is better than cure

Stressful situations arise naturally in life, prompting mental and physical reactions enhancing the ability to meet and overcome them. When a stressful situation is prolonged, or the situation causing the stress is repeated or perpetuated, then the prolongation of any accompanying reactions can become damaging. Similarly, when the source of the stress is imaginary or anticipatory rather than imminent and real, again, prolongation of the physical and mental changes brought about by the stress can by harmful to health.

Stressful situations arise from the way in which we see ourselves relative to situations and people we encounter, or think we will encounter. Stress hinges on our assessment of how competent we feel we can deal with a situation.

Stress is a feeling of fear or anxiousness based on self-doubt and an imaginary perception that results in a loss of confidence. This loss may be momentary or persistent. We feel anxious when we anticipate the demands of a situation or person will exceed our capabilities. Stress is also a fear of failure, personal failure and the humiliation or negative judgement placed upon us following that failure. Not only are we fearful, we are afraid of looking weak or stupid. All is stress.

Frustration, anger, injustice, fear of criticism and the unrealistic demands of other people, are all common causes of stress. Too easily the goals, hardships, desires and fears of other people are introduced into our lives. How much we take on board or the degree to which we become emotionally (and stressfully) involved, is determined largely on how we see ourselves and our role in society as a whole and as individuals. Ultimately, the amount of stress to which we expose ourselves is a matter of choice, though it may not always seem that way.

The two classic symptoms of stress are those of *flight* or *fight*. Whether we take these feelings to their extreme points of action is another matter entirely. While we might feel like lashing out or running away, seldom do we act literally upon our feelings.

Instead we let our feelings simmer and in frustrated resignation or miserable depression, suffer the effects of 'stress'. Sometimes we reach breaking point when an outburst of words releases the stress, the energy that has been building within us.

Variations of fight and flight include *avoidance,* when we go out of our way to avoid a person or situation we find stressful to think about. *Neglect* is another substitute reaction, when we become negligent of duties and responsibilities we find stressful. When we give up and bow to the weight of our stress, we *succumb,* and lose self-respect, another flight or fight substitute.

Because of the changes it brings about in body chemistry and hormone activity, stress weakens the immune system. The successful management of allergy problems and therapy is reliant on effective stress management.

Many life events are naturally stressful because of the almost unavoidable effects they bring. These include: death of a spouse or partner, divorce or separation, jail sentence, illness, marriage, loss of job, retirement, pregnancy, sex problems, major change at work, large mortgage, in-law problems, change in living conditions or residence, Christmas... and many more.

Essential to change and the adoption of a less stressful way of life, or of looking at life, is an admittance to be stressed. As this also amounts to an admission of being unable to cope with some aspect of life, or simply of life in general, such an admission may not come easily. It is also an admission of fear and of admitting and defining our limitations.

It is perhaps at this point we should remember that the ordinary person who does not know fear has not yet been born, recognised or not, no one is without limitation,.

Ways to avoid 'everyday' stress.

1   Identify people who make you feel uneasy, who create anxiousness, anger and resentment. Then detach yourself, or your thinking from those people. Adopt a philosophy by which you accept other people just as they are. Not by agreeing with them or their behaviour, but acknowledging they exist simply because they do. We each have a path to walk, a life to lead, leave them to

theirs and resist their impinging and impositions on your own, physically or mentally.

2   Avoid pessimistic anticipation. Live in the 'now' of time, not in a future of problems or in a past of old hurts and grievances – both are unreal.

3   Discriminate between fact and fiction; news and speculation; the possible and the probable; your reality and the realities of other people. Know what you know, hold your truth and be true to your truth and your ideals. Live in peace with yourself.

4   Accept your personal responsibilities and recognise your abilities.

5   Stop presuming and assuming – ASK!

6   Feel equal to other people because you are, not because you think you should be. Equality is not ability. Each to his own ability and expertise. Equality is a common respect among people, respect for one another regardless of ability, seniority or social position. Respect yourself.

Rank of seniority exists because the job exists; aristocratic and social positions exist because they are allowed to exist; equality exists through birth, death and that bit in between that is common to all. A human life.

7   Be realistic in your expectations and forgiving in your judgements, of self and of other people.

8   Examine personal values, needs and beliefs: feel useful as well as fulfilled. Find purpose in your life and satisfaction in your acts.

9   Compromise. Find the path of greatest harmony, the solution benefiting everyone. Nobody has a monopoly on being right.

10 If you need help, ask for help. Friend, neighbour, therapist, counsellor or guide all exist for such a reason – that is their role in life, to help. Find you own role in life and within it feel useful and recognise that in some way you are helping other people.

and more....

Work no more than ten hours a day. Slow down and get more done.

Have at least a day and a half free from normal work each week.

Eat slowly. Allow yourself adequate time to enjoy each meal.

Cultivate the habit of listening to music, not just as a background sound.

Walk, talk and move about gracefully – don't rush about.

Smile and respond cheerfully when greeting other people.

Plan and take an 'away from it all' holiday each year or when you can.

Take exercise of some kind, out of doors and in daylight, every day.

Sort out emotional, relationship or sexual problems, seeking advice or help if necessary.

If you are unhappy, take stock of your situation, arrive at a conclusion and live with it.

Work methodically, finish a job but don't be afraid to leave a job unfinished.

Express your feelings, without antagonism or hostility.

Don't set or accept unrealistic deadlines.

Don't rely on drugs, coffee, alcohol and cigarettes to get you through the day.

Do some things just for yourself.

35.   The Enemy within

De-stress by sorting out your thoughts.

Seven things you can do to help get rid of those doubts, fears, worries and frustrations

1   Make a list of things you dislike, or once disliked, in your parents.

2   Without feeling critical, write down what you see as their negative traits; those you were aware of as a child and those you see now. Now ask yourself how much applies to you.

3   Take seven pieces of writing paper. Every day for the next seven days, take a fresh sheet of paper and write on it five things with which you are blessed and for which you can be thankful, never putting down the same thing twice.

Keep to hand a small notebook. Whenever you find yourself with a worrying thought, or getting angry or frustrated, or otherwise distressed, write down how you feel, why and what or who brought it about. Use your notebook as a diary, keeping each day's worries and annoyances on separate pages.

Keep the entries going for at least four weeks. At the end of which look back and see what you wrote on day 1; write a comment, reflecting how you feel now about that event.

4   Using a small notebook. Whenever you have the thought that you would like to do something for yourself, anything at all, make a note of that thought. Your thought could be about anything, joining the library, taking up swimming, having a week-end away, buying a new coat, write a letter. From the merest whim to the serious though. write it down.

From time to time look back and see how many thoughts you have turned into actions. Contemplate on those things that you once, and may still desire, but which remain, undone.

Everything begins with a thought.....

5   Keeping your notebook to hand... Whenever something or someone your find you resent or dislike or upsetting, write about it. Keep a separate page for each occurrence, though you need not say why you feel resentful or upset, just describe what it is that you dislike. Do this for at least two weeks before looking back at what you have written. After (at least) two weeks has passed, consider each entry and write beside it the name of the person you feel is responsible for causing or creating the situation and arousing your feelings.

Should you let this person know how his or her actions affect you?

Is there an injustice or mistake that deserves you attention or intervention?

Do different people, in different situations arouse similar feelings for similar reasons?

Do you think you may be over-sensitive or have some unrealistic expectations

6   In the evening, write down the names or descriptions of everyone you have met during the day, those you have spoken to, those you have not spoken to. Take your time and include everyone you can remember. How does each little memory, each meeting, make you feel; is any meeting especially memorable. Who has come into your day and what have they left with you?

7   In your notebook, keep separate pages for making a note of those things with which you strongly agree or disagree.

Just how much of what annoys you or satisfies you, brings you to express yourself openly?

The enemy within.

Within us all is an enemy who, unless opposed, can bring misery that is without purpose. Knowing who you are, what you want and recognising those parts of your thinking that do not reflect your true desires is of paramount importance.

The little exercises described above can help, but it is more than that, it is the ability to think freely within one's own mind. Of clearing away the rubbish, sweeping away the dust to have true clarity of sight.

Beware the enemy within, the enemy that binds with cords of fear, each binding tautened with each fearful thought: fear upon fear in suffocating, terrorising oppression.

Fear of the fear that comes unbidden to the mind; fear of the fear that clings and claws despite each desperate, pleading wish and inward cry that it would go; go, disappear and leave a mind at peace.

Question follows question in unanswered torment; dark clouds that overwhelm the sky, no light to show the way. Why me? Why now? Why this? Why that? Oh no, no more, what have I done that I should suffer this?

Why can I not be happy once again when happiness is all I want, so very much, so very badly....is that too much to ask?

Nobody understands. Nobody wants to know, nobody knows how I feel, how can they when it is all inside my head? They think I must be mad. I must be – no, I must not say, I must not tell, how can I tell? There must be something wrong with me, to have these fears, these frightening thoughts. Why do they come? Where do they come from? I don't know. How can I shut the door against this enemy within?

YES, ENEMY is what it is! It is the voice of non-sense. The voice that says, "What If?" and "If only." "But...." Behold this is the voice of un-reason!

The voice of un-reason speaks un-reason from an un-reasoning mind. The voice that comes from deep within, from that place into which has been swept since earliest time the ill considered and misunderstood, each cutting word and hurtful look, words, pictures, feelings of a bygone age that would be best left lie like some old pile of autumn leaves, to rot away, as nourishment for coming spring.

So see your enemy, its menace crumbling into dust. Un-reason and un-truth.

No longer need you be afraid; no longer can you heed to untrue when you know the true.

Truth is the blade that cuts the bonds the untrue ties.

Reason is the wind that blows away the clouds and lets the sun shine once again.

Love is the hand which soothes and heals.

Look up, not down; look out not in because in truth you are now free from that which kept you captive in your fear.

The enemy within has no place in which to hide and is powerless in the light of truth. The darkest depths made bright from radiance of reason, truth and love no longer sanctuary for that which withers and dies in the light.

No longer hurt or hurting, by unkind words or deeds,

No lies or accusations, jealous disbeliefs or seeds

Of doubt that grow uncaring in a garden full of weeds.

Loved, loving, and in that love sharing,

Happiness and hope, for one another caring,

A flower filled garden's sunny mantle wearing.

36.   Choice and Decision - Problem or Opportunity?

Faced with a problem or choice, in searching for a solution, past, present and future perspectives will be encompassed. In this way, experience, present circumstances and prospective outcomes will be considered, perhaps in the light and bias of a desired or preferred outcome.

The Past affects us in several ways.

Memories of personal experiences creates an wealth of knowledge upon which we can draw. Less obviously, the subconscious memory of our experiences provides us with reactions based on *how* we behaved and felt on previous, similar occasions. In addition there are the shared experiences of other people as conveyed by them or related to us by other means, leaving much interpretation to our imagination. The past is a mixture of fact, fear and fantasy, all of which becomes part of our decision making processes.

The present, inextricably connected to the past, affects us similarly in a number of ways.

The moment in which we are make our choice is in always in present time. Decisions are only made in present time, in the moment within which they are enacted. In the moment of choice, which is not necessarily the moment of decision, associated memories are resurrected consciously and subconsciously, together with the reactions and responses connected to them.

From the moment of choice, the process of decision making initiates the imagination to project possible consequences based on our understanding of both past and present.

The future brings additional opportunities to those presented by past and present time.

In our imaginative search for a predictable outcome, future prospects can be viewed with fear or enthusiasm, hampering or encouraging our search. Prospect of the new and unknown may be viewed with fear or excitement. There may be dread of dire outcome, or optimism with hope of betterment. There may be apprehension or non-acceptance in the light of some fearful prospect, or cautious acceptance of a future truly unknown.

Many influences are at work as we come to make the choices facing us as we go through life. Some choices demand an immediate decision, many will, if ignored, simply disappear as circumstances and the consequences of the decisions of other people play out around us. In this way, all manner of situations come full circle and to what we might call, their natural conclusions, our inactivity being part of the process by which this happens.

There is only one NOW, the moment in which we enact our decision is the NOW in which we choose to do so. NOW is that fleeting moment in which we fling from us the seeds of change, to be carried into the future by the winds of time. Where and by what means these seeds take root we cannot truly know; only hope that with good intent, they harvest well.

Options of Choice are not always clear, inevitabilities are sometimes difficult to accept, and the future can seem bleak if past experiences are our only guide. In this confusion we may become overwhelmed by contradictory thoughts, making any decision seem impossible. At such a time, it is the moment of NOW that offers us a firm foothold from which a more positive stance can be taken. The moment of NOW offers us tangible reality and clarity unclouded by what-if's and may-be's. It offers us the space in which we can decide in which way we should look for our solution. It gives us time in which to decide when we need to make our choice.

The moment of NOW gives us control and freedom.

Choices

349

Choices are presented to us constantly and continuously. No matter where we are or what we are doing, alternatives present themselves in every respect.

Do you stand, run, walk, sit or lie? In every aspect of your life, no matter how limited or restricted your life may be, choices are there to be made, should you so wish, or should they be demanded.

We pay little heed to many of the choices we make, accepting them as foregone conclusions. Those choices we make out of habit and to which we give little thought. Because of this, many of the real choices presented to us go unrecognised; as do the consequences of our habitual decisions.

Some choices require very little effort of thought, demand little motivation and are made passively, with little real interest or commitment. Decisions we make at a time of preoccupation when we settle for an easy answer, or one that is expected of us.

When a person's particular pathway in life becomes established, routines become adopted and preferences and prejudices ingrained. Many choices then follow predictable patterns. The result may be contentment or boredom, or something in between.

Someone who feels his or her life is boring, repetitive and who lives a fairly predictable existence may find himself apathetic in his adherence to an almost ritualistic routine. Someone who feels unable to make any serious changes or decisions. A stagnation due in part to a lack of confidence in his ability to make decisions, have not exercised that ability to any great extent; partly from a fear of the unknown when so much of his life is lived with tried and tested repetition and regularity.

Yet there is a paradox for someone in this position may use his or her brain a great deal. Someone who thinks very carefully about making even the most trivial choice; someone who, when taking action, does so with serious deliberation. A person who needs to feel in control of life and the narrow that life is, the less there is to control.

A person who lives his life as best he/she can, within passively accepted, self-imposed restrictions that deny any real prospect of serious change. This fear of change denying serious original or imaginative thoughts; thoughts that might run out of control if let!

Value Decisions.

Value decisions are those which bring about fundamental change. Value decisions are acts of commitment and for the purposes of examination here, fall into three categories. 'Big' decisions, 'Ordinary' or advised decisions, and 'Personal' decisions.

The value element of each type is reflected in every aspect of daily life – personal, social and business. It is the way in which a choice, or problem, is approached that determines whether an individual sees it as Big, Ordinary or Personal. The way in which a choice or problem is approached is determined by the personal psychological characteristics, intelligence, bias, and so on, of the individual.

The Big Decision approach.

The basis for all big decisions is firstly to question the need for the question, or opportunity itself. Put in the simplest terms, *Do I need to do this, and if I do, do I need to do it now?* Answer 'no' to either and the question is denied.

Upon validation of the question, the next step is to question the need from which the question sprang. That is, if the answer to the former question is yes, *Why do I need to do this, is there an alternative?* If the case for change is upheld, and the need for change is accepted, the process of decision making can proceed.

A Big Decision perception is based on a genuinely perceived need and the acceptance that that need must be satisfied. Only when it is firmly established that a need is genuine and must be satisfied can the means of its fulfilment be addressed. Serious consideration coupled with strong motivation leading to finalisation.

The conclusion of the Big Decision process is reached when the value of the need is established, its urgency assessed and means of its completion devised. In a business context this might be a policy decision made at the highest level.

The Advised Decision, or ordinary decision approach.

Advised decisions are those that often involve other people, their management, integration or opinion, or all three. In a domestic situation a typical example might be the choices made in household management and child care. Who does what, with whom, where and when?.

The 'need' element in advised decisions is usually obvious and decision making focuses on *when?* and *how?* the accepted need will be met. The factor of *when?* overlaps with the Big Decision approach and so the timing element may be pre-established, leaving the secondary *how?* element to be considered. 'How' is the substance of the Advised Decision. The answer to this question poses the further question of *who?* Look again at the typical domestic situation above. In a business context this is an administrative decision: a manager using his resources.

The Personal Decision approach.

A Personal Decision is one which affects the person making the decision directly, though not necessarily in a fundamental way. The consequences of a personal decision may affect the lives of other people, even though they have not been involved with the decision making process. Even though a personal decision may not result in any significant change to a person's way of life, the freedom in which to make personal decisions is highly valued. Unfortunately it is a right too often denied by the presence or actions of other people.

Most Personal Decisions are to do with the ways in which we live our daily lives. The minutiae that satisfies the uniqueness within each one of us, telling us who we are. Decisions that are concerned with the satisfaction of personal needs, which may be on no interest to other people. These needs may not be seriously questioned and the timing of their satisfaction is concordant with the sequences of everyday life.

The acceptance of one's position and the limitations that

position may impose, i.e. work, focuses upon the satisfaction of immediate personal needs, comforts and preferences. Decisions based on ways of making the best of whatever situation currently exists, and those that will bring most satisfaction and contentment.

In a business context, these are Skill Decisions made by operatives.

Any process of decision making will incorporate *all* three levels of thinking.

Individual bias and ability coupled with the opportunities and demands of circumstance direct the focus to favour a particular level or aspect of the decision making process.

Every aspect of life is encountered in the overall process of decision making. We can see this commonly when comparing the choices of different individuals faced with the same problem. Extremes of difference, resulting in very different choices, reflect differences of many kinds. Differences between the strong and able-bodied and the weak invalid; or those between someone of wealth and one who is in poverty; and those between men and women, the single and the married. Regardless of what each would like or wish to do, his or her abilities and circumstances become over riding factors in the decision making process.

The persistence of conditions disadvantaging a particular person may result in that person's apparent passivity, apathy or subservience. However, such appearance may disguise suppressed feelings of resentment, frustration. This person may find comfort in making small personal decisions, the only avenue of self determination left open to him/her and here there is a risk. Small though these choices are, their satisfaction is important and significant, in a personal sense. The right to make small Personal Decisions is greatly valued, resulting in what other people might regard as a minor matter becoming a source of major discontent. An example of this would be the personalisation of one's work-space, for example a placing a personal photograph on the desk.

Unfavourable self-comparison with other people, envy and jealousy can all be motivating forces behind endeavours to exert greater control over one's life. Effort and self-discipline drive personal decision making and the realisation of goals, with demanding persistence. If decisions subsequently fail to bring realisation, any feeling of control and self-determination becomes illusory and the underlying dissatisfaction and resentment remains.

Failure to take Big Decisions when they are necessary; or mistaking Personal or Advised Decisions for Big Decisions can lead to anxiety and depression, which may be long-standing. A reflection of both circumstance and personality, the resolution of which can require extensive counselling and therapy.

Decision making means accepting responsibility, taking responsibility and demonstrating responsibility. To avoid being overwhelmed by something that is beyond your capabilities, questions you should ask yourself include: *How much responsibility do I want to accept? Am I the best person to take on this task? Am I capable of undertaking this task? Is this really my responsibility? Am I being rewarded sufficiently for taking on this responsibility?*

Avoid being a square peg in a round hole.

What do you do best?

Are you comfortable making Big Decisions, happy to accept responsibility for the consequences of decisions that may affect many people's lives? Or are you a natural organiser, an Advised Decision maker. A planner who likes nothing better than the challenge of making best use of resources and getting a job done? A manager of situations and opportunities, someone who sees his role as finding solutions for other people, rather than taking responsibility for them?

Alternately, are you someone who enjoys simply getting on with the job? Someone making Personal Decisions, who takes pride in his work and who enjoys puzzling the detail and crafting a work piece, working conscientiously to a high degree of personal satisfaction no matter what the task?

Some people feel they are poor at making decisions and avoid any commitment to do so. This may be a reflection of the individual alone, it may point to resentment at being asked to do something in particular, or resentment toward the person asking.

Your view of yourself is based largely on how you think other people see you. This is, in part, a self-fulfilling expectation as you assume, or at least hope, that people will see you in a particular way *before* you have met them. Your manner and the way in which you act, projects your anticipation leaving other people to mirror that projection.

Other people have their own opinions, prejudices and agendas and so it does not always work out quite as expected. Self-image can be changed by another's expressed opinion, even when that opinion is coloured by that person's bias or is ill-judged. Individual reactions may be to countermand that person's view by reasserting the preferred image; or undertake a submissive self-image reassessment.

Only by being yourself, by asking rather than assuming, and by self examination and self questioning can true self-value be established. With a naturalistic and philosophical sense of self-value, self estimation, and self-esteem, Value Decisions can be made naturally and confidently.

There can be no worthwhile comparison with other people. Life brings to the individual personal responsibility and freedom of spirit, of Self, in which to find fulfilment

You are entitled to say *yes* as easily as *no*, without explanation.

You are entitled simply to *be*.

Decisions.

Decision making, or taking, is inevitable. Not making a decision requires the decision not to do so. Making a decision today that is not demanded today, and that might better be made tomorrow reflects an anxiousness surrounding that decision.

Every problem has a solution that is an opportunity awaiting the time of its enactment: it is inopportune to harvest green corn.

Every problem has a solution, every solution contains within the seed of a problem.

Choice is everywhere: every decision reveals another choice.

Choice and decisions are as natural as they are essential to happiness and the expression of free-will. Because we have choice, decisions always lie ahead. A desire to be free from the 'burden' of decisions is a denial of the self and the choices life presents to all people.

We may be tempted to look back to a time of choice and say that we made the *wrong decision*. It maybe truer to say that, given the opportunity or choosing to delay making that decision, we would have chosen differently. Perhaps at that time the problem or choice weighed heavily, prompting a premature decision; or inaccurate or questionable advice resulted an equally ill-advised choice.

To conclude that by making a decision that with hind-sight seemed *wrong*, the person making it was incapable of making the *right* decision, is erroneous. There are too many underlying factors for that conclusion to hold water. Similarly, it is extremely unlikely that anyone deliberately chooses the *wrong* option, or goes out of his or her way to make the *wrong* decision. Someone may be able to make a decision but not able to see it through!

Presented with a choice we assess the options as carefully as we can and arrive at a decision. The best time to do this is when our decision must be enacted. If the time of enactment is not imminent, optional contingencies can be considered.

Procrastination has certain benefits, one of which is time for consideration and the development of the prevailing situation.

Drawing up a list of options is a way of satisfying the need to remove much of the pressure an impending decision can exert. It also satisfies the imaginative mind with the knowledge that nothing is yet fixed. A decision has been made, yet all options remain open and far from being over, further options come into view.

Any decision results in a change of some kind and it is on this basis the following options are considered: to change, to not change, to wait and see – indefinitely.

To Change One's job?

Will our decision to change be based on:

    A.   a desire to change in order to escape or get away

from something or someone?
Positive action based on negative reasoning.

B. A desire for something regarded as being better, to go forward?
   Positive action based on positive reasoning.

In [a] the motivation leading to change is wanting to escape, to run away, to leave a situation, or person. The direction in which one 'runs' is a consequential or secondary consideration. Such prime motivation can lead to acceptance of the first opportunity that offers extrication from the present, which may be no better than that left behind. Out of the frying pan into the fire, resulting is self-questioning, a loss of confidence and resentment at having been placed in such a position.

In [b] the change is brought about with enthusiasm based on a desire to create something better and new. The result is a sense of achievement and satisfaction that reinforces self-confidence.

To stay with it?

Once again not a single option. Do we

A. go along with things just as they are, feeling obliged or pressured to stick with this choice.
   Negative action based on negative or absent reasoning.

B. Make the best of the present situation; trying to make the best of something that is presently unsound.
   Positive action but negative reasoning.

In [a] factors that are additional and external to the matter in question may cloud the picture and confuse the process of otherwise simple problem solving. This may give rise to dissatisfaction, resentment and a tendency to blame other people for feeling trapped in a situation that could have been resolved. The long term outlook is poor.

In [b] there is initial enthusiasm to seek a solution through compromise and ingenuity. In a work situation this might be achieved through promotion or eliminating those aspect of work that are problematic, such as by redefining responsibilities. There is potential for progress but always the risk that goals amongst individuals may clash. The ultimate risk is of feeling unable to get out from under and submitting to the needs of the establishment. Suppressed resentment will prove a formidably destructive power.

Wait and see before deciding?

Accepting that change is going to be made, but delaying the timing. Here one may:

A. Wait until the opportunity to move coincides with an opportunity to leave.
   Negative action and negative reasoning.

B. Feeling unable to change immediately but intend moving at some time.
   Negative passivity and negative reasoning.

C. Be undecided finding sufficient positive elements to make the present situation acceptable but remain unhappy about other less satisfactory elements.
   Indecisive passivity and negatively absent conclusion.

In [a] responsibility for the timing of implementing a decision is placed on other people, and denies the self implementation of the chosen action. Because there is no clear goal, there is also no clear path ahead. Procrastination robs impetus.

In [b] there is recognition of real limitations and little opportunity for change makes it seem impossible to do so. This disguises the existence of a far greater choice than has yet been addressed: hinting of avoiding real issues and using superficial circumstances as an excuse.

In [c] with an awareness of the opportunity to take time to assess the present position further the risk is in letting opportunities slip by. Avoiding the fact that a problem is known to exist, a desire to play things carefully may result in damaging procrastination. If a problem exists, its solution may be sought, found and planned. Not to do so can be deeply unsatisfying.

Conclusion.

A detailed and analytical examination of the processes of decision making may reveal nothing more than the ability to do exactly that – examine, analyse and detail.

People are more than this and weaving throughout human decision making are the subtle energies of imagination, intuition, experience, and philosophical understanding that make the most practical, intellectual and logical analyst despair!

The presence of goals is essential to sound decision making. The principle of going toward something rather than running away from something is a sound principle. The desire to run away points to an underlying fear that inflames the imagination and gilds the prospect of change.

The presence of a clear goal or objective is essential in steering the challenge towards an appropriate solution. Change arising from a desire for something better or more appropriate; identifying that something and finding a path toward it; looking ahead and choosing the direction travelled; arriving at a conclusion in attaining that which is sought.

Patience and the belief that all people have a place that is naturally appropriate for them, that all people can move with fluidity within their circumstances and situations to attain an inner harmony reflective of outer peace.

Patience and the belief that one can realise the nature of discontent and, in acting accordingly, attain happiness and fulfil one's destiny, make change an inevitability.

Problem solving is a process of taking steps.

Recognise that a problem exists: accept and admit that some kind of change is necessary.

Admit and accept that you want, need and are entitled to change aspects of your life.

Look at what options are available.

Think about what options might be available if the present were changed in some way.

Identify the elements contained in your ideal solution.

Investigate opportunities more deeply, be imaginative in viewing prospects.

Consider compromises and the benefits and disadvantages of goal adjustments.

Plan a path of action, set out a time table, put those plans in motion.

In this way action is taken.

Step by step progress is made in clear vision of the goal ahead.

The first step is perhaps the most important as without this, nothing further will happen. From the first to last, each step is an achievement and the product of decisive action. Each step builds confidence making further actions increasingly decisive.

Everything we see about us is the result of the power of the Mind, the result of thoughts, decisions and actions. Everything is a result of choices being made, free-will being exercised, desires being fulfilled.....and the starting point for all things is thought.

Problem solving and decision making.

Solving a problem may call for a decision but it will not necessarily bring about a change.

Taking a decision may mean solving a problem that makes change unavoidable.

Before assuming a particular change is necessary it is essential to identify, examine and analyse the perceived problem. In effect this is a problem solving process as in identifying the elements of situation, their relativity to any change becomes obvious.

What is the problem?

Is it a large problem comprising several smaller ones, or a small one creating or created by other problematic elements within the bigger picture?

Does identifying the problem also identify its cause and if so, does this change the nature of the problem?

What part do individual people, including one's self, play in the creation of the problem or in creating the circumstances by which it has come into being?

Has a change in your awareness, or change of objective, created a problem that otherwise did not exist? And so on....

Once the true nature of the problem has been identified, working towards a solution can begin.

The goal may be clear if an objective has been set, but the means by which it can be achieved remain unclear. Whatever the case, nothing will come without imagination, Mind Power. Activate your Mind and draw upon its suggestions freely. In a group this is known as *brain-storming,* where people put in their ideas regardless of how bizarre that might seem; the same process works equally well for the individual. Write down whatever thoughts come to mind. Follow links and chains of thought: sometimes a solution just jumps out, or alternative piece by piece solutions are formed.

While compiling a brain-storm list try not to judge or criticise any suggestions. The knack is to let the mind run freely and engage the subconscious which will in any case have been trying to find a solution for you. Don't shackle your Mind with prejudice, criticism, false logic or fear of failure. Allow yourself plenty of time and continue until you can come up with nothing new.

Consider the list of possibilities objectively and talk through possible consequences. It may seem obvious that some will not work or are totally impractical. Others will look odd and perhaps fire the imagination further. Some potential solutions can be evaluated and expanded. New ideas will sit beside the more familiar, patterns may emerge. Don't rush, let the process move ahead at its own speed.

Keep your mind open, let it work for you. Stop the *Its hopeless, there's no way out, it won't work, what's the point....*mentality dead in its tracks!

Eventually one particular solution crystallises and you begin to feel that this is the way ahead. Write it down, the very moment you know, even if it is in the middle of the night. Writing is an act of commitment and confrontation.

Why should you do this? The human mind is capable of working at phenomenal speed and with absolute accuracy at many levels of awareness simultaneously. You may be consciously thinking about one thing while subconsciously dealing with a completely different matter. Even while you sleep your mind continues to work. Going to bed with a problem and saying your will *sleep on it* is sound practice.

Your mind is a computer second to none in its accuracy, speed, reliability and complexity. It is using all the information at its disposal, constantly and continuously updating its records – your memory. Always trying to provide you with solutions to EVERY choice and problem you encounter. Sometimes answers are instantaneous, those times when you come up with an answer to a question so quickly that you wonder where it came from. Only when we question ourselves do we go wrong: second thoughts are usually second best! Sometimes you have to wait a little while to get an answer you feel is right: so wait!

There are three very important factors to take into account.

Firstly, your Mind will give your result based on the information and facts is has been given. If these are inaccurate the conclusion will be flawed. The most brilliant Mind cannot make a decision without knowing what the decision is about or without having sufficient detail from which a conclusion can be drawn. No one knows everything. Expect not to be able to make a 'sensible' decision on occasions simply because it is about something unfamiliar to you.

Secondly, your Mind is logical in its critical and reasoning processes and it is this mode of thinking that is able to express itself verbally. However, your intuitive and reflexive Mind processes see things differently and may be unable to convey their conclusions adequately in words. This is what we call gut feeling, instinct or intuition.

Thirdly, a logical solution may be found emotionally or reactively unacceptable because it causes a conflict of conscience or provokes an inhibitive reaction based on some innate or deep-rooted fear.

Theoretically, and subject to individual physical and mental soundness, everybody is capable of clear and concise thought; everyone is capable of reaching accurate and sensible conclusions leading to direct and positive actions.

The reality is a compromise between conclusions drawn from incomplete information, doubts concerning the reliability of intuitive feelings and seemingly unsubstantiated answers, and the barriers to action that are created by personal inhibitions.

Hurry up slowly.

The fastest way to an answer is to let the mind work at its

own pace, which will be many times faster than when one *tries* to think.

Do not make a decision when no decision need be made. If a matter can wait until Friday, so can any decision. A forced decision on Wednesday serves no purpose as until Friday arrives the option to change that decision will still be in mind.

Too much time spent in pondering over this and that, slows down the mind, introduces distractions and tends to put thinking into a repetitive track. Use the conscious mind to gather information and deal with matters of the moment and accept that when sufficient information is to hand and other considerations evaluated, a moment of knowing will arrive.

Where no deadline is imposed or necessary, choices come and go, with or without specific attention. In an ever changing world, today's options disappear to be replaced with tomorrow's alternatives. Similarly problems come and go without their being paid any special notice.

When you have your answer, act. Do not delay. Show your Mind that you appreciate *its* hard work. Ignore answers too often and your Mind will cease to work so diligently: ignoring the answers its gives is ignoring yourself.

Today's answer to yesterday's question may be different from yesterday's answer.

37.   Self Determination – The Power We Have.

All that we are, all that we have created, is the result of what we have thought.

The relationship between Mind and Body is absolute. Changes brought about by either, upon the other are also absolute by cause and effect.

A fearful perception results in physical changes in the body brought about by the reality of the perception, not a reality of fact beyond the mind. An anxiety of mind without basis in worldly reality.

Bodily changes, such as those brought about by physical exercises or in adopting certain breathing techniques, can stimulate brain function and bring about altered states of awareness, mood and perception. Mind and body, body and mind integrated and inter-responsive.

The following process makes use of the way in which Mind, Brain and Body relate and function and how paranormal activity, rather than being unusual, is an integral part of our make-up. The process describes ways of self-management that help in the achievement of personal objectives.

The structure of the process, or technique, appears simple and, set out in the form of ten separate, progressively interlinked stages, it is simple. The changes brought about through using the technique may themselves be simple but their effects reach far beyond any imagining. One touches one, touches all.

Judgement, or more correctly, evaluation, may only ever be made on one's achievements. There is nothing to judge in failure, not even failure itself. In the evaluation of results, success is in the belief that even an apparent failure will ultimately bring benefit.

Do not be deceived by simplicity. The means by which simplicity is achieved is often complex and this final distillation of thought, these final instructions reflect little of the understanding of their perception, preparation and completion.

Fear of failure is barrier to all.

The relationship between how we feel, what we think and

the circumstances in which we find ourselves can be used constructively to our benefit and our progression through life. We can make things happen, though not to the cost of another.

The techniques described combine two particular factors which work at many levels of being to bring about changes that shape your future. These factors include heightened states of awareness and an enhancement of your communication abilities.

It is important to accept that you can and want to control your future to a far greater degree than at present. You may have an immediate and pressing need, or simply wish to take greater personal responsibility and self-determination in placing yourself in the world.

The process begins with the thought of what it is that you want.

Step One - What do you want from life?

What do you want?

Want do you want from yourself? How do you want to be? Where do you want to go? Stop now and ask yourself, seriously, what do you earnestly and sincerely desire?

No idle whim of the moment, to be forgotten and ignored; no wild imaginings dismissed in the assumption of impossibility but the deep-felt need and desire for something essential to your future happiness.

It might be a new car, a better job, a change of behaviour or presentation; it could be a move to another house or area, or to feel confident in meeting a situation you find especially challenging. There are no limits on what your heartfelt wish might be but whatever it is, your desire must be deep and sincere; something you feel is right for you, the achievement of which is not to the detriment of another. In the case of getting a new job, your success is not detrimental to other people also trying for the same job. Your achievement will be on merit and suitability and the achievement of a state of harmony. This benefits all people, especially those who have not yet found their best place.

IT IS NOT ENOUGH TO HAVE AN IDEA OF WHAT YOU WANT.

You must be specific and you must believe that what you want is truly important to you and to your future happiness.

I truly want.........

Step Two - Picture what you want.

Having settled on your goal, the next step is to form a very clear picture of what it is that you want. See clearly and in detail what your goal entails.

Set aside some time when you will not be disturbed. Sit comfortably, close your eyes and build in your Mind a mental image of your goal. Omit no detail, take your time, walk the walk. For example, your goal might be to present yourself well at a job interview. Picture how you will dress, what you will wear, what you will look like wearing it, every detail. See yourself as you will be when you present yourself for the interview. Hear what you will say, how you introduce yourself and how you reply to questions, not what the answers might be but the manner in which your will respond. It is unnecessary to know where the interview will take place or who will be present. YOU are the focal point, YOU control how you will behave, not other people.

From this exercise you give your Mind the plan you want it to follow. If you do not know the answer to a question, your response is careful and considered: *Is that an area in which I will be expected to work?* Or *That is not something I had considered, please tell me more about it,* and so on. There is nothing in prospect you cannot handle, your ultimate goal is to put yourself in a position where, in the light of what you have learned, YOU can decide whether you want the job. You may not.

Now you see the importance of being clear in your mind about your objective. Not a job at any cost, (if that is the case then your objective should be focussed on the state of mind which brings you to think in that way) but the right job at the right time.

Step Three - Keeping your objective in view.

Keep your mind in tune with your objective. Your goal might be something attainable in half an hour's time, or tomorrow, or next week, or next month or further distant. Where the need or prospect of achievement is not immediate, it is necessary to remind yourself of your goal. Keep your mind in tune with your objective and remind it of the detailed plan your gave it through your visualisation in Step Two.

With that visualisation in mind, and the goal itself, take several small cards and write on each a word or two of your choice, representing either the goal or a key part in its attainment. For example 'Interview', 'Blue tie', 'Relaxed'. Place these card where they will act as reminders – in your wallet or bag, on bedside table, in sock draw, in your car, on fridge and so on.

Each time your eye catches sight of a card there will be a subconscious recognition of your visualisation. You may also be consciously aware of the forthcoming event, at times perhaps not want to be reminded of it, but quite quickly you will accept the presence of these reminders and the inevitability of your plan.

This will happen automatically and there is no need to dwell upon any aspect of your visualisation or think further about the interview on these occasions. Familiarity is the name of the game here, combined with your gentle acceptance of what is happening.

Step Four - Keep It To Yourself

Do not tell anyone what you are doing.

A very important part of this technique, this process of thought concentration, is not revealing what you are doing to anyone. There will be exceptions and while you may tell someone close to you, or who shares your goal, what your objective is, you need not reveal to them the method by which you are achieving it.

This is your goal, share it with a few people as possible. This is your method – keep it to yourself and there are several reasons why you should.

First and foremost is to contain the energy and enthusiasm you have built up in working through the preceding three steps.

There is truth in the saying *A trouble shared is a trouble halved.* We do feel better having given away part of the problem, or more correctly, part of the anxiety accompanying the problem. It works for other feelings too.

Think of a time when you were so ecstatically happy you were bursting with joy and couldn't wait to tell someone. When that time came, suddenly, in that moment of sharing so your joy diminished. The intensity of the moment passed.

So it is with your goal. Keep the mental picture safe, hold onto the energy of your enthusiasm and the intensity of your eagerness. Hold your future safe. It can be the difference between he who talks about doing something and he who actually does it.

Another reason for not putting thoughts into words is to do with the way in which the human brain works. The brain is divided into two hemispheres, the left and the right. One hemisphere, usually the left, deals with language, detail, analysis and logic, breaking down words and thoughts to examine them, critically. The other hemisphere, usually the right, works quite differently and sees the whole picture, gets the feel of problems and works intuitively. This hemisphere blends together words and thoughts and gives a balanced view of the overall picture; a broader and deeper perspective placing the objective in a broader context.

Your earlier silent visualisation took place almost entirely in the intuitive, non-language brain-hemisphere. By not putting your goal into words and engaging the critical part of your brain, you avoid introducing unnecessary doubts and self-limiting thoughts.

A further reason for privacy is to avoid unnecessary criticism and allowing other people's doubts and envy to detract you from your objective. You will also avoid any deliberately obstructive intervention to your plans by those who might gain by your failure or who are jealous of your enterprise, especially those who might see your success as a measure of their own failure.

By not putting your right-brain visualisation into left-brain words you go far in avoiding doubt, damage and self-limitation.

Step Five - Believe!

Hold on to the belief that you really can now achieve your goal, success is within your grasp. Your belief cannot be half-hearted and it must not be either aggressive or arrogant: simple acceptance is sufficient.

You may ask why believe now, at stage five; why not earlier, at stage one or two? The answer is very simple. Only now, at this stage, when you have considered your objective carefully, also the means by which you will go about achieving it equally carefully, let it rest in your mind and kept it quietly to yourself, only now can you look again at what you are doing and reaffirm your conviction. I am entitled to ask this of myself, to go for this, to achieve this – it is important to me.

Consider this. Are you aware of any reason why you should not achieve your goal? Before answering consider further. If what you want had been achieved by others, you know that it is possible. If what you want is totally original there is no precedence for it being unattainable. If your goal is something you have tried for before and were unsuccessful you benefit from valuable experience and can approach your effort with greater confidence.

Time and place change otherwise unchanging circumstances.

A salesman may knock on nine doors only to have nine occupants decline to buy. His popular product offers good value for money and the absence of sales reflects that, for various reasons, nine people did not want or could not buy at this time. Understanding this, the salesman can approach the tenth door with the same optimism as he had when approaching the first. After all, the salesman could have begun at the other end of the street, beginning at number ten.

The lesson is that an offer declined is not a failure. The offer is not devalued, the product is not devalued, neither is the salesman. There is simply an incompatibility between offer and need.

Step Six - Stop Trying.

You have now reached a point beyond which you find a new sense of mental concentration building. A reflexive awareness and feeling of confidence that helps you 'let things happen' grows within you. Whatever you do requires less effort and it becomes increasingly obvious that you no longer have to *try,* you simply *do*. This is your right brain hemisphere at work.

As you allow your right brain work for you, you become increasingly aware of opportunities that may hitherto have gone unnoticed. You will start along paths you never knew existed, not necessarily knowing where they will lead, but knowing it is right for you. Some may seem to lead nowhere, or end abruptly but there will be reason enough in journeying them, even if it is not immediately obvious.

A greater consciousness is aware of your needs and intentions and requires you do nothing more than fit into a pattern of harmony of which you are not fully aware. Your needs can only be met when they mesh with the needs of others, people you may never know, but whose needs are equally important to your own. Letting it happen for you is letting it happen for all.

Step Seven - The mirror technique.

Your bearing, appearance and expressions reflect your determination and self-opinion. Care is needed in the way in which you present yourself to other people.

This step is the only step which need be repeated. All other steps, once completed and to which you become committed fully are then set aside. The importance of the positive action you take in carrying out this part of the technique cannot be emphasised too strongly. It involves looking at yourself in a mirror.

Choose a mirror in which you can see yourself reflected from (at least) head to waist and from which you can stand about 12 inches/30cms distant.

Approach the mirror, taking stock of the person approaching you. Regard your reflection as you would someone you were just meeting. Walk up to the mirror and stop to stand about 12inches/30cms away from it.

Look directly into the eyes of your reflection. Look at this face for a few moments before returning to make eye-to-eye contact with yourself. Say aloud what this person is going to do, or how this person is going to feel or behave, or where this person is going.

Using one short sentence, using the fewest possible words, repeat your goal over and over for a few minutes.

You will handle your interview in a calm and relaxed way.

You will remain calm and relaxed during your interview.

You will get that car, you will have it.

You will make yourself understood.

As you carry out this exercise several things happen.

We each place around us an imaginary fence that determines what we consider to be our *comfort zone*. The precise distance this fence is from us is determined largely by our mood, our outlook. The more hostile we feel, the larger to zone and the further away from us is the fence. The more friendly we feel towards people, the nearer to us the fence and the closer we allow people to get to us, physically. When two people feel very friendly there are no fences and touching is allowed.

The average distance from people going about their normal business is about 24 inches or 60 centimetres and only when people invade this space, come inside the fence, do we begin to notice and perhaps resent their presence. In this process you cannot ignore the person (reflection) you face you. As you then hold eye-to-eye contact, something associated with truthfulness, you cannot ignore what this person is telling you. Because your concentration is exclusively on yourself and your goal, you stimulate the mental images created in Step Two.

By repeating in a single sentence, the essence of your objective you condition your subconscious mind to accept the process of by which you can achieve your objective as inevitable.

Your mind is already tuned in to your objective by the completion of Steps Two and Three; the certainty of Step Five is now deepened and accepted as you invoke the subconscious response completely.

A phenomena of image switching may take place during this

procedure, where you experience a momentarily loss of self, not knowing on which side of the mirror you are standing. Do not be concerned if this happens, it is an aspect of self-hypnosis in the absence of activity by the critical brain. It is good!

Furthermore, you will develop a natural ability to hold close eye-to-eye contact with other people, increasing your powers of communication and persuasion.

When your objective is distant, carry out this procedure daily. If your objective is imminent, a few minutes in the wash room and some well chosen words can do wonders for your presentation.

Step Eight - Subtle Communication

As you practice the technique, and especially if your goal is something you are working towards over a period of time, you will become aware of the ease by which you seem to communicate with others. You may find that other people seem to go out of their way to help you, without you having to ask and without they knowing in what way they are helping.

There are more happy coincidences in your life and people seem more helpful, even those who are not especially friendly toward you.

You have an inner energy centred around your objective. Your subconscious mind is now working continuously to bring your search for happiness to a conclusion. Remember that happiness is a universal goal and the harmony brought about by your success brings greater happiness to all.

All these things happen as your inner enthusiasm, belief, awareness and focus align your entire being with the achievement of your goal. A purposeful harmony of being that enhances your powers of communication at *all* levels, including the paranormal. Powerful energy streams from the subconscious levels of your mind influence those around you whose behaviour is being influenced by your desire.

Proof? Think of the childhood game played when, on a bus, staring at the back of the neck of a passenger in front of you eventually made that person turn around. If you are a woman you will know the feeling of being watched or stared at, usually by men, as you walk through town. Even though you cannot see who is watching, you can feel their eyes on you, their desire energising their thoughts.

Had friends round and wish they would go home as you want to go to bed? Quietly focus on one and in your mind suggest he is tired and can now go. It works!

Step Nine - Your image is not your appearance

Everyone you meet responds to the image you present them. This image is essentially one of sight and sound and, in the context of this technique, you have chosen what you want people to see and hear. From this you are creating the impression you leave with people, but you may not always be able to do so. Accidents happen and you may not always look at your best.

Fortunately, what we say and what people hear us say is ultimately more important than how we look. You have the advantage of knowing just who you are and what you want. Regardless of how you may be disadvantaged by circumstance, your naturally positive and focussed approach can flow easily over others who, for the most part are preoccupied or unfocussed. Your certainty and reassuring and happy enthusiasm will be picked up by other people who will then act in appropriate ways without thinking.

You may be aware of this and deliberately guide conversation in a particular direction; at other times your guidance will be automatic and more subtle.

Do not feel disadvantaged on those occasions when the visual image you present is inappropriate or ideal. What you say and the way in which you say it is far more important. The fact that you seem unconcerned at your state of dress will make other people feel comfortable and take their attention away from that aspect of your presence.

Step Ten - Waste neither time or effort.

Do not waste time or effort on pointless thoughts, fears or side issues. Try not to dwell upon thoughts that could diminish your mental powers. Anger and vengeful thoughts are natural reactions but should be let go of as quickly as possible. They are inappropriate – a thought is either working for you or against you – you choose!

Look forward, not backward for yesterday has gone.

Summary

1

Decide what it is that you truly want.

2

Picture your goal clearly in your mind.

3

Remind Yourself

4

Keep it to yourself.

5

Believe

6

Stop trying

7

Look at yourself

8

Subtle communication.

9

Image

10

Waste not, want not.

A limited perception creates boundaries impossibility.
An acceptance of the unknown opens the mind to infinity.

38.   Points to Consider

A GIFT – Something for nothing, something given without expectation of reward, free and without obligation.

A gift is such a simple thing but one which many people find difficult to accept freely, without it creating a sense of obligation to return the kindness.

Gifts come in many guises, commonly as inducements, the implementation of which is intended to create a feeling of guilt or obligation in the mind of the recipient. The danger is that in not succumbing to those pressures, that which incurs no cost may be deemed to have little or no value.

Real values and personal values become matters of perspective, opportunity and need. Something regarded as a personal treasure by one person may be disregarded completely by another. Value is in the eye of the beholder. To a thirsty man alone in the desert, what value has a gold bar?

The thought of getting something for nothing is generally found attractive, evidence for which is seen throughout society. Desire has more to do with acquisition and the accumulation of 'wealth' in any form, than of true need, but of course there are exceptions. Many disadvantaged people rely on gifts in order to survive.

A personal gift has worth in itself as well as representing and displaying the motives of the giver, for example gratitude, love, respect etc., but what of other kinds of free gifts?

A company seeks to increase the sales of a product. In order to do so the product must be made to appeal to people, for example being more useful, bigger, better, stronger and so forth, but if none of these things are possible, or have already been tried, another form of inducement to buy must be found. The 'free-gift' is one such way.

The 'free' part may be an add-on gift that comes included with the product, an additional amount of the product for which no charge is made, or a discount for buying more than one item. But where do the resources to fund this free gift come from?

The cost of the promotion, the free gift, comes from the

company, by way of investors who fund the marketing inducement on the premise of sharing in increased profits. Or from the company's advertising and marketing budget, itself the result of previous sales profits, or from the cost of the promotion being part of the purchase price of the product, i.e. the customer pays for his own free gift. Ultimately it is always the customer who pays for the free gifts.

Free is a magic word that stirs the emotions and the stirring of emotions is what marketing is all about. Carefully presented advertising is designed to affect us emotionally rather than logically simply because under scrutiny, the true cost of products, and their profit margins and risks, becomes clear.

Fear is an emotional reaction used to effect by insurance companies and manufacturers of any product offering the promise of safety and security. The potential buyer's response to clever advertising is likely to be disproportionate to both risk and product. The risk appearing greater than it really is, the product seeming more beneficial that it really is. The ability to remain purely rational is diminished as a direct result of an advertiser determined to manipulate the unwary.

Football pools, bingo, raffles, lotteries, horse and greyhound racing are some of the many ways in which people are invited to take a chance, a risk and gamble on getting 'something for nothing'; though the stake money parted with in order to take part in the gamble is not 'nothing'.

A common way in which promoters encourage gambling is to make the 'gamble' appear as entertainment or amusement, or a game of skill, as a result of which it becomes either trivialised or challenging.

Amusement arcades are designed to be seen as places offering harmless fun knowing the appeal they will have to certain people, some of whom will become hooked on the challenge or the promise of financial gain. Unfortunately many of these people will also be poor and spend money they can ill afford.

Gaming machines are cleverly designed to engage players with a combination of sequences, sounds, lights and rewards that ensure the attractiveness and long-term use. Here nothing is for free.

Gambling is just one way in which people take risks, sometimes extreme risks resulting in suffering and deprivation. There are many theories and psychological explanations why this is so but one basic fact is unavoidable. Gambling exists to exploit a natural human characteristic for gain.

Gambling in its many forms sells internet space, newspapers, television programmes and all manner of media to which the public are exposed, public of all ages. A vast network of industries rely directly or indirectly on some form of gambling or another, from the stock market to the housing market, government finance and taxation to the corner shop. A vast parasite whose tentacles reach from the heart to the very fingertips of society.

Money and personal wealth are seen not only as the rewards of success but as alternatives to work or effort. Even the gambler who gamblers for the thrill of gambling wants to win, to be successful, that he may gamble even more.

Money or wealth is regarded by many as the yardstick of success. The opportunity of being able to win instant success is therefore attractive in itself but when allied to the prospect of being able to escape relative poverty, the combination is very attractive. The poor are an easy target as they feel they have a need to win, rather than simply a desire to play.

The prospect of being rich offers the prospect of freedom and equality to anyone who feels trapped or disadvantaged.

For whatever reason, gambling is *waiting for something to happen* little short of an atheistic expectation of the second coming. Each week, millions of people wait for the gambling saviour to favour a disciple and pluck the fortunate being out of his or her misery.

To gamble, to seek something for nothing is to give up a part of one's personal responsibility, to beg without need, to seek a crutch where there is no lameness.

The best that can be said of gambling is that it is a uncreative waste of time while closing one's eyes to the destructive, draining of humanities collective resources. A sign of inequality and dissatisfaction that holds a mirror to society.

What of the few who win? Will their new found wealth bring happiness, peace, health and contentment, who can know? Wealth is relative to want, need and desire. For one person, sufficiency is enough. Freedom of mind cannot be bought or sold, fears persist despite every reassurance and the more one has the more one is afraid of losing that which one has.

Freedom of mind is freedom of spirit, a freedom unparalleled in life.

Investing money in stocks, shares and savings accounts of various kinds is not regarded as gambling, even though there are elements of risk and the possibility of loss. Investors who win, do so at the expense of those participating in one part or another of the cycle. Investor, entrepreneur, manager, intermediary, customer or whoever. People who 'invest' time and money furnishing the system, and society with its needs.

There is no shortage of societies and organisations waiting for investors. The products, or opportunities provided by banks, building societies, insurance companies, government bonds, unit trusts, commodity traders, antiques, futures, paintings, pension funds, property holdings, diamonds, gold, oil, loan companies...the list is limited only by the imagination.

A vast array of ways to tempt the would-be investor to part with his money. A global network of inter-related and inter-dependant opportunities created and managed by an army of people whose existence depends solely on passing money from place to place; and of course convincing us they alone can best give us a profit, ' something for nothing'.

We know that this is impossible. As well as paying for their time and expertise, any interest, or profit, subsequently paid must come from someone, somewhere. For one to take, another must give, whether the giver does so knowingly is another matter.

The question is, not how much can you get but how much are you willing to give?

A building society can only pay higher rates of interest to its investors, or savers, if the people to whom it lends pay higher rates of interest on their loans.

A mutual society is able to spread its share of share wealth in a way that benefits both savers and borrowers closely. Beyond its establishment and operational costs there is no requirement for additional profit.

A non-mutual society or bank, owned by shareholders, operates to provide those shareholders with a profit, or dividend, an additional cost placed on those to whom it loans AND to its investors, who are offered lower rates of interest on their savings.

Interest paid on government bonds comes from government resources, part of which comes from tax revenue. Money borrowed in this way enables a government to spend money it does not have and which it cannot otherwise justify from raising by taxation. Such government borrowing creates a future liability of repayment financed by future borrowing or from tax revenues. A dangerous precedent for future irresponsibility and unaccountability. A burden of liability is passed from one generation to the next, without the willingness of the latter.

The ability to borrow is the ability to have power and the ability to form a regime supportive of itself. The alternative would be to raise revenue through increased taxation, which would likely prove unpopular, but which in fact offers the prospect of greater governmental accountability. Beware governments who offer ever lower direct taxation.

This is just a flavour of the ways in which money becomes anonymously used while providing rich pickings for the few along the way.

From pension funds to savings accounts, investment fuels property prices, chemical plants, fuel prices, food prices, and almost everything you could think of, including the manufacture of armaments sold for profit to foreign powers.

Even money seemingly innocently spent funds massive armies of paper-pushing clerks, call centre operators who do nothing but pass your money from place to place and person to person. As they do so drawing on huge reserves of energy and other resources that would otherwise not be needed or which could benefit us all far more than it does. In thousands of offices all over the world, millions of people who produce nothing but consume much.

The age in which we live is one of virtual money, – the age of the credit or other kind of transfer card.

Before the widespread introduction of credit cards, the ways in which loans with which to buy goods was very limited in heavily restricted. When it became apparent, to governments, that public spending equalled brought greater tax revenue the ways in which people could buy goods became less important. Credit restrictions were lifted and the responsibility for credit management handed over to lenders and individual members of the public. No bad thing, idealistically, but people deprived, or who felt they were deprived, of all manner of consumables found their appetites insatiable. Governments and lenders rubbed their hands gleefully while Jo Public paid up in taxes, interest and charges.

Impatience and greed have their price. The true cost of both goods and borrowing the money to pay for them becomes obscured. Accountability is also obscured, nobody is at fault, nobody is to blame, except – yes, of course, the individual.

Both left and right of political extremes deny individual personal responsibility. Add to this the phenomenon of computerised control and authority delegated to programmed responses, the real governing power becomes limited to an anonymous elite. Heads of state down to heads of departments may feel they are in control of what is going on but they are not. The implementation of their edicts relies on the ability and willingness of those who write and operate computer programmes.

Recent history shows us that many an idea has collapsed under the weight of its own deficiencies, even before it has become implemented.

How when faced with a faceless world of seeming inevitability, does one retain a sense of personal responsibility and enjoy the sense of freedom that brings?

One way is to hamper the system while working with and

within it. By legitimately using formal procedures, red-tape, in a way which restricts the system and uses its resources, rather than those of the individual.

Another way is to work legally outside the system as far as is possible. Use cash instead of passing money through card or banking systems, which also has the benefit of denying prying card companies and shops the ability to know what you buy, when and where you buy it, from which they may draw up a personal financial profile – yes it happens all the time. This is a time of fluidity in financial and government circles and no doubt a more balanced approach, a compromise solution will complement future unseen needs and lifestyles. Devolving everything to electronic digital formats will at the same time go a long way towards reducing world energy usage.

Use a mobile phone and you whereabouts is known. Walk down a street and you are on camera. Use a credit card and your whereabouts and needs are known. Drive along a highway, travel by train or air or bus and your whereabouts is known.

Just be yourself, be responsible, patient and happy.

In holding personal values dear, in pursuing the goals of truth and understanding, by creating rather than destroying, and supporting only those things in which we believe, our influence is felt.

Be happy in the truth of who and what you are.

39.   Gifts of the Happy Self

1 - The Visitor

You are where you know yourself to be, where your mind and your body tell you are. Your body grounds you and fixes you to a place, the location in which it happens to be. Your mind may have directed your body to that location, or simply witnessed its movement from one place to another. Now, in mind and in body you know where you are.

Your mind takes you to the realities of its perception of fact and fantasy. Your mind holds you in its preoccupations and journeys you in its imaginings. Your body recognizes where your mind is and shares its consciousness. Mind and body share their realities.

You are not only your body and you are more than your mind. That part of you which is beyond both mind and body sees mind and body and their actions and perceptions in the context of that place in which they live and with an understanding of their needs and limitations. You are this observer.

You use your body and the facilities it offers you. You use your mind to explore the world in which you live in partnership with your body. You use your body to experience the world about you, the world your body knows and your mind sees as reality. In mind and body your are the explorer.

You may feel that your body imposes certain limitations upon you; you may feel a prisoner in your own body but do not reject your body nor fail to heed what it is telling you. You have come into the body for a reason, a purpose you can know only when you are not your body and when you are more than your mind. Even your perception of your body as a prison and your mind as jailer reveals that you are much more than both.

In this deepening perspective lies the insight which brings you into your true Self; that invulnerable Self who visits, journeys and observes.

Soon you will move on, travelling to distant places yet unseen. You may return, to do that left undone, or to give a helping hand to others. Or you may not return but you will carry the wisdom of your journeying always.

Only in journeying through your time in this world can its revelations be understood. Only in your journey's end can you know the path that you have walked and that which lies ahead.

Your body and your mind are the vehicles of your passage and a means to your enlightenment; gifts of your creation to be cherished and nurtured. Treasure them, guard and guide them, reassure them and in harmony of partnership come safely to that place of all tomorrows.

2 - Hidden Gifts

It was Tuesday and market day came warm and sunny. Outside a cafe on the market square sat two old men, where they had met each week for many years. All around the market bustled with activity. "Just look at it, all the buying and selling, the money passing from hand to hand. Many needs will be satisfied today, " said one.

"Yes, happiness for some, disappointment for others," replied the second, "Look how those two standing in the corner bargain over a box of fruit, how they argue, bartering down to the last penny so seriously. Yet see the happiness in the face of the child nearby as she eats her apple."

"Every market day the same and every one different. People travelling from miles around to buy and sell, meet old friends and strike a bargain. The Farmer and the labourer, the rich the poor, the honest and the cheat, all drawn together by their various needs, each in need of the others for without them all there would be no market."

"A thousand people and a thousand hidden gifts," replied the friend.

"Hidden gifts, how so?" enquired the other.

"Whenever people meet there is an exchange of gifts. Of course the giving is often without thought or intent and the receiving are without recognition or thanks, but gifts are exchanged none the less."

"Go on," urged the friend.

"Well it's like this. We give away our words and our deeds - they are our hidden gifts. Words and deeds which leave their marks upon the world, marks which once struck can never be erased. Gifts that last forever carried by another all the rest of his days."

"Yes, words that firstly touches those around us and then go on to touch many more. To think that the power of a word or some slight act can be so great but this is the source of our history. We are each the product of others who have gone before and who in many ways surround us now."

"Such a pity then how the kind and thoughtful acts of selflessness are so often scorned by those who see no further than the advancement of their own position and who measure success in profit and possession. Whose short lived gain is often to another's cost, whose carelessness spreads so much unhappiness."

"Come come," replied the other, "While what you say is true, the kindly act is never lost Treasured in the heart it soothes away the hurt, sustains and builds again the good for good outlasts the bad a thousand times and is so valued."

"Thank you. Thank you dear friend for your gift today."

"And you for yours."

And as the market cleared two friends rose and went their separate ways, each richer for their hidden gifts, the measure of their friendship.

3 - THE WRITER

The writer sat at his desk staring at the blank sheet of paper before him. Pen in hand he searched his mind for the inspiration that would bring forth the words of wisdom for which he was renowned.

Nothing happened.

Outside the house the sun rose higher in the sky. He felt its heat creep across his hands and forearms as they rested on the faded mahogany desktop. The sheet of paper became dazzlingly bright, reflecting harshly its unaltered state.

Nothing happened.

The longer the writer sat the more difficult it became. His thoughts no longer made any kind of sense, his mind wandered. He had to write, he just *had* to.

Nothing happened.

He felt unsettled. Then a strange, uneasy feeling that he could not place crept over him. Unsettled yet not restless, his fear was that of an unwanted anticipation. Perhaps he would never again be blessed with the inspiration and flashes of insight that had flowed so effortlessly, until now.

Nothing happened.

The greater his uncertainty, the greater his fear became. Not just the uncertainty of some distant tomorrow but here and now uncertainty. That which had previously been viewed with clarity was suddenly obscured; the obvious became invisible as the brilliance of the sunlight on the still blank page burned everything from his mind. Where was his wisdom now?

No abstract philosophy, no bold words or grand treatise could match the concrete solidity imprisoning his mind. A mind now starved of reality save for a small white rectangle, now the mocking window of his imprisonment.

Nothing happened.

Absorbed in timeless solitude his vision gradually cleared and he knew that in his fear he was not alone. He knew the fear of those whose expectations brought them to find comfort in his words and direction in his teaching.

"Fear is my inheritance. I was born free into this world, to exist in my own right. Endowed with every gift of nature, the joy of existence bestowed upon me. Only humankind denies me these riches and in expectation seek to rob me of my joy.

'I must resist such impositions and remain free in thought and deed. Even though I may continue to know fear I must rise above its miserable deception and keep free the joy and love in which I was created."

He took up the piece of paper and began to write.

4 -Value for money.

The old man sat by the fire, comfortably enveloped in a rather worn armchair; a cushion at his back, a little foot-stool raising his slippered feet above the drafts of cool air drawn to the hot coals glowing before him.

He looked down to his upturned palm in which rested a solitary coin, the firelight catching its bright edges.

"All I have in the world," he mused to himself, "All I have in the world."

In the silence of the darkened room the old man's thoughts wandered, guided by the coin to which his eyes were drawn ever more intently.

"What this small coin must have been exchanged for in its short life. Touched by many hands and rested in many pockets it has journeyed far, little doubt of that. With each exchange its value surrendered and renewed at the hand of its new keeper.

'The value of the coin unchanged but then in passing never twice the same.

'This which now rests in my hand has been a reward for labour, a bringer of happiness, a source of nourishment, the creator of profit and the seed of failure.

'Passing from one person to another it has brought satisfaction, security, promise, and regret, elation and despair.

'Yet this simple piece of metal is much more for it has brought to me all that it has been and all that it is yet to be, enjoining me to so many people whom I will never know but in whose lives I share.

'And then tomorrow, when I place my value on this token of men's dreams, this source of rich imaginings, our parting will make possible another's play."

Slowly the old man and his thoughts drifted into the night.

5 - Faith can move mountains

Faith leads us to that path of destiny by which we shall arrive safely at our journey's end. Faith is the finder of solutions, the bringer of enlightenment. Faith is the acceptance of destiny's hand.

Faith sees not with the eyes of the mind but with the vision of the Spirit. Faith is of the Self, by the Self and for the Self in its realization of purpose, place and time. In Faith life is a journey embarked upon willingly in the certainty of its destination, a journey that will be completed despite mountains.

Two men of Faith, together journeying the same road, found themselves confronted by a mountain beyond which lay their destination.

One man decided to travel a path that lead over the mountain. A difficult and demanding climb which passed through wild and windswept places, barren deserts and rock strewn wastes: a lonely path which offered little shelter from the violent storms for which the peak was renowned.

The other traveler chose a way of greater length that skirted the mountain. A path which meandered as it followed the banks of streams and rivers, passing through fertile plains and lush valleys, offering sustenance and shelter among its trees and bushes.

On reaching their destination the two were pressed for tales of their travels by friends who marvelled at the strength and endurance of two who would make such journeys.

"It was magnificent," said one, "Sights of overwhelming beauty and splendour, the world like a carpet beneath my feet. I could see into the very depths of eternity and feel the raw power of creation all around me. In abandonment I was at one with my journey. The path I walked became my strength and in it I found the love of my Creator."

"It was magnificent," said the other, "Sights of overwhelming beauty and splendour, the world like a carpet beneath my feet. I could see into the very depths of eternity and feel the raw power of creation all around me. In abandonment I was at one with my journey. The path I walked became my strength and in it I found the love of my Creator."

6 - The Wise One

In a certain town lived a Wise One of whom those in need

sought comfort and counsel. As in all towns there were those who would seek an audience out of curiosity or to relieve the boredom of their days; there were those who wished to be seen in the company of the Wise One thinking it fashionable and that their own reputations would be enhanced.

There were those who were impatient to be seen and those who were reluctant. There were those who wanted to listen and those who wanted to talk: those who would accept those who would take, and those who would share.

On leaving, some took with them happiness, others contentment; some found enlightenment, others guidance and encouragement. Some could find only disappointment.

A visiting friend of the Wise One, witnessing the comings and goings of so many people, asked if some did not take advantage, greedy for time given freely, abusing the kindness they received and offering no recompense for the hospitality they were offered.

The Wise One replied.

"Those who feel they have taken advantage of me do so only in their own eyes. From me there is no gain to steal. That, which I give, I give freely as I choose: that which I withhold cannot be taken.

'We each can give only what we have and what we are able but we may not know what we have until another demands it of us. Each teaching is a precious gift to giver and receiver.

'If I give that which is demanded of me I have satisfied a need. If I cannot give that which is sought; or if that which I offer cannot be accepted, then he who makes such a demand may question his need or look elsewhere. In either case he will have taken a step toward enlightenment.

'I can only give someone that which he is capable of receiving. If he is unable to accept all I offer he may feel cheated or disappointed that he has been given less than he deserves or desires. If he seeks more than I can give and still feels disappointed he will see me the lesser and in resentment fail to find value in what he has received.

'That which I give is in response to the need which I

recognize, not necessarily to the question that is asked or the answer or solution that is anticipated.

'He who speaks ill of me, or who feels he has stolen from me or taken advantage in some way, steals only his freedom. In self-knowledge of his words and recognition of his deeds, he surrenders freedom to become a prisoner of guilt. The key to which lies within his heart.

He who seeks forgiveness from me need only forgive himself, his guilt is his own and not of my creation, and in self-forgiveness he will know the love I have awoken in him."

7 - The Smallest Thing

No matter what I do, the smallest thing will leave its mark upon this world. The least significant of my acts, the seemingly innocent and unimportant words and deeds of my days have effects the magnitude of which I may never know.

A thought, a look, a word, a touch, a turn, a smile, whatever way.

For as the waters of the river change and mould the lands through which it runs,

So too do I change all around me and mould the world through which I travel.

From the mountains and forests, the plains and the seas,
to the creatures they hold, from the air that I breathe
and the people who I meet; all are changed, just by me.
I too am changed as are each one and all,
each of us river, each of us shore.
Take nothing for granted, not one single act.
Do all with a purposeful trust that no harm may follow my turn of hand,

but should it be so then I pray you forgive me, I did not understand.

Then I can take pleasure in all that I do and find joy in my acts.

and delight in a life that I now share with you.
To build or destroy, to take or to share?

To smile or to frown, laughing face, furrowed brow?

To do or leave undone, each act its sum?

A thousand choices in each day and on each one the weight of all eternity,

for one by one and all in all, you too will know my journey through your land.

Within each act there lies reaction's, sown first for Self,

and then for others, and for all.

In every heart a love which stirred, awakened, and embraced, embraces self,

and others all.

And I am you and you are me, together, here we stand before eternity

8 - Little Truths

The hustle and bustle of the street market was hushed suddenly by quite the loudest noise that anyone had heard in a very long time. All eyes turned to where the sound had come from. Men and horses, coughing and spluttering staggered from a cloud of dust hanging over the remains of what had once been two rather large wooden carts.

Looking down from a window high above the commotion, two women paused from their work to take in the sights and sounds of the market.

"What happened?" asked one of the other.

"I don't know," replied the friend, "I think two carrier's carts have collided. Look you can see the horses and drivers there now, wandering about in a daze....what a mess, look at all those broken boxes.."

The two watched a little longer before returning to their work, not mentioning the incident again until their families returned for the evening meal. Around the table opinions came thick and fast.

"I heard that a carrier had overloaded his cart which then leaned over and pulled his cart sideways into another," said one.

"Well, two carts drove too close together and one broke a

wheel in separating was what I heard," said another.

"No, the load was too heavy and one cart ran backwards into the other."

"The empty cart was travelling too fast, or so it was said," added a fourth voice.

"I thought a rope broke causing a load to spill," said a child.

"A pile of boxes stacked by the roadside was blown over by a sudden gust of wind and that made the horses rear up," added yet another.

"Well," said one of the women, "I'm none the wiser, everyone with a different tale."

From his place at the head of the table, grandfather had been watching and listening without comment. Now came his time.

"That is not really so daughter," he began, "There may be truth in all that has been said for nothing in one view need contradict the substance of the others.

'Little truths may seem confusing but they are usually all we have. Little truths can be added together to make bigger ones, or subtracted to cancel each other out; or simply left as they are for what does it matter what they appear to be, each right in part and in their moments.

'In drawing together our truths we learn but in contradiction and confrontation we remain ignorant. That which has gone is fixed in time and in its own truth for eternity, to value or dismiss and to do with as we will we build today with bricks we take from yesterday."

A thoughtful quietness descended as the family began their meal.

9 - A Matter of Opinion.

One hot day in summer two friends sat in the shade of a large Plane tree, the dappled sunlight moving to and fro as the lightest of breezes rustled the leaves in the gently swaying branches above them.

"Why is it," began one, "That although we often disagree we

never argue?"

"Because there is no point," replied the other.

"Perhaps so but there must be more to it than that," replied the first, "I have never known you argue with anyone, even when what has been said to you was contrary to your view."

Neither spoke for a while. The silence was broken only when the questioning friend returned to the subject.

"Do you not think it necessary to take a stand on a point of particular importance, especially when not to do so could be interpreted as a betrayal of your belief or worse, leading another to conclude, wrongly, that you are in agreement?"

"I realize that some might see me as trying to be all things to all people," replied the second, "But do you agree that we are all entitled to our opinions?"

"Of course I do. A cornerstone of freedom and free speech."

"In which case must I not accept the opinions of others as being as valid as my own ?"

The companion nodded in agreement.

"Further, that unless I am asked for my opinion should I not assume it is not sought? Contradicting another by offering that which is not sought could be regarded as an unwelcome interference, giving rise to feelings of resentment and seen as an attempt on my part to invalidate his or her point of view."

'This also I can see."

'Would I be right to refute every statement I find disagreeable knowing that doing so might be thought to be intolerant, judgmental and critical?

'Acceptance is not agreement and to see it so reveals a mind or more precisely an ego, seeking reassurance rather than insight. With acceptance comes the acquisition of knowledge, the opportunity for change and growth through deeper understanding through unity.

'In unity lies strength, a drawing together of natural forces. Is this not preferable to confrontation and argument; the disharmony created by the intolerant bigot whose blinkered view sees naught but one reality?

'Acceptance offers neither criticism nor support. The false, the reckless, the ill-conceived and the futile wither and die without support: aggression grows weak where it lacks the testing nourishment of opposition."

The two fell silent once more, the sun shone and the shadows flickered.

10 - Valuables

As night approached, a wayfarer found himself on a lonely country road far away from the city. The evening wind chilled his face and he looked forward to arriving at his place of shelter, some way off.

Suddenly from out of the deepening shadows stepped two fearsome looking men who quickly made it apparent they were intent on halting the traveler's progress. Catching him roughly by the arms, they forced him to his knees, demanding his money as they did so.

"I have no money, what is it that you want?" asked the traveler.

"Everything, we want your valuables, all that you have."

"Then everything is what you must take."

So saying he proceeded to remove his clothing. He took off his hat, handing it to the man standing to his left; then his coat, offering it to the man at his right. He had just begun to unfasten his belt when the robber holding the hat shouted at him, as he did so, throwing the hat to the ground.

"What are you doing? I don't want your hat and he doesn't want your coat either."

"I'm undressing. You said that you wanted everything."

"No you old fool, we want your valuables," said the other as he put the coat aside.

The old man looked at them and shrugged his shoulders.

"Enough of this, where is your money, where are your valuables?" they demanded, becoming increasingly impatient.

"I have only what you see. I am returning from the city, which I visit twice a year to attend to certain matters and am now quite without money," he said, turning out his pockets and tipping his bag upside down.

Cursing their misfortune the robbers threw the man to the ground and vanished into the night as quickly as they has appeared,

The wayfarer rose to his feet slowly, wiping the mud from his new leather shoes as he did so. Standing up he dusted off his new trousers and brushed his new coat clean. Putting on his warm new hat he turned and set off for home, taking his riches with him.

40.   Bread

When two people exchange vows, committing themselves to each other and to their future together, each brings to the table a loaf of bread. Bread to sustain them through the coming years. Bread to be shared generously and never taken greedily.

Loaves made from wheat refined over many generations; from seed sown in a certain way, brought to maturity in its own time. Each harvest distinct, each loaf unique in flavour, colour, character and style.

loaves to be revered, each delicate nuance of flavour thoughtfully tasted. Each morsel savoured and eaten with passion, relished with a growing awareness of the loving essence it contains. Loaves that are respected and appreciated as gifts exchanged between two friends, graciously enjoyed piece by piece, never consumed in haste or taken without regard.

Two loaves, two plates.

No single loaf placed in between, thence to be shared by two but two people, each eating of the bread they bring and of each other's; but old loaves do not last. New fields must be sown for bread that will be eaten in the coming years.

With change of years come change of needs and circumstance demands that recipes evolve. Some old ingredients are set aside in favour of the new but nothing can conceal the way in which the seed is sown, the diligence and care with which the field is tended and kept free from weeds; and the rightness of its harvesting.

In times to come loaves may be tainted with the bitterness of wild seeds sown in haste or their goodness depleted by the inclusion of corn gathered before its time. Far better they be enriched by ears plucked in golden fullness, gathered patiently, selectively from here and there, grain that is sweet upon the tongue, for sweetness sought is sweetness surely found.

There will be times of abundance and times when resources are stretched to their utmost. There will be times when one must plant for two and times when two must eat as one. Yet no matter how thin the harvest, no matter how stale the few remaining crumbs may be, when seeds are sown with trust and hope, when seedlings are nursed with loving care, then even the most barren field will yield a harvest of goodness. Bread there will always be upon *this* table.

Season upon season passes until there comes a Spring that sees the planting of a solitary field. When Autumn's softness sees just one loaf drawn from the oven. A loaf still baked with care and filled with love but baked for one alone. A solitary loaf that will be eaten slowly and thoughtfully, each silent meal now measured to the last. Each slice, each precious crumb bringing to life some treasured memory; of dreams from which bright futures once were to be made, of dreams no longer dreamed; of hope and fresh spring rain, bright sunshine and green shoots: of harvests, storms and rainbows over sunny fields, of days unceasing in love's eye. Dreams, journeys, memories and loves that live forever and are forever shared.

by
Tony Beckett-Hester

41. Tony Beckett-Hester, a short biography

Tony was born in Marlow, Buckinghamshire, England, in 1940. He is a widower with a daughter and a son.

On leaving Art School, the early part of a varied career that included design, technical writing and creative advertising culminated in Tony running his own company. He also worked as an independent trouble shooter and personal counsellor.

In 1980, he and his wife Pat moved to Wales where they established a private counselling and therapy practice. An unexpected encounter brought Tony to work also as a spiritual healer. Led by demand, Tony focused his attention on anxiety management, providing help to people with personal problems of all kinds, including those related to the use of prescribed drugs.

He specialised in relationship counselling. Helping patients understand their problems was an essential part of his approach. To compliment this work, and as an adjunct to therapy he wrote extensively, producing papers on more than 100 subjects and conditions and privately publishing three books. Based on his personal experiences, including those of spiritual healing, they focus on case histories, spiritual and philosophical guidance.

In 1995 Tony travelled to Germany to see the Indian Avatar Mother Meera.

Tony retired from practice in 2005 and in 2009 he and Pat moved to Lincolnshire. Four months after their move, Pat died suddenly and unexpectedly.

Tony continues to live in Lincolnshire and to write.

Tony Beckett-Hester